Look What You Made Me Do

For many years, Helen Walmsley-Johnson was the author of the *Guardian*'s 'The Vintage Years' blog, which had 65,000 regular readers, and she is still a regular contributor to the *Guardian* and the *New Statesman*. Before beginning her column, she worked for the *Daily Telegraph* and as Alan Rusbridger's PA at the *Guardian*. Her book about middle age, *The Invisible Woman*, was published to great acclaim in 2015. Her experience surviving coercive control is powerfully told in her personal memoir *Look What You Made Me Do*. She lives in a village in the Midlands.

'Compelling . . . A hard book to read, harder I imagine to have written. But absolutely necessary if you want to understand coercive control. Read it.'   Suzanne Moore, *Guardian*

'At first, Helen Walmsley-Johnson was so desperate to please her boyfriend Franc that she overlooked his exacting standards, his overbearing interest in what she wore and who she saw. But before long, her every move was controlled by the man who claimed to love her. The scariest part? How easily such behaviour – and worse – became her new normal.'
                                                    You Magazine

'A piercingly accurate depiction of being in a controlling relationship and how difficult it is to leave'
                              Dawn Foster, *Guardian* columnist

Also by Helen Walmsley-Johnson

The Invisible Woman: Taking on the Vintage Years

Look What You Made Me Do

A Memoir

Helen Walmsley-Johnson

PICADOR

First published 2018 by Macmillan

This paperback edition first published 2019 by Picador
an imprint of Pan Macmillan
20 New Wharf Road, London N1 9RR
Associated companies throughout the world
www.panmacmillan.com

ISBN 978-1-5098-4875-1

1 3 5 7 9 8 6 4 2

A CIP catalogue record for this book is available from the British Library.

Printed and bound by CPI Group (UK) Ltd, Croydon, CR0 4YY

Visit **www.picador.com** to read more about all our books
and to buy them. You will also find features, author interviews and
news of any author events, and you can sign up for e-newsletters
so that you're always first to hear about our new releases.

For my girls

We've got something in common, you and I. We are both alone in the world.

Daphne du Maurier, *Rebecca*

Introduction

Why did I do this?

Why did I decide to write a book charting my progress through two relationships with controlling, abusive men, exposing all my guilt, humiliation and shaming mistakes; why have I revisited painful workplace memories of a controlling, abusive woman and why have I made myself remember things I would much, *much* rather forget? Why have I put myself through that?

I have asked myself each of those things, many times, while I've been writing *Look What You Made Me Do* and especially on the days when I felt it was all too much and couldn't bring myself to get down more than a handful of words. The answer is because I had to . . . because I am not alone, because I am one of many and I want to know why.

I can trace the origins of this book to a mild obsession with *The Archers* on Radio 4, specifically the moment at the beginning of 2013 when Rob Titchener first turned up in the fictional village of Ambridge. His charming manner, and the way he claimed to have fallen so quickly and helplessly in love with single mum Helen Archer, generated a queasy feeling of recognition. The programme is broadcast daily (except for Saturdays) but work commitments meant I had to catch up with the week's events by listening to the Sunday-morning omnibus and joining in the #thearchers Twitter feed

– a sizeable part of the fun. As Rob swept Helen past all the usual relationship milestones with reckless speed, almost all my fellow tweeters seemed to strongly approve of this turn of events (*so* romantic), delighted that at long last Helen had found the One. I kept my doubts about Rob to myself but I had a niggling feeling that I'd met him before and began combing my own history for clues.

Helen's story progressed through real time, which made it all the more powerful because it showed very clearly how insidiously the form of domestic abuse known as coercive control takes hold. My *Archers* Twitter timeline became punctuated with 'Why does she stay?' and 'Leave him, Helen.' By the point where she had been rushed into marriage, agreed to Rob having parental responsibility for her son, been told how to dress, tracked on a mobile phone, isolated from her friends and family, raped, slapped, disempowered and humiliated, the omnibus tweet-along had changed to 'I can't listen to this anymore' and disbelief that an intelligent middle-class woman who ran her own business in a close rural community could be suckered like this. Then inevitably some listeners began referring to Helen's previous mental-health issues at about the same time as her husband.

With the benefit of first-hand experience and hindsight, I realized that there is a basic misunderstanding of how domestic abuse, and coercive control, works, and I began to feel an overwhelming compulsion to set something down about what had happened to me, despite having tried to ignore the fact that it *had* happened for a decade or more.

It took me almost a month to wring out a 2,000-word article and the only way I could find to start it was to muddle this real Helen's story with that of the fictional Helen. I didn't formally pitch the idea to anyone – I wasn't even sure I could write it. It was only towards the end that I came out with it and wrote, 'That happened to me too' – not 'this' but 'that', still distancing myself, still hiding. Whenever I tried to articulate what I had been through, I felt paralysed by shame. In this, again, I am not alone.

By the time I was ready to send the piece out, the 2015 Coercion and Control law[1] was beginning to have an impact, making what I'd written reassuringly apt. Nonetheless, it was turned down twice before the *New Statesman* took it and to their credit, printed it exactly as it was.[2] It went viral.

Then something remarkable happened. One of my Twitter followers, Paul Trueman – @paulwtrueman – got in touch. He also listened to *The Archers*, had read my article and wanted to do something to raise money for victims of domestic abuse. He asked me if I thought it was a good idea (yes!) and where the money should go. Send it to Refuge, I said, thinking of all the times I'd almost called them and never found the courage. Paul's initial target was set at £1,000 but topped £7,000 in the first twenty-four hours. Within a week the Helen Titchener (née Archer) Rescue Fund had reached £50,000. At the time of writing the total stands at a staggering £173,000. The messages left by hundreds of donors show the reach and effect of domestic abuse. I am *really* not alone.

Domestic abuse is like cancer: everybody knows somebody. It's only when you start to speak about it that you find out just how many women have been through it and carry that burden about with them. It affects the everyday lives of hundreds of women. It affects mine.

---

1. Serious Crime Act 2015, Section 76: *Controlling or Coercive Behaviour in an Intimate or Family Relationship.*
2. *New Statesman*, 'Helen's story of abuse in *The Archers* reminds me of my own', 2 February 2016.

Of course, men can be victims of domestic abuse too. I choose to say 'women' because the majority of those affected *are* women, and by quite a substantial margin:

— The volume of domestic abuse prosecutions completed rose in the year 2015/2016 to 100,930, the highest level ever recorded. Where gender was recorded, 83.3 per cent (71,706) of victims were female and 16.7 per cent (14,406) were male. In 18,081 cases the gender was not recorded.[1]

— Every week, in England and Wales, two women are killed by a current or former partner[2] – that's one woman every three days.

— One in four women will experience domestic abuse in her lifetime.[3]

— In one study 95 out of 100 survivors of domestic abuse reported experiencing coercive control.[4]

The 2014/2015 Crime Survey for England and Wales found that 63 per cent of female abuse victims had experienced non-physical abuse (emotional or financial) in the last year.[5]

---

1. Crown Prosecution Service (CPS), *Violence Against Women and Girls* (VAWG) *Crime Report*, 2015/16, p. 5, p. 32.

2. Office for National Statistics, *Crime Statistics: Focus on Violent Crime and Sexual Offences, England and Wales: year ending March 2016.* Chapter 2, 'Homicide'.

3. Office for National Statistics, *Intimate personal violence and partner abuse* (February 2016).

4. L. Kelly, N. Sharp and R. Klein, *Finding the Costs of Freedom: How women and children rebuild their lives after domestic violence* (London: Child and Woman Abuse Studies Unit, 2014), p. 19.

5. Office for National Statistics, *Crime Statistics: Focus on Violent Crime*

Bearing in mind the suggestion of one report that a woman is assaulted thirty-five times before her first call to the police, these figures are a glimpse at an undiscovered country. Women suffer in silence for years and – because the very nature of abuse is control through fear, shame and guilt – some never speak about it at all. But by *not* speaking, women who have suffered leave control in the hands of the abusers. Speaking about it is problematic but it strips away the stigma and robs what has been done to us of its power. It is, trust me, both a relief and a release. But most important of all, it helps us to identify this form of abuse and protect ourselves against it.

But how do we recognize the pattern of an abusive relationship, which starts like any other and somehow slowly twists out of shape? The key is that word 'pattern' because there *is* a pattern and it's always the same. The similarity is the thing that strikes me most when I talk to other survivors, and most of what people know about domestic abuse is told from the victim's point of view. The story in this book is told from my point of view – it is, as it says on the cover, a memoir. But I hope it also supplies the missing voice – that of the abuser. You can tell people you've been disarmed, frightened, loved, confused, desperate and despairing but how do you explain how that happened when you don't understand it yourself? You need the words.

I have an archive of material because 'Franc' (not his real name) and I wrote to each other. Dozens of notes, emails and letters. Thousands and thousands of words and I kept them all, or most of them. What he wrote meant so much to me

and Sexual Offences, 2014/15. Chapter 4, 'Intimate personal violence and partner abuse', Table 4.36.

that I squirrelled everything away, and when he cast aside what I had written to him I kept those letters, too. I also have my diaries and they allowed me to construct a timeline. I began by sorting and filing everything into chronological order. When I'd done that I went to work with a highlighter pen and tracked the path of our relationship – the pattern. I saw very clearly what had happened to me and how it had been done, and I saw both sides.

You would have thought that having this well-documented insight into our relationship would make it an easy story to write. In one sense it did because it's all there. In another sense it worked against me. These are not letters I read every day, or have read since . . . or at all. I don't know why I kept them, unless it was for this. I soon found I needed strategies to deal with the truth that emerged.

At the end of each working day I learned very quickly to be careful about what I left in my head overnight. The afternoon I spent reading through one of our epic email rows left me unable to sleep, tangled in a blanket of self-loathing and negativity, pretty much the way he used to make me feel in life. Hatred of my defensive, grovelling, snivelling, self-pitying, cowering former self was a dominant theme. I saw how pathetic I was in the nauseating prose I wrote, desperate to calm him. I saw too that the way I tried to big myself up, to show him that he couldn't hurt me, in fact only made him worse. Remembering all this made me afraid to write, to put my voice on paper.

When I was with him my world shrank. It shrank again while I was writing this book – the fear and inadequacy I felt then came back as I re-read his words telling me I did not love, could not love, that I should do as I was told, instructing me to be 'a good girl'. Words asking where was I, who was I with, was I fat, was I thin, what had I eaten, had I been writing, had I written about him, had I been to the gym, how much money had I spent this week, not to do this, say that, wear that, behave that way, speak to that man, breathe that way. The words that said I was hopeless, disorganized, mad, fat, old, frigid and above all, that I treated him badly, after all he had done for me. He said that I was cruel and that I made him do what he did. 'You did this. You made me do this.'

He still held the power to shock me. I would feel my heart swell when he said something lovely in a letter or an email and collapse in on itself when he turned it bad. Things I thought I remembered but wasn't sure I remembered accurately were indeed true and reading about them put me back in the place where I first read them. Some things he'd written were as much of a punch as if he was standing here in the room with me. He wrote almost nothing about his violence, but when he did he made it sound logical, defensible: 'A slap is nothing compared to what you did to me'.

As long as such things remain hidden they fester. They help no one. In tipping them out into the world I hope they will help others understand what happened to me, and, in some cases, understand what is happening to them, too.

All I ask of you, the reader, is that you approach this with an open curiosity and try not to judge us, that you bear in mind the psychological scars which domestic abuse, coercive control and workplace bullying leave behind, and perhaps understand why I am occasionally hard on myself and others.

Finally, this book is not about revenge. It is about understanding and about how we can forgive the unforgivable. It's about wanting to alter perceptions. To that end I have changed names, places and anything else that might identify the protagonists. Everything else is as it was.

Home Office: Controlling or Coercive Behaviour in an Intimate or Family Relationship – Statutory Guidance Framework [December 2015]

The types of behaviour associated with coercion or control may or may not constitute a criminal offence in their own right. It is important to remember the presence of controlling or coercive behaviour does not mean that no other offence has been committed or cannot be charged. However, the perpetrator may limit space for action and exhibit a story of ownership and entitlement over the victim. Such behaviours might include:

— Isolating a person from their friends and family;

— Depriving them of their basic needs;

— Monitoring their time;

— Monitoring a person via online communication tools or using spyware;

— Taking control over aspects of their everyday life, such as where they can go, who they can see, what to wear and when they can sleep;

— Depriving them of access to support services, such as specialist support or medical services;

— Repeatedly putting them down such as telling them they are worthless;

— Enforcing rules and activity which humiliate, degrade or dehumanize the victim;

— Forcing the victim to take part in criminal activity such as shoplifting, neglect or abuse of children to encourage self-blame and prevent disclosure to authorities;

— Financial abuse including control of finances, such as only allowing a person a punitive allowance;

— Threats to hurt or kill;

— Threats to a child;

— Threats to reveal or publish private information (e.g. threatening to 'out' someone);

— Assault;

— Criminal damage (such as destruction of household goods);

— Rape;

— Preventing a person from having access to transport or from working.

This is not an exhaustive list.

If you drop a frog in a pot of boiling water, it will of course frantically try to clamber out. But if you place it gently in a pot of tepid water and turn the heat on low, it will float there quite placidly. As the water gradually heats up, the frog will sink into a tranquil stupor, exactly like one of us in a hot bath, and before long, with a smile on its face, it will unresistingly allow itself to be boiled to death.

Daniel Quinn, *The Story of B*

Prologue

I have been living in London, in my rented flat, for nine years. It is my own space and that is important to me. I have been a high-level personal assistant since I moved from the Midlands, leaving behind me an ageist job market and some personal ghosts, coming somewhere no one knew me. My life is pressured, busy, social, creative, a success, and I am – I *really* am – happy. I am at the top of my profession in a life I want. Since coming here my primary motivation has been to prove to myself that I am good at something, *very* good . . . the best. Proving it to anyone else is secondary because at this stage the only opinion that really matters is my own. I am fifty-four years old and my experience of life so far has shown me that people in general are unreliable and that some are downright dangerous. Since my move to London I have repaired my self-esteem, taken some knocks but built up my confidence. I can believe in myself. I tell myself I am a strong, independent woman.

This August day – the 10th – is hot. South-east London thrums through the haze of pollutants that streak my curtain linings grey but above that there are clear blue skies and bright shining planes on their approach into Heathrow. I am on holiday. For the newspapers, which are my working life, August is the Silly Season, dead news time. Almost everyone I know is on holiday, including my boss, so I am too. This is sensible because apart from Christmas it's the only time emails dwindle, the work phone doesn't ring and I can relax properly. I have decided to spend the time at home doing my own thing, imagining future plans, writing, taking pictures and just drifting about London. I am, I think, entirely content. And in my little tucked-away flat, intercom security-protected, double-locked and up six flights of stairs, the sun is definitely shining. I remember that.

And then my phone rings. The landline.

A familiar voice says, 'It's me.'

It is my ex. My insides squeeze and when I speak my voice – tellingly – is higher than usual. I try to keep myself level: 'Hello . . . you. How are you?'

'Fine. I'm fine. I'm outside.'

Then, inevitably, 'Can I come in?'

No explanation, no reason, just the fact of him being there, as though there is nothing at all unusual in standing outside my front door. To the casual observer there isn't. But he lives hundreds of miles away; he's been to my London home just once and that was seven years ago – I haven't seen him in five.

I know better than to answer his question with one of my own and 'no' is a word I have always struggled to say to Franc. He knows that and now he knows I'm here, too. That's why he called the landline and not my mobile, so I would be trapped and unable to lie.

'Sure. I'll buzz you in.'

I didn't mean to say that. I didn't want to say that. I have to remind him which flat is mine . . .

Chapter One

Of all the days you *wouldn't* pick for a blind date, Halloween would surely be a no-brainer. Even if there wasn't a superstitious bone in your body you would still be tempting fate. There was, as I recall, an element of fate-tempting about me at the time. Nothing I did, no prayer to the Almighty made the slightest bit of difference to anything so why bother with playing safe. I was stuck in a never-ending cycle of shit. Someone would ask, 'How's it going?' and I would say, 'Oh, y'know . . . *fine*,' and all the time, inside my head, a small panicked voice was wailing, 'Fuuuuuuuuuck!' on a loop. I felt I was living on borrowed time with a sense that the next disaster was already coming. So when Jeannie at work said, 'Let's have a night out and I'll introduce you to my Franc,' that was exactly the kind of diversion I was up for. Franc was her boyfriend's boss and she went on and on about him and his delicious sexy French-ness to the point where everyone rolled their eyes whenever he was mentioned. She wore him like a badge.

The hospital where we worked was holding a Halloween party (8 'til late, £2 in advance, £3 on the night – I still have the ticket) so we made a plan to meet at Jeannie's where I would also stay the night. We'd be a big group so inviting Franc wouldn't look like a set-up, but when I arrived there was no sign of anyone else. There was just Jeannie, her boyfriend

Dave, and the fabled Franc, lurking in the kitchen pretending to stir something.

After all the hype I was a little underwhelmed. He was perfectly nice – tall, slim and well dressed (a suit on a Saturday night!) with a neat goatee. (I don't like goatees – they're camouflage for a weak chin.) With his crisp dark curls and glasses he looked like a cross between a university professor and a surgeon. He was clean, though, always a plus, with a nice smell (Acqua di Parma?) and a nice voice. His English was slightly imperfect, conspicuously lacking the letter 'H'. When he said he was pleased to meet me I became 'Ellen', not Helen. He was a company director and therefore intelligent (one would hope), and seemed polite and courteous. His precise way of placing his hands, his cutlery, napkin and wine glass suggested a reserved, fastidious man. Apart from his eyes which were a deep, delicious blue, he looked young and ordinary – the kind of man you'd probably pass in the street without a second glance. Definitely not a psychopath. He gave every impression of being nice and a gentleman . . . but I wasn't looking for 'nice'.

Perhaps I should explain about my birthday the week before. I got very drunk, won the pub quiz and was comprehensively snogged by a fabulous Russian half my age who sidled up to me and murmured, 'Ellen, I give you buurrthday keess,' breathily into my ear. *Na zdorovie!* I thought. For some reason (achieving the great age of forty-three?) I kept thinking about Brenda-behind-the-bar and her defence of random physical encounters that might otherwise raise eyebrows: 'At my age, if a bus is passing I hop on.' Amen to that.

Weaving an unsteady route home, I remember lying on the grass in the churchyard (as you do) looking up at the October stars and experiencing the early signs of a midlife crisis. 'Is this the beginning of the end?' I said out loud to nobody. I suppose churchyards are natural midwives to the birth of this kind of thing. In this one I conceived a sincere wish to avoid 'dull' or 'nice' for the foreseeable future, or until 'dull' and 'nice' became fatally unavoidable. I remember it very clearly. It was a pivotal moment.

Fate duly delivered 'nice' Franc and there must have been something about him (I think it was his eyes) because that Halloween night at Jeannie's – based on no evidence of mutual attraction whatsoever – I decided to see where it might lead, which only goes to show that I don't even listen to my own advice, never mind anyone else's.

Later, at the party, we could have been forgiven for thinking we'd got the wrong night. It was dismal, depressing. The sparsely populated room echoed with 'Love Potion No. 9', 'Monster Mash', 'Bat Out of Hell', 'Thriller' – not loud enough to hide the half-hearted shuffle of feet but too loud for private conversation. There were two pumpkins, a 'Happy Halloween' banner and a handful of orange and black balloons. Disappointed, I thought I was owed this night out so when Franc suggested that the two of us might go on to a club I said yes, not too enthusiastically (I was aiming for 'sophisticated') but flattered that he'd shown any sort of interest in my company. I wanted other people to see that he liked me – at the time I was always looking for approval. When Jeannie's crowd opted to stay I was pleased – it meant I had him all to myself.

Franc drove us. He held doors open for me, including the car door – this was unusual in the Midlands and I liked it. I don't remember whether we danced or not. There was none of the lightning-bolt mutual attraction that I had been hoping for. Two recollections from the club have stuck. Franc could light a pair of cigarettes in exactly the same way Paul Henreid did as Jerry in the film *Now, Voyager*, which was super-sexy and romantic and then, when he came back from collecting our coats and I was chatting to another man, he leaned in and whispered, 'Ellen! I cannot leave you alone for a second.' Then he grinned, which made him look much more attractive. It was a flash of that other man – the one Jeannie talked about in the office.

Yes, of *course* we went back to his place. He intrigued me. That made the choice between Jeannie's spare room and hanging out with him an easy one. Perhaps a bit reckless but that was my middle name back then. He made us coffee (proper coffee, so Brownie points) and put on the television to watch the Grand Prix (cancel the Brownie points). Not great but still better than a bunk bed and a single pillow. In any case, given that I'd been drinking all evening, had no money for a cab and my car was parked outside Jeannie's house, how was I going to go anywhere but here? I could have asked Franc for a lift but aside from hoping Jeannie would think we'd spent the night together (shame on me), I knew about men and sport – if I really wanted him to like me, then being the reason he missed the last race of the season was not the way to go about it. This, I understood, was 'give and take' and I was fine with it.

Apart from holding my hand briefly when we were introduced, Franc hadn't touched me, and he flirted more with Jeannie than with me. My prior experience of dating ran somewhat contrary to this. The Franc approach – or non-approach – was something new. It raised questions. If he didn't like me he wouldn't have asked me to go to the club or come back here with him, right? I found myself looking for signs that he at least fancied me but I found none. Franc was inscrutable.

To demonstrate my indifference to his indifference I curled up on the floor next to his feet, sat back against the sofa and rested my head on his knee, like a spaniel.

In Japan the Grand Prix ended. At about 4 a.m. in a rented suburban Midlands semi Franc leaned over and kissed me. It was lovely and definitely worth waiting all evening and half the night for. Then he told me that he had a fiancée at home in Paris, which explained his reticence. I couldn't think of an appropriate response, and perhaps my lack of disapproval encouraged him because he took my hand and led me upstairs. He didn't say another word except to ask my permission. I remember putting my hand over his to stop him switching on the light – I didn't want him to see the marks of age and motherhood on my body – and saying that I didn't want him to look at me naked. That says a lot about self-esteem. Nonetheless, we had good sex, but we didn't 'make love'. I thought we enjoyed a physical transaction between two adults who respected each other. We comforted each other with sex.

On Sunday morning I stayed in Franc's bed longer than was strictly necessary although he wasn't in it. There was none of that lying around in a lovely intimate tangle of sheets and limbs. I could hear him moving about downstairs and when he appeared round the bedroom door a few minutes later wearing a blue-and-red tracksuit I thought he looked like a complete prat – neat, matched, wrinkle-free and lined up is not how you wear a tracksuit. I looked again at the man I'd just spent the night with, taking in his serious face; the pronounced feminine curve to his upper lip; the intelligent dark-blue eyes (which I now found unexpectedly captivating); posture so upright he was almost leaning backwards; and a mug of tea – which was for me. I had a flash of something

I might describe as intuition which said, this man will break your heart.

Why would I think that?

Even before we had been introduced, I'd decided I would sleep with him if the opportunity arose – a combination of the Brenda-behind-the-bar school of thought and Jeannie making him sound like Luc in *French Kiss*, a film that put having a Luc of my own at the top of my romantic wish list. I would be able to look back on this encounter with pleasure when I was eighty-five. At forty-three, you're inclined to think this way and it prompts that feeling of I-haven't-done-enough-of-anything. When we met, my intentions towards Franc were completely dishonourable. There would be no commitment. It would be a one-off, a fling, a gift to myself, one of Erica Jong's 'zipless fucks'. I was not looking for a life partner, nor was I hooked. He would not break my heart because I would not give him the opportunity.

Without anything being said, it became clear that Franc had plans for Sunday that did not include me, which was fine because I also had things to do. As soon as was decent he drove me back to Jeannie and Dave's to fetch my car.

'Do you have any French in you, Helen?' asked a smirking Dave.

'Erm, no. I don't think so. English through and through.'

'Are you sure?' Exaggerated wink.

'Oh, stop it.'

I felt curiously pleased.

I walked back with Franc to his car to say goodbye and thanks for the evening. I offered him my phone number but he refused to take it. Instead he said, 'You will call me.' And gave me his. A prickle of irritation. I would not call. I would not be told what to do.

Three days later I called.

In my diary there is a cursory note: '7 p.m. – Franc.' If I was excited about meeting him I didn't say so. I didn't even make a note of where we went. I have a vague memory of a cold, wet retail park and something about him needing to buy office supplies so I went with him. I think he said he wanted my advice on something. So, definitely not a date then and a piss-poor effort. The implication seemed to be that it didn't matter whether I was there or not – not very gentlemanly considering we'd already slept together – but I thought, OK then, I'll play your games.

At the back of my mind and in spite of the unpromising start, a thin hope piped up that here might be my holding-out-for-a-hero hero, my port in a storm . . . my Maxim de Winter, my Jerry, my Luc, who would sweep me off my feet, rescue me and take me home to Manderley . . . Washington . . . Provence . . . to a better life. It's not a very modern thought but then we daughters of the 1950s grew up with this guff. We were drilled in the art of sidestepping responsibility for ourselves. We were absolved from it, encouraged to occupy the same gender hierarchy as our mothers before us. Woman's theatre of operations was the domestic one; man's was to decide everything important. Woman deferred to man. In the rural Midlands I was not exposed to feminism until my teenage years and by then it was too late. I already contained a dangerous fault line.

I met Franc straight from work that evening, unhappy about my scuffed heels and seen-better-days black business suit. We stopped for something to eat in a chain restaurant – I don't remember which one. There was nothing remarkable about any of it, although he did do the two-cigarettes trick again and took my hand briefly across the table, cradling it gently inside his own while he picked up his fork and ate one-handed. It was a tenderly casual gesture that could have meant something or nothing, but the thin hope grew fatter on it. He kissed me goodbye (properly) and I went home. He was courteous and kind – still the dreaded 'nice' – and somehow he lodged in my head.

At the weekend, he invited me to stay over at his house for a second time. He explained that things with his fiancée, Sophie, were not good, although he added that they had been together for twelve years. (Twelve years and not married – what's wrong with her?) It felt too pushy to ask questions, and not my business. Franc was the one in a relationship; I was as free as a bird and I wasn't being unfaithful to anyone. I felt no moral obligation to the absent Sophie, justifying my behaviour by choosing to believe that whatever-it-was with Franc was a temporary thing, despite simultaneously changing my mind. I wanted the hand-holding and laughter (we did a lot of both). I wanted to be understood and to belong to someone, with the intimacy of a proper, grown-up relationship. Most of all I wanted not to be on my own anymore. And then there was the whole French thing. I'd been married to a Scandinavian for fifteen years, divorced for seven. I did not find Franc intimidatingly foreign as some might, but comfortingly familiar. I don't know exactly when I began wanting him to be more than just a distraction but it was very early on. And I can't imagine for a minute he was unaware of that.

Only a week after our first meeting, Franc and I began a correspondence that would last almost a decade. I did not own a mobile phone (although he did) and email had scarcely begun. It's easy to forget that twenty years ago communication was much slower and you had to think about it. It's lucky for me there was no Twitter or Facebook, no Snapchat or

WhatsApp, or the mess I made might have been far greater. And I wouldn't have had Franc's letters. He wrote what he didn't say. He was softer, more open, romantic, funny and often filthy. He wrote the things he knew I wanted to hear. I hadn't ever had a single love letter until then. When they started I looked forward to his letters and I kept them. Later, when the gilt had definitely worn off the gingerbread, I kept those too.

And that's how it started. No pressure, no ownership, no responsibility. Just a grown-up thing, which, whether it worked out or not, I was sure I could handle.

*

I am a chronic hoarder, the Smaug of personal ephemera with a dragon's hoard boxed beneath my bed. I sleep on memories, dusty parcels of baby shoes, school swimming certificates, cards I made for my own mother as a child and cards my children made for me, a kangaroo-skin handbag bought in Australia by my father for Nana when he was demobbed from the navy in 1945, my mother's wedding veil. Given life's calamitous course, it is a wonder that any of this survives at all.

Amongst all this are my diaries from the last thirty years. They tell me what I was doing and when I was doing it. They are factual and contain little emotional content, which makes coming across the line, 'DM – Can't do things for kids anymore', unusual. It is a coded message from the past. I pause and think . . . before checking this recollection against two other caches of documents. DM was my line manager at the hospital where I worked, Doreen Milson. She was telling me where to draw the line with my family, as if it was any of her business. I made the note to remember what she said and when she said it. I felt it would be important later.

These papers and diaries are all bound by those odd little connecting threads that a personal history sometimes throws out: they are from a time when I found myself simultaneously trapped between two abusers, with a history that included a third. What are the odds? Well, actually, quite high – Crime Survey for England and Wales reports show that domestic violence 'has a higher rate of repeat victimization than victims of any other crime'.[1] Again, I am one of many.

You might call these people bullies but to me it's not a word that accurately reflects what they did. 'Bullies' and 'bullying' are terms that belong in the school playground, not in the adult world of work and love affairs and marriage, although such people do exist in every walk of life. Nonetheless, I prefer to call them abusers and what I experienced, abuse. Having initially all seemed harmless, friendly, these three wreaked havoc, not just in my life, but in the lives of those I cared about most of all. Between them they nearly killed me although they would not have been called murderers in a court of law.

One stack of these under-the-bed papers concerns my relationship with Doreen and work. The other comprises all the notes, emails and faxes Franc and I exchanged over the course of our relationship. A relationship that extended – extends – far beyond its physical ending for reasons which will become clear with the telling.

Ask any woman who has experienced one of these relationships first-hand – and is prepared to talk about it – what happened to her and you will almost certainly find it hard to comprehend. You will most likely be left with feelings of confusion and anger. 'Four years!' you shout (it helps to punch

---

1. Office for National Statistics, *Improving estimates of repeat victimisation derived from the Crime Survey for England and Wales* (October 2017).

something). 'With that bastard! Unbelievable!' It is, and actually you've hit the nail on the head. Suspension of *dis*belief is how it works.

In a nutshell, domestic abusers and workplace bullies are weak but they like to feel strong – to achieve which they need to be in control, to dominate. There is nothing new or original in this; it is the same method used in interrogation and brain-washing techniques the world over. Put very simply: *I'm nice, I'm nasty, I'm nice again. You must love me when I'm nasty because then I'll be nice but if you love me when I'm nice I can still be nasty.* It's highly manipulative and very successful. In this maze of contradictions it is very easy to lose sight not only of reality but also of yourself.

An abuser will project a beguiling charm and conceal themselves behind it while they confuse, undermine and foment doubt, not just in their target but in their target's friends, family, anyone whose advice and support they are likely to listen to and draw strength from. This cannot happen overnight – it requires time and patience – so first they have to behave in a way that will make you want to spend time with them. They need you to like them so you won't see, or can't accept that you see, what they're up to.

You'd think you would spot these people a mile off but they're very good at knowing what you yourself hide behind. If you're having a terrible time an abuser scouting for their next victim will offer you a shoulder to cry on; if you're at a crossroads in your life they will offer kindly advice; if you're miserable they will go out of their way to make you feel better. Perhaps things have been so bad for so long that you feel you can no longer impose your misery on your true friends, that they must be as fed up with it all as you are. Feeling like a burden to others makes you feel terrible. It lowers your self-esteem. Crucially, it isolates you. A stranger with a sympathetic face relieves you of that burden, provides you with an opportunity to go back over the whole story again – they don't know it and they want to hear it. With your mind on your problems, you are unlikely to ask yourself why they are doing this, what's in it for them. *You* are 'what's in it' – that's why they chose you. If they weren't so accomplished at being lovely and making you feel good about yourself; if your life wasn't giving you so much grief, if you didn't feel quite so alone, if you didn't need someone, anyone, to be nice to you just for a little while, you wouldn't go anywhere near them.

*

Now that I'm in my sixties, and unintentionally but very contentedly on my own, I know my future happiness is not – nor was it then – dependent upon finding a man to 'attach' myself to. But in 1955, when I was born, that's what a woman was expected to do – find a good man (or have one found for her) who would look after her, and in return she would fulfil her wifely duties: keep the house nice, cook his meals, look after him, provide (formal) sex, have his children and so on. Men, for their part, understood this was the deal but, I think it's fair to assume, were a little cagey about the mysterious power of women to 'capture' them.

When I was growing up the generally accepted view was that a woman who chose to remain independent, single and childless, or be a single mother, or who divorced herself from an unpleasant husband, or attempted to provide for herself in a male-dominated world, was somehow incomplete, even an aberration. Women were urged to fulfil their 'biological destiny'.

For young women in the 1950s, '60s and beyond, the patriarchal message was presented as a kindly intention to protect us, the so-called weaker sex, from unspecified nastiness. The paradox is that the greater part of what we required protection from was perpetrated by the very people who wanted to protect us. It's the kind of circular argument one often stumbles across in dealing with a ruling majority. Instead of being provided with the tools to look after ourselves, my generation was wrapped in an over-protective blanket of tutored helplessness. Ignorance is its own form of control.

The 1950s, in a reaction against the egalitarianism of the 1940s, saw the beginnings of a concept under which women continue to labour to this day: a constricting belief in 'perfection' – women were women and men were men, women served men, men looked after women. Except that it was, of course, a lie. It's still a lie. Women and girls toil away striving to achieve perfection in ways that beggar belief. Everything about us must be flawless. Anything that reminds the world in general of the messier aspects of what it means to be a woman must be removed, obliterated, glossed over. A continual barrage of mixed messages emerges from the media but the main directive seems to be that we should, at all times, be sexy, feminine, available and above all, perfect.

Each age has its own definition of what constitutes the perfect woman and very occasionally that definition coincides happily with freedom – the 1920s, for example, when fashion became far less restrictive, or the 1940s when women found freedom in conscription to the war effort and a wage packet – but more often than not it involves some form of imprisonment, whether that's fashion, lifestyle or politics and religion, and frequently a combination of them all.

For every step women take forward it feels as though we take two, if not three, backwards. The gender pay gap and the glass ceiling still exist, sexism still exists, misogyny definitely still does . . . Fighting for women's right to simply be women feels more and more like battling the hydra – cut off one head and two more spring up in its place. The list of demands we are told to make on ourselves is endless and baffling and mostly to do with the way we look. We must not look old or even middle-aged but eternally youthful, smooth, hairless, prinked, stretched and uplifted with full lips, long lashes, white teeth, and we hand over countless billions to the (mostly male) cosmetic surgeons who will give us what nature hasn't, even to the extent of 'tidying up' our labia or 'rejuvenating' our tired vaginas. Such unrealistic ideas about women, where you must have your bikini body back one month after giving birth to twins and skip through menstruation with no outward sign, surely have their origins in the rise and rise of pornography.

The exponential growth of computer technology has helped, of course. We have a society in which a woman who needs to be taken down a peg or two (mouthy, opinionated, not submissive) can be hunted through wi-fi to be bullied, harassed, trolled and revenge-porned into compliance. Witch-hunts these days happen through social media and the tabloid press. Women's bodies are held up for ridicule – pictures of any of their constituent parts that fail to meet the standard are published to shame and control. Punishment threats of rape and death have become commonplace and are sometimes carried out. Women can more easily be stalked and tracked. Children learn about sex through watching porn, which gives them the wrongest of wrong ideas about what constitutes normal sexual relationships.

It is perhaps, then, unsurprising that we are now witnessing an increase in violence against women. Year on year the reported crime figures demonstrate that it is a constantly evolving threat. Despite decades of progress, an increase in the platforms which give women a voice, a real empowering through education and legislation – all of which have at least nominally given women some sort of parity with men – we are still seen as somehow inferior, subjects to control rather than genuine equals.

Chapter Two

It's time I gave Franc a voice. This is the first letter he wrote to me. It arrived in an envelope, with a stamp, brought by the postman. The method of delivery was quaint, old-fashioned and romantic:

11 November

Darling Ellen,
    Thank you very much for your love letter. I enjoyed reading it . . .

He said he was looking forward to seeing me that evening and to cooking a meal for me, his 'special guest'. He wrote some hugely enjoyable but blush-making French stuff and then asked if, 'by a terrible mistake', he faxed the letter to me in my office, 'would that be a problem?'

> *Can't wait.*
> *Love, kisses and . . .*
> *Yours forever*
> *xxx*

Yours for ever, my arse – we'd known each other all of ten days. As for faxing a letter to my office, it looked like teasing but was, I know now, a gentle exploratory threat. He was testing me and I reacted exactly as he had hoped – I was horrified. I'd been in this job only two months and was still settling in.

I don't have the letter Franc is replying to, my first. Perhaps he didn't leave it behind as he did all the others, but I imagine I was responding to something he had done in the best way I knew, with written words. Knowing me it would have been an honest statement of what I felt, not especially flowery, not over-sentimental, but true. I do, however, know what he did to prompt it – he listened. We'd seen each other half a dozen times and each time he encouraged me to talk about myself. It was such a relief to tell someone about the awful time I was having that I told him where my strengths and weaknesses lay. I was completely open with a man I barely knew. Why did I trust him? Because Jeannie did. It wasn't as though he was a complete stranger I'd met in the street. He was Dave's boss and my friend's friend. Of course it was OK to trust him.

There was one other thing. That weekend he had woken me in the night, pulled me into his arms from my side of the bed and whispered, 'I need you, Ellen.' Something flared in my heart and I fell in love. That was the exact moment.

I remember talking to my close friend Nina about it. She had also met someone who might be described as 'spoken for'. I think this was the only time I voiced concern about the speed with which my feelings for Franc had deepened. After that any reservations I had seemed to melt away.

So what did I tell him about myself in that first couple of weeks? *Almost* everything.

He knew I'd been married and divorced – that's not something you can gloss over, especially not when you have three almost grown-up daughters. But I didn't, for example, tell him I had ended a long-term relationship a couple of years earlier for fear of dying of boredom. I didn't tell him about my ill-advised dalliance with a married man that summer either . . . or the Russian birthday kiss. My love life was, for the time being, off limits.

I told him that having teenagers in the house is a continually evolving crisis, but that the issues tend more towards minor than major. I confessed, bravely I thought, that I was already a grandmother. He laughed at that.

Number 1 Daughter had fallen pregnant within weeks of finishing her college course. It was quite a shock – I threw up when she told me. But then we talked about it and I said that whatever she decided to do I would support her. Nine months later I held one hand and her boyfriend held the other as she pushed my first grandchild into the world.

As soon as my grandson was born, the midwife took my arm and said, 'Don't go anywhere. I have something to show you.' She came back a few minutes later with a tiny plastic ID bracelet bearing my daughter's name. She had been my midwife seventeen years earlier, helping to deliver the baby who had grown into the young woman who had just become a mother herself. She had kept the bracelet because it had been an unusual birth of an unusual baby. We had both almost died. I hadn't been in any position to thank her at the time and so it's hard for me not to read some deeper meaning into her being exactly where she was at exactly the moment we needed her again. It was, she said, quite wonderful to see that the tiny scrap of very sick baby she had worked so hard to save was now a mother herself, tall, healthy and beautiful. And then we hugged each other and cried. It was the strangest and most amazing thing. I didn't tell Franc about that; it was far too personal.

But I did tell him that my daughter and grandson came

home to us a few days later and her boyfriend moved in too. For a while our rented house on the hill felt a bit like an episode of *The Waltons*. I thought it was a nice story, showing how we coped and held together as a family. It showed I was a good mother.

I told Franc, too, how it all came crashing down and we had to leave. Our elderly landlord became ill and his niece, with one eye on her inheritance, served us notice to quit. We loved that house, and thought we'd be there for ever.

I told him about the practical difficulties of finding a new home for us that would come even close to the one we were leaving. I was very upfront about struggling to find something we could afford on my income. The problem with renting your home is that when your landlord decides to have the house back you aren't given much time to find a new one. That narrows your options considerably.

Then I told him about a happy thing, which was also a bit sad – Number 1 Daughter married her boyfriend the following spring and they moved into their own home. I told him about the peculiar loneliness I felt sitting by myself at the top table amongst the groom's family.

I explained that our new landlord had asked how I would feel if he moved back into his house, with us – my two younger daughters and me. This felt wrong. Why would he want to do that? I decided I didn't like or trust him so I put my foot down and, just like that, he decided we had to leave. We'd only been there six months.

Now we were living in our third home in a year – a cramped two-bedroomed house on a new estate. We all hated it, but it was the only thing available, and it did at least have the benefit of being in the right place for schools, friends and shops. Most importantly, it was affordable.

We'd only been there a couple of weeks when, out of the blue, my ex-husband reappeared after an absence of eight years. It wasn't as if he'd been looking for us; his reappearance was pure chance. Number 1 Daughter was at a local garage when she spotted him. 'That's my dad,' she said to her husband.

He followed my ex-husband into the kiosk and asked him, 'Are you—?'

'Who wants to know?'

'Because if you are that's your daughter sitting in that car over there.'

He hadn't even recognized her.

When she told me, I felt the fabric of our lives tearing again. She hadn't wanted to mention the encounter because she didn't want to hurt me, knowing that even after all this time I would still feel the sting. She had, though, told her sisters and they wanted my blessing to pick up contact with him. They knew I would give it. He was their father. They – and he – had every right to see one another. Our eight years' exclusion from his life hadn't been my choice and I felt he owed them something. We'd weathered so much together but I knew, I just knew, that this would be the end of us as we were, as a family. The time we'd had, growing together and being happy, was coming to an end.

It was a nasty shock and one I certainly didn't tell Franc about. It felt too soon.

But while we were cuddled up on his sofa I did tell Franc how my life seemed to be turning into a series of leaps from one frying pan into another. I had to tell him that. I wanted him to think I needed him but, of course, he already knew that. Everybody needs to be needed, though, don't they?

I told him about how I had been earning a living, that my

income came from several freelance jobs. One of them was as a bank secretary at one of the city hospitals, which was how I knew Jeannie. This was the job with the biggest and most reliable wage packet and I enjoyed it enormously. I'd recently applied for – and got – a permanent secretarial post there. All that was by way of explaining how I'd come to meet him. Wasn't that lucky? I finished my tale of woe determinedly upbeat with a big smile which said, And now there is lovely you so everything will be all right.

*

Looking back at my stash of work papers tells me something I had forgotten – that I was *invited* to apply for the role when no suitable candidate had emerged from the formal recruitment process. The invitation came from Doreen Milson, who would become my line manager – the same Doreen who told me I could do no more for my 'kids'. At the time I remember feeling intense relief at the promise of some necessary security: holiday pay, sick pay, regular hours . . . such riches. Thinking about it now, this invitation and where it came from should have sounded alarm bells – I'd heard rumours – but I didn't stop to think about that. Stability was what we needed and stability was what I would provide.

Much later, I recalled one of my colleagues mentioning that working on site was a lot different from freelancing, adding something vague about office politics. Office politics are a given, we all know that. But had I known then what I know now I might have made a different decision – although my choices at the time were pretty limited, by which I mean I didn't have any.

Looking through my old diaries I see a woman who in spite of a shitload of catastrophe was doggedly persevering, organized and more or less on top of it all. This surprises me, because I came to believe that I was an accident waiting to happen.

In fact, despite everything being a bit seat-of-the-pants at times there is steady common-sense neatness about the entries. I've marked down Number 1 Daughter's antenatal appointments. There are entries for school timetables, sports days, parents' evenings, concerts and exams, periods. I have a regular appointment at the hairdresser and occasionally I have a facial or a manicure. I have a social life and I'm running a very efficient parent taxi service. I know precisely when my TV licence quarterly payment of £25 was due. My father came to stay for a weekend and the rugby Six Nations championship is marked down with the scores. Pets go to the vets. I take the children and their friends to see *Jurassic Park* and *Independence Day* at the multiplex twenty miles away. The girls go to parties. I drive all over the place in my old blue Metro following up on commissions for wedding dresses, evening gowns and hand-painted murals, and collecting freelance secretarial work – the hours I've worked on the various jobs are meticulously itemized. My blood pressure, unsurprisingly, is a tad on the high side (it still is) but I am across everything – on it like a bonnet. I am lost in admiration for forty-three-year-old me. And dismayed at what I know is coming.

What my diaries don't show is how I felt the very second I woke up at the start of each day, even before opening my eyes – the knotted stomach, hands curled tight into fists, the gut-crunching terror that everything would unravel. The family doctor had prescribed antidepressants to help me cope but still every hour of every day was lived in fear of a blow that would finally finish us off. It wouldn't take much. That fear left me vulnerable.

In fact it took three blows to do the job. The first was the reappearance of my ex-husband. The second came much sooner than I had anticipated and it brought me to my knees.

When I got home on Sunday evening after my third (lovely) Saturday night with Franc, Number 3 Daughter told me straight out. Some things are so terrible there is no other way to tell them.

'Sally's dead.'

Sally was a close friend to my girls, almost an honorary daughter. This couldn't be right. She was only a teenager – teenage girls did not suddenly die. I made her say it again in case it wasn't true.

'Sally's dead.'

I recall slipping down to the floor and folding up in a corner, my back against the wall. My daughter tucked herself in next to me and we held each other for a very long time. We were too shocked to cry.

There had been a car accident – Sally in the front with the driver, Sally's friend sitting in the back. The car had been going too fast, caught the kerb on a corner, flipped over and as the rear window burst outwards the friend in the back went with it and into a thick hedge, which saved her life. She told us later she remembered picking things up – a shoe, a CD, a bag – as she walked back through the rain to the over-turned vehicle. She looked inside but Sally wasn't there. She was some way off, lying in the road. That was the moment she knew.

I needed to round us all up, get the wagons in a circle, know my girls were all safe. How could I have been away for a whole twenty-four hours? Bad mother. Where was Number 2 Daughter? Did she know? No mobile phone, no contact, a void. With the reappearance of her father she had wanted her own space away from our tiny cramped home and the fractious hole he'd punched through our lives. At seventeen she was staying with her boyfriend's family. She was close enough for me to keep an eye on her and I'd thought we were OK but now I didn't know where she was. They were all so close – this little group of friends. They'd grown up together. I didn't know what to do. What *could* I do? What did I do? I can't remember.

On Monday morning we did our best to carry on as normal. All the young people who'd known Sally wanted to be together and their school provided the support for their sorrow. I was content that that was the right place for them to be. I went to work but left at lunchtime on compassionate leave, too distraught to concentrate. I drove back to see my friend Quinn, an artist and a New Yorker who lived on the road where Sally had died. Quinn was eighty and I wanted to break the news to him myself, for this heavy blow to fall gently. He knew us well, we were close and I loved him dearly.

'Oh, pet lamb. You're all beat up. Come in. Come in.' He had a rumbling, cigarette-roughened voice. He told me he had seen the blue lights from the emergency services on Saturday night but had not known they were for Sally. Grateful that I'd come to tell him myself, he made me sit down, opened a bottle of vodka and we held a two-person wake. That was Quinn – always the right words, always knowing what was needed. It was Quinn I turned to at this desperate time – not Franc. I didn't feel I knew him well enough yet.

Sally's funeral was the following Friday. Our instructions were to wear something she had liked with as many birds as possible. I'd been to see her mother and father, sitting on their sofa and trying but failing to find the right words. Her mum told me she hadn't known Sally had a tattoo until she'd seen her at the hospital and noticed the tiny bird inked onto the side of her foot. It matched the one on Number 2 Daughter's foot – they'd had them done together in secret. I remember still not believing what had happened, even as I held the order of service in my hand, even when the coffin, smothered in white flowers, came into the sunlit church. I remember the courage and steadiness of Sally's parents and her brother, of a tight group of battered young friends. I remember dear, lovely Quinn, who I'd never seen in anything but jeans and a T-shirt, wearing a suit – pinstripe, *circa* 1945 from the look of it. When the vicar began the service by talking about God's great plan, he muttered, 'Bullshit,' and I squeezed his hand. Afterwards we stood on the churchyard path, smoked cigarettes and talked.

What happened next is fogged in my memory. A friend invited me over for lunch and managed to give me food poisoning with an overripe pheasant. The following day I was weak and fragile and my daughters needed me so I didn't go over to Franc's until Sunday – a whole week since I'd last seen him. Others having a claim on my time seemed to have irritated him, but I chose to see this as an outward manifestation of his need for me. I called him a heartless bastard, although I said it with a smile. A warm hug of a letter arrived for me by post the following week. It was dated 23 November.

The letter began with his usual 'Darling Ellen', and in it he told me that he had enjoyed spending Sunday with me 'even if it ended . . . well . . . you know'. He said he understood how I felt because he had been 'in the same situation'. He said he would do his best to take care of me and make me happy and he ended by saying that he couldn't wait to see me again, to kiss me and hold me and 'well, this is it'. He signed it,

Your lovely irresistible bastard.

How did our Sunday end? Once I started crying I found I couldn't stop.

Two days after Sally's funeral my youngest had her fifteenth birthday. My diary tells me that we did what she wanted most – had a takeaway, watched a video and went shopping – proper Mummy-and-sister time. Then she had some proper Daddy time – weekend visits had quickly become part of our routine. I never saw him because he picked her up on the corner of the street. Though this was painful I thought it was right. They had a lot of time to make up. I especially thought this when she came home with the CAT boots she had been longing for but which I couldn't afford.

Our family was fragmenting and a treacherous vacuum forming in the spaces between – spaces into which Franc slipped with nonchalant ease. I saw him three times that week and he deftly changed the subject whenever I began to talk about Sally.

After a week – on 30 November – he sent me a fax at work. I wasn't sure about this but Jeannie, whose desk was beside the fax machine, was also receiving one, two and sometimes three faxes from Dave almost every day. And he worked with Franc. Jeannie said not to worry, so I didn't.

At the moment I can't fax you for one hour (or more) as usual. So just a quicky one.

Then he phoned and asked me to book a restaurant in my neck of the woods for the following night. I remember he picked me up in his car – a proper date – and over dinner we talked about him. He told me how when he'd moved from France he'd spent the first two weeks staying in a motel room and how lonely he'd felt. He told me about arranging with Jeannie's boyfriend, Dave, to rent a house he owned and how

lonely he'd felt there too. What he didn't tell me was why he
was here in the first place or why he took a job so far from
home. Then he told me that Sophie, his fiancée, was coming
over to spend the weekend with him – *that* weekend, so obviously I couldn't be there. He was very matter-of-fact about it
but understood that I felt hurt, despite pointing out that it
wasn't as though he hadn't been straight with me. He even
tried one of his jokes. He said he'd had to make a thorough
search of the house for my long red hair. I was a nuisance and
moulted like a bitch, he said, smiling and pleased that he knew
the English word for a female dog. I laughed too. When he
took me home, Aerosmith's 'I Don't Want to Miss a Thing'
was playing on the car radio and he held my hand tightly all
the way. Then he drove back to his empty, lonely house. The
way I felt when he left me hadn't been part of the deal I had
made with myself when I first met him.

Years later, the wreckage Franc left behind contained several of my letters to him including this one, written the day
after the 'Sophie' dinner:

2 December

My darling Franc

 I wanted to write to you again before the weekend . . .
I want, if I can, to explain to you how I really feel about you.
That way there can be no doubts, on my part or yours, and
you will know exactly what you mean to me, which I hope will
help you to sort things out in your mind.

 For me this is a very difficult situation, as I know it is for
you too, and it seems even more strange to be writing to you
like this when I have only known you for such a relatively short
time. However, we are both adults and as such we should know
our own minds . . .

I really look forward to seeing you and, like you, it feels as though the time we spend together is too short. We have so much to talk about, being so similar we would, we are never short of conversation. It doesn't matter what we do or where we go, being with you is a constant delight and I love it. You are a kindred spirit. A lot of the things you do and the way you do them are exactly the same as the things I do when I am at home . . .

I feel for you this weekend and, because I am a little selfish, I feel somewhat hurt and confused myself. I will deal with it but when I think you might go away from me . . .

You asked me if I was sure I loved you, I hope this letter answers the question for you. You also asked me to say what I was thinking. I hope this letter does that too.

I do not know Sophie and I do not know what is, or has been, between you. I cannot hate her or say bad things about her but I am jealous, I can't help that.

It IS too soon to decide anything . . .

Please try not to hurt me, Franc, I feel things very deeply and I feel very vulnerable over the way I feel about you. I would risk or give up a great deal for you.

Helen xxx

I can't understand why I said any of this.

But reading between the lines tells me quite a lot about Franc and his methods. I sound measured and a little formal – perhaps mirroring him (wanting him to like me). I have played down my own hurt at a fairly brutal disappointment and I have called us 'kindred spirits'. I have hinted at what I feel but held back from expressing it. Franc has played the 'alone' card and I have empathized because I am alone too, not in the sense of having no one – I have several good and trusted friends as well as my children – but because my circumstances at the time are isolating. Franc is making it him and me against the world. He is making himself my ally and events in my life have conspired to help him. I have said I am 'selfish' but at the same time it sounds like an apology – 'I'm sorry I feel this way but . . .' when in fact I have every right to feel concerned for myself. I have suffered enormous loss, a terrible shock, and my family life is balanced on a knife-edge.

It is unfortunate that Franc happened along at precisely that moment. It wasn't simply that I was naive – I was caught up in a series of personal crises, exhausted and distracted. I was looking for someone to prop me up and he was there, so as a default I cast him in the role of rescuer. Given that was exactly how he saw himself, he was more than happy to oblige.

I thought I knew who I was but it turns out I didn't know myself nearly well enough, or at all. Perhaps that's the question – not 'how' but 'who'. When I met Franc, who was I? To understand your present and future you have to know your past. In my quest to understand the woman I was and am, I have to know the girl.

*

I was a people pleaser, always have been. It was only when I reached my late fifties that I made an effort to put a stop to that nonsense but it's proving surprisingly difficult – what you might call 'work in progress'. Ingrained habits – like nail biting, eyebrow pulling, hair twiddling, chewing my bottom lip and saying 'yes' when I mean to say 'no' – are the deep-rooted knotweed of my psyche. Performing my womanly duty of making sure that everyone is happy, that I get a great big beaming smile and a 'well *done*' at least once a day, was something I assimilated into myself without protest or question and it became an excuse for not asking what *I* really wanted . . . me. My life was a carrot-and-stick exercise, which narrowed my outlook and made me no more self-reliant than one of Pavlov's dogs. Along with so many of my generation I was coached, disciplined and moulded into that most desirable of creatures – an eager-to-please, biddable young girl who would grow into a woman whose most fervent wish in life was to not draw attention to herself ('don't show off, darling') or to offend anyone, ever. I learned to keep any disobliging thoughts to myself, or I'd squash myself into the family dog's basket and confess all to her (she was wonderfully discreet). If I'm angry now it's because I have realized far too late that I seem to have spent a great deal of my life striving to live up to the expectations of others and I did this without even thinking about it, complicit in my own mediocrity. That thought and the fact that for much of the time I have failed are profoundly distressing. It feels like a shocking waste.

But then people don't always tell you when something has gone wrong. I didn't know, for instance, that my father wanted to disown me after my divorce when I changed from my married name to my mother's maiden name rather than the family name. I did it with the best of intentions – my mother was the last of our Walmsley-Johnsons and I wanted to preserve the name and her memory a little longer. I only found out about the offence it caused (but not why) in a late-night pub conversation with my older brother while our father was slowly slipping away from us in a hospice. It was a painful thing to hear at a painful time and I wasn't able to contain a small sob. My brother, embarrassed, excused himself until I'd regained my self-control. The men in my family have always been contemptuous of feminine tears.

For twenty-five years I'd had no idea and yet it explained

a lot, made sense of some distances and coolness. That said I still don't understand it. There is, I am sure, some other long-forgotten thing connected to the name but nobody ever talked or talks about it. I can't carry the blame for something I didn't know about (an unknown unknown) and yet it nags – a conspicuous, if unconscious, failure to please on my part, an extra parcel to add to the burden of a lifetime's guilt for not being perfect. It hurts. It shouldn't but it does.

I have a photograph of a smiling little girl in a frilly frock, a wreath of flowers in tightly curled hair, carrying a posy. Standing in a snowy churchyard I am a bridesmaid at the wedding of my parents' friends. It's a black-and-white picture but I remember the dress was pale yellow and it had a little cluster of silk flowers at the waist, trailing ribbons, and the skirt stuck out just like my mum's favourite star-sprinkled navy one. I think that was 1960 or '61 and I still love pale yellow and lilac together. And sticky-out skirts that rustle when I walk . . . and heels that tap . . . and stars. I am happy because everyone else is happy and this is what little girls are supposed to do and be – a credit to their parents. An early success in the art of pleasing but at a cost: I was freezing cold, the dress prickled and for most of the time I was bored silly.

Ten years or so later I am a bridesmaid again and this time my dress is burnt-orange Crimplene with a high lace collar and bib. It is fitted over the bust and then flared to ankle length. My hair, long by now, has been teased and back-combed and sprayed and with the addition of not one but two hairpieces it is piled high on my head and has a large velvet bow pinned at the back. And ringlets. It feels like hell. Again the dress prickles and again I am freezing cold and bored silly only this time I don't put up with it because I am a teenager. As soon as I am reasonably sure it won't cause offence I take down my hateful crispy hair and change into something I like better. Every time that photograph comes out I get, 'Do you remember that? You were a right little madam.' I still think ringlets are ridiculous and I hate Crimplene to this day, although over time I've found it in my heart to forgive burnt orange. I didn't enjoy the feeling that I'd let everybody down. On the whole, I decided, I preferred it when everyone was happy and pleased with me.

When I was thirteen, my French teacher had the bright idea of teaching us a song – in French, obviously. Once we'd all had a jolly lesson singing together, she decided to go around the class at random and whomever she chose would stand up and sing one verse, solo. She picked me first and I refused out of shyness so she made me stand up for the rest of the lesson *pour encourager les autres*. It was a summer's day, we were in a Portakabin and it was very hot. The sun streamed through the windows, chalk dust drifted and danced. I remember my skin prickling and sweating; I was sure everybody could tell I had my period. Every so often she would turn to me and ask again and each time I shook my head, mute with embarrassment, and disappeared into a towering, shaming blush. I've never been able to sing in public since, and in church I mime. In fact, any kind of performance has me reaching for the sick bucket, which makes taking to the stage professionally at various points in my life really very surprising. It was a game effort to beat the handicap. Eventually, though, I had to stop on account of the vomiting.

That French teacher wasn't the first to render me incapable of functioning. Chadwick, Chadfield and 'Sparky' preceded her – a sequence of maths teachers so terrifying that I've been number blind ever since. At one point I persuaded my mother to cut off all my long hair in the touching belief that Chadwick wouldn't recognize me in the next day's mental arithmetic class: 'And what's *your* name, new little girl?' Aside from being shit at maths, a large part of my confusion was that what I was being asked to do ran in direct contradiction to everything I'd been taught about being a girl. I was so inculcated with the rule of not drawing attention to myself that I became effectively paralysed when all eyes were, legitimately, focused on me.

When Franc and I had been together for a few months I began to brush up my French. I had an idea that he would be pleased if I was able to chatter away to him in his own language. The first time I tried it he hooted with laughter, rather unkindly I thought. He said my accent was '*tragique*'. I misheard him and thought he'd said '*très chic*'. It was awful. My throat closed up and my larynx froze when he explained my mistake and I never uttered as much as a '*bonjour*' to him ever again.

These are unhappy things. Some of it is, of course, about good manners and being kind and considerate to others but quite a lot of it isn't about that – it's about choice. I didn't choose not to stand up and sing; I didn't choose to be a brides-maid, I didn't choose to upset my father when I changed my name. I *did* choose to get married although I knew even as I was doing it that it was a very bad idea. I *did* choose to sleep with Franc on our first date and he chose to do that too, which makes it a bit rich that he brought it up in almost every argu-ment we ever had – 'I wish you hadn't done that, Ellen' – as though I was a tart and he had nothing to do with it. I didn't choose to get myself raped by a work colleague in 1976 but I *did* choose to go back to a dinner date's house in 2002 and then I chose to go along with what came next because it seemed to be the safest option, and anyway I had only myself to blame.

As I go through life I sort of hope my choices will be understood and that I will be forgiven for an occasional blunder because blunders happen to everyone. Most choices are fine but some are a little bit wrong and others catastrophic. So what? I'm quite philosophical about my mistakes now but there wasn't really room for failure and human error when I was growing up. It's taken me a lifetime to understand and embrace the concept of 'freedom to fail'. The first time someone said that to me I nearly fell over: 'You mean it's OK to get it *wrong*?' Getting it wrong certainly wasn't the philosophy in my family. I was pushed and pushed to be better, to be perfect, to be an exemplary young woman, and all my girlfriends were pushed too. It must have been an awful shock to my parents when I reached my teenage years and hit back – they must have felt as though they had an alien in the house. It's not that I was particularly wild – a good many of my school friends were far worse. I was always the one to wimp out if things looked like they were getting too lairy, although I did (don't we all) get outrageously drunk one night; that was down to inexperience and I discovered that drinking whisky and cider together in a pint glass will always end badly. Many years later I learned that my paternal grandfather had been a violent alcoholic but no one thought to mention it at the time – I expect from shame – even though it would have brought understanding. I flouted my 10.30 p.m. curfew (obviously). I started smoking (badge of honour in the early '70s). I had boyfriends (mostly unsuitable). But I remained a top-stream grammar-school girl (playing down my academic achievements to boys because they didn't like swots) and a virgin, earmarked by my headmistress for Oxford. Not that much of a lost cause then.

The last time I got a good hiding was when I was fifteen. I don't remember what I'd done but I was in my bedroom with my Marc Bolan posters, my Dansette record player and the blue-and-silver psychedelic flowers I'd painted over my wardrobe doors. I remember my father's rage and the stinging red handprints on my leg; I also remember him then turning and putting his fist through my bedroom door. I was terrified and whatever it was, it was all of it *my* fault. But I didn't cry. All I wanted for a long time afterwards was to have everything happy and normal again, for all the tension and terse conversations to be over. Not that my father was habitually violent – he wasn't – but he and I shared the same red-headed temper, quick to flare but equally quick to subside. It was more usual for Dad *in extremis* to walk slowly down the garden, thoughtfully pick up a rake and then break it over his knee. Afterwards he'd sit behind the greenhouse for thirty minutes or so; pipe smoke would be seen curling upward – like a papal signifier that all was well. When he reappeared the crisis would be over. Having said that, I remember a good walloping with the back of a hairbrush for climbing up onto the porch roof and not being able to get down again. I can see the house and the porch and I can see my father reaching up to lift me down. To then be roundly spanked gave a bit of a mixed message. I was five years old.

At one point in my fifties I tried seeing a psychotherapist because I thought it might help me to deal with a few things that had been bothering me. When she asked me how I felt about having a violent father I was furious. 'My father was *not* violent!' I yelled. Then I walked out and never went back.

It's too easy and frankly, lazy, to apply our enlightened early twenty-first-century awareness to events that happened decades or centuries before. I was angry with my therapist because I remember my childhood as a broadly happy one but I grew up in an age when corporal punishment still existed in schools and if, as a child, you transgressed you could expect and would probably receive six of the best – 'the best' referring to the strength and efficiency of the administering member of staff's downswing. Inside the home punishment was usually physical too. 'Wait until your father gets home,' was what mothers said to their disobedient children, imprinting the message that discipline fell within the sphere of male responsibility. Women were not allowed to hit but men were. If it was decided that the man in the family should beat you then you took it as fair punishment, without complaint. It was, as they say, a different time. These punishments were only outlawed in the United Kingdom's state-run schools in 1986 and in private schools in 1998. A parent is still perfectly entitled to smack their child – just as long as no implement is used or bruises left. The difficulty comes with individuals deciding what constitutes bad behaviour and what constitutes 'reasonable punishment'.[1] Bearing those two parental curbs in mind, it's not too hard to see how with some people, the issue of not leaving bruises becomes less of a restriction and more of an invitation to use their imagination.

Calling up these memories reminds me that much about the 1970s was troubling. Often described as 'the decade taste forgot', for those of us facing our transition to adulthood it was a decade forgotten by a lot of other things too. It also marked a deep fracture between the inhibiting values of our parents and a new and freer society. My internal fault line juddered up and down like a tectonic plate.

On one hand girls had the mind-boggling possibilities of second-wave feminism, women's lib and freedom, but on the other we had the status quo very much reinforced by the

---

1. Children Act 2004, Section 58.

magazines we read, the media and culture in general. The world, our world, was still run by men – which perhaps goes some way to explaining why the Equal Pay Act passed into law in 1970 but didn't actually take effect until 1975, men being in charge of legislation – and they told us what to think. I loved the idea of feminism but anti-feminist propaganda, and especially the right-wing press, informed me that all feminists, without exception, were unfeminine, or lesbians – or both – and it wasn't desirable to be either if you wanted men to like you, which of course you did because men were your future security and not having one to look after you was, as we were told, *ad nauseam*, unthinkable.

There were no female editors of national newspapers, and in 1973 at the BBC fewer than 6 per cent of senior posts were held by women. Women's magazines were still overwhelmingly concerned with domestic matters and appearance – girls' magazines were junior versions of the same. *Woman's Own* dealt with life after marriage, *Jackie* with life before it. Having a boyfriend was your A+ at being a girl and a husband the ultimate endorsement of your 'empowering' femininity.

The 'Cathy & Claire' problem page in *Jackie* magazine (which I loved) shows how innocent we were. I wouldn't have had the faintest idea what to do in the unlikely event of finding myself alone in a room with Marc Bolan but I hoped he would, which casts an interesting – and sinister – complexion on the centuries-old 'men take the initiative and women are passive' train of thought. It's still funny to look back on the things that concerned our teenage selves but with hindsight (that word again) I can see how really, seriously, unhelpful it was. There is a deceptively innocent gloss over everything because for all we are told it wasn't a remotely innocent time but a very dangerous one. Young girls were sent out into the world as ready-made victims, clutching tightly to their Playtex Cross-Your-Hearts a mixture of fairy-tale romance, the rewards of domesticity and the necessity of finding a boyfriend to take charge. For the more adventurous there was *Cosmopolitan*, which spoke of the excitement of female sexual liberation, but no one told us about the darker side to all this and how to protect our naive selves from predatory men. 'Free love' was neither free nor love but sex without responsibility for men. We were only 50 per cent equipped to deal with real life and extremely vulnerable. Feminists did explain about male shortcomings but these were the same feminists who were condemned for having hairy armpits, burning their bras, being 'man-haters' and in some way unnatural. Germaine Greer was obviously held up as 'chief witch' and an example of what women should *not* be, but in the provincial Midlands I would no more have been seen reading a copy of *The Female Eunuch* as walk down the street naked. Such balancing influences, however radical, were therefore limited. It is the oldest trick in the book to pillory a woman for 'transgressing' (look at what they did to Joan of Arc) and in the 1970s the majority of us fell for it because we didn't know any better, so the status quo remained just that.

As it was, in the 1970s, to be a woman or a girl was to be at daily risk of a groping or worse. In my first job barely a week passed without an uncomfortable encounter with the office sex pest and his perpetually wandering hands. New girls were warned not to attempt the filing without a winger. We laughed uncomfortably about him to diminish his horribleness but when he found out he became much worse. He wouldn't have lasted five minutes in today's work environment but in 1973 none of us breathed a word because that was the way it was then. Women and their wiles were invariably seen as being at fault in matters relating to men and sex, an assumption that had barely changed in five hundred years. Men were helpless should they encounter a woman wearing a short skirt or a low-cut top or, God forbid, hot pants. You reported an assault or a rape at your peril. Assuming anyone did believe you, you could then expect to have your private life held up for scrutiny with an implication that you had done something to deserve it. As if anyone would deserve that.

In 1986, in her own home at St Mary's vicarage in Ealing, London, twenty-one-year-old Jill Saward suffered a horrifying gang rape during a burglary. Her father and boyfriend were beaten and tied up in another room. The case became notorious not just for the nature and violence of the crime but for the way it was handled both by the media and by the judiciary. Just a few days after the event, the *Sun* newspaper, edited at the time by Kelvin MacKenzie (yes, *him*), published a photograph of Jill Saward, which obscured only her eyes and effectively revealed her identity. He asserted that a rape victim only earned the right to anonymity once a suspect had been charged. When the case came to trial a year later the presiding judge, John Leonard, gave longer sentences for the burglary than for the rape, telling the men involved, 'Because I have been told the trauma suffered by the victim was not so great, I shall take a lenient course with you,' a comment for which he later apologized. His remarks would have been disgusting applied to any rape case but Jill Saward had been a virgin at the time of the attack. Given that this was how such crimes were regarded then, it is little wonder that rape and sexual assault were massively under-reported. They still are.

That said, *reported* violent crime against women is, at the time of writing, at record levels. Domestic abuse, rape and sexual assaults have risen by almost 10 per cent, stalking prosecutions by just over 7 per cent, child sex abuse by 15.4 per cent, and a 32 per cent rise in cases involving the sending of grossly indecent or offensive messages. There have been 206 cases of revenge pornography,[1] a relatively new addition to the abuse lexicon. All of which begs the question of what a true picture would look like. Recent reports suggest it is even uglier than we might have thought:

— Since the publication of Her Majesty's Inspectorate of Constabulary, Fire and Rescue Services' (HMICFRS') first thematic report on domestic abuse, *Everyone's Business*, in March 2014, recorded crimes of domestic abuse have increased by 61 per cent (12 months to 31 August 2013 compared to 12 months to 30 June 2016).[2]
— The approximate number of women raped in England and Wales every year is 85,000 (which works out at roughly eleven every hour).[3]

More worrying still is the rise in the number of young women experiencing controlling behaviour in a relationship,[4] which the domestic abuse charity Refuge says is one in two. Is it just that we're more aware of what constitutes abuse and can put a name to it? But if we are then why are so many women suffering in this way and why are so many of them

1. Crown Prosecution Service, *Violence Against Women and Girls* (VAWG) *Crime Report*, 2016.
2. Her Majesty's Inspectorate of Constabulary, Fire and Rescue Services, *A progress report on the police response to domestic abuse* (November 2017), p. 4.
3. Ministry of Justice/Office for National Statistics/Home Office, *An Overview of Sexual Offending in England and Wales*, 2013.
4. Refuge and Avon UK, 'Define the Line' study (March 2017): https://www.refuge.org.uk/our-work/affecting-change/campaigns/define-the-line/

young women? Why do so many of us still ask if what we are experiencing is actually abuse? Today, we are more educated about what's OK and what's not, so you would think we'd know how to avoid it, how to be less vulnerable, less susceptible, less easily trapped. Yet it's not the case, and the reality seems to suggest that we haven't come very far at all in terms of raising awareness and at the very least substantially reducing the number of cases. How can we make people understand that not all abuse is measured in bruises?

Chapter Three

At the beginning of December – the weekend Sophie was staying with Franc – I drove to Heathrow to collect a friend who had been working in New York for a few months. She had lent me her car and I owed her a favour so at least my mind was on things other than love triangles. A week later Number 2 Daughter came home. I gave her the bedroom that had been mine and moved my duvet onto the sofa, which I finished up sharing with the dog and an assortment of cats. These were the pets which had been part of our established happy lives in the old farmhouse where space and country-side for walking were not an issue. That way of life did not fit easily into an estate semi with two tiny bedrooms and a postage-stamp garden. Everything felt wrong, and I didn't have a clue what to do about it, or the strength to do it.

Then the third blow fell: our new landlord, the third in eighteen months, put our rented house up for sale. We still had unpacked boxes from the last move. Aside from the obvious upheaval and disruption, the problem with moving so often between rented properties is the expense and I was broke. I'd sold my old Mini to help pay for the last move. I had nothing left to cash in.

Over the next few days, a workable solution emerged: Franc said I could stay with him during the week and Jeannie (who lived a short distance away and drove to work) would give me a lift every morning. That meant I could keep my job and my income for the time being at least. As a temporary measure it wasn't perfect but it would do. I even had a Plan B: if the house sold quickly before I had time to find another, then Number 2 Daughter said she would stay with her boyfriend's family again and Number 3 Daughter would stay with Number 1 Daughter or her father. Friends offered to board our pets until we sorted ourselves out. We just had to weather the storm. Franc even offered to clear a corner of his company's warehouse so that we could store our stuff, free of charge, if push came to shove.

Although we'd known each other for only six weeks, I already thought of Franc as a friend and ally. Whenever I needed something there he was. I remembered a line from my O-Level English Lit, about Gabriel Oak in *Far From the Madding Crowd*: 'And at home by the fire, whenever you look up there I shall be – and whenever I look up, there will be you.' I thought, I love this man who knows what to do, who is considerate and strong and can put things right again without complaint. When Franc took charge everything was fine, better than fine.

His weekend with Sophie had been, he said, a disaster. He couldn't have sex with her because all he could think about was his 'Ellen', and he was on the point of finishing with her. He said he liked the house better with me in it.

I said, 'I love you, Franc.'

I might as well have painted a target on my back.

As I spent more time with Franc, I began to notice little details about him. He liked things to be a certain way, for example. That was fine, I like things a certain way too, I can't think of many people who don't. Dizzy with relief I did my best to make things lovely for him.

I noticed too that his sense of humour was a little out of whack but I put that down to cultural differences – people from different countries laugh at different things. It made sense that a French sense of humour would be different from an English one. That said, I wasn't very keen on his jokes about taking me on as a housekeeper, but I didn't say anything. He liked to have dinner ready at a specific time, which was OK because my dad had been the same. He said he hated onions and garlic (unusual), which meant that our meals were, for me, a bit bland but I worked around it and made a joke of my own: this Frenchman is broken – please send one that works. I liked walking around with bare feet but he said it was dirty and insisted that I wore slippers. He liked to know what he was going to do at the weekend by Thursday at the latest so I would draw up a schedule, bearing in mind that he wanted to see something of the UK. He didn't enjoy being at home all day. I began to worry about that, in case I suggested something he didn't like; not that it should matter but I preferred it when he came up with some ideas of his own rather than leaving it all to me.

Going along with all this wasn't even a conscious decision. I just allowed it to happen because I am by nature quite easy-going – and I was happy when I was with him. It's the simplest thing in the world to drift on life's currents, especially when we feel contented. Neuroscientists tell us that our unconscious brain orchestrates everything we do – you and I might refer to it as being 'on autopilot'. When I think about that I realize there are things I do out of habit, but not out of *my* habit. There are little triggers that spark actions. I haven't been able to stop lining up cans in the cupboard with the labels facing outward. I can't sleep if the bedroom curtains aren't hanging straight. I can cope with stuff like that. I can't cope with staying in other people's houses because every morning that I wake up in a strange house I want to cry and when I do it in front of people it's awkward and embarrassing. It happened once when I went to my dad's for Christmas. I almost did it staying at my boss's house. I don't even think about it; it's a kind of reflex, as though somewhere inside my head a button has been pushed. I know what it is now – it's anxiety. Panic. And I know who put it there but it took a long time to work it out because I'd just got used to it. Abuse sets its roots slowly and over time they go deep.

At the beginning of our relationship I did think about what I was doing but it was more of a 'This isn't really my thing but we love each other, right?' and wanting to make things perfect. I told myself it was just Franc being Franc and I felt very much in his debt. On the other hand, there's something about going around with an attractive French guy that puts you on a bit of a pedestal. I felt a little guilty about enjoying that. After a long time of nobody even considering me, I was suddenly in possession of something covetable. I'd forgotten what that felt like.

In the second week of December, Franc took me shopping – he said he wanted to buy me something nice to wear for Christmas. Where I would usually creep in and hope no one noticed me, he walked into a smart shop as though he owned the place. I hated that moment when a sales assistant appears at your elbow and you feel like a fraud because you're sure they know you can't afford anything, but there was none of that with Franc. He went along the rails and picked things out for me. Then he sent me into the changing rooms with instructions to come out wearing each one to show him how it looked. While I did that, feeling a bit hot and embarrassed, he pulled over a chair and sat there, holding court. Staff fussed around him, returning clothes to racks and showing him things they thought might suit me. I'd never seen anything like it – it was less a shopping trip and more a takeover. Nobody asked me what I wanted, though I suppose it was a mercy because I hadn't the faintest idea.

In the end we, or rather Franc, settled on a midnight-blue evening coat. It had long sleeves, a Nehru collar and was fastened with a row of tiny silver buttons. It was elegant and gorgeous but utterly impractical – I mean, I could hardly go to work in it. In the car I slid my hand into the bag and stroked the velvety softness, as I would one of my cats.

Then, when we got home, Franc said, 'Let's have a *défilé*.'

'A what?'

'A fashion show. You show me your things and put them on. I tell you whether to keep them or not. You have terrible clothes. You need to organize.'

Coming from a well-dressed Frenchman this seemed an entirely reasonable thing to say. By now I'd got quite a lot of clothes hanging in a wardrobe at Franc's place so this took some time. I went along with it a bit sheepishly but quite happy because he was showing an interest and he'd just bought me that beautiful coat and I liked dressing up. I don't think anyone had done anything like that for me before. My last Christmas present from my husband had been an unsolicited garden hose.

At the time I had a fondness for slightly hippyish, off-the-wall stuff. Most of it was cheap, but pretty. There was a forest-green full skirt edged with tiny silver bells that tinkled when I walked (which the girls liked because they could hear me coming), tie-dye T-shirts, Doc Marten boots, a pink-and-blue patchwork dress that reminded me of one I'd had in the '70s . . . all of these went onto Franc's reject pile. I sacrificed it all for the blue velvet evening coat and possible future treats of a similar nature, and was left with a sad, boring little heap of the conservative stuff I wore to work where I had to conform. Although there was one dress – navy and covered in tiny white stars – that I stuffed secretly into the back of a drawer because it reminded me of my mum's favourite, the one with the nipped-in waist that rustled when she walked.

He didn't have to explain. I understood that the way I looked was important to him and that there was also room for improvement. I was painfully aware of that. Before my divorce I used to make a lot of my own clothes, which meant I could dress well with originality. I owned things no one else had, and though I missed that I no longer had the time or money. I liked the compliments that came with it and I wanted those from Franc – affirmation that I was attractive and worth a second look. I wanted the sudden flash of a smile, the one that came with, 'Ellen, you are beautiful.' When he said that, I would glow. I spent cash I couldn't afford on a new dress – black, fitted, sophisticated – and he wrote to me:

> *You looked stunning and I feel sorry we ended up in Pizza Hut – and . . . for me it was not so bad, was it?*

He said there was 'something special between us'.

I was horribly overdressed for Pizza Hut – he knew that – but he took me there because he loved pizza. There was a blonde waitress – 'Kerry' according to her name badge – who flirted outrageously with Franc the whole evening (he did tend to have that effect on women) and to my utter disbelief he encouraged her. At one point she was practically sitting in his lap. I felt uncomfortable, embarrassed. Anger rolled up my spine and I fell silent. Was he expecting me to do something? Say something? Every time Kerry hove into view – which she did far more than was strictly necessary – he turned and fixed those amused dark-blue eyes on her. I might as well not have been there. 'You know I love you,' he said, as we drove home, taking my hand gently and kissing the inside of my wrist. If I felt a spark of doubt about that statement (and I think I did) it was snuffed out when he said 'love' – drawn-out, potent, heavily accented, sexy. I loved him for it. I tried to forget about Kerry (and Sophie).

*

Three days later a fax arrived from Franc:

> *I did enjoy my pizza (a special one) last night even if I missed your smile.*
> *Regards from Kerry.*

I didn't like that.

A week later, at 11.30 a.m. on 10 December, Jeannie handed me another fax:

> *As I have already told you, you should try to remember that you have to close the doors only, not close the doors on your hands (maybe I am asking too much for a woman).*

He added something about 'one of the places a woman is supposed to stay' being the kitchen and another bit about how well I expressed myself in bed, which was nice to know. But a PS at the end ruined the rest of my day:

> *Had a lovely pizza yesterday with some gorgeous young . . . cheese.*

He'd been back without me – twice.

This wasn't the Franc I thought I knew – putting me in my place, teasing me with Kerry. It upset me. As for the doors and hands thing, that was my fault. We'd both gone to close a kitchen cupboard door at the same time. It was an accident. Don't go reading things into it that aren't there.

I can take a joke. I can laugh about a spot of woman teasing (my husband used to do it all the time) – it's just banter, isn't it? All couples do it. But this time Franc's laughter was unkind. He was laughing at the way my face registered hurt and the way I could be so easily embarrassed. It amused him to over-step the mark and I would turn scarlet at the drop of a hat, which made it even funnier. Perhaps I shouldn't have said any-thing about Kerry (I offered to boil her head) when it seemed he enjoyed the idea of us 'fighting' over him. Competition for his attention made him feel important. It didn't work both ways, though. In another letter he wrote, 'I am so jealous about you and I want you to think only about me and forget everybody else.' To 'win' him it seemed clear that I would have to make him the centre of my world and do as I was told. He said as much: 'You are so important to me and I would like to be the most important person for you.' My marriage had been the same, so whilst now and again I would bridle at it, it was something I was accustomed to. I was on the point of moving in, spending most of my time with him, and I could have backed out but then what would I do? I loved him and I know this because it is a fact. But I don't know what I was thinking other than that he appeared to be the answer to everything. I knew life would be far less exciting without him. It would only involve a small sacrifice on my part. Give and take. That was it.

I remember that as well as feeling happy I was also mud-dled and dreadfully tired. I remember holding in lacerating grief for Sally – Franc had told me to try not to think about it – and feeling desperate sadness and worry about my home, my children and our pets. When the office Christmas party came around I was fragmenting, off balance and all over the place. Partners were not invited, so just when I could have done with a steadying hand there was no Franc to provide one.

My diary tells me I went to the hairdresser and had a manicure in the morning on the 17th so I started off the right way. I had a couple of large glasses of red as soon as I arrived to take the edge off. Then my boss began topping up my glass before I'd finished and I started to feel all lovely and fuzzy and sort of went with it. I got a lot drunker than I meant to get – I missed 'comfortably numb' by a mile. I was sick in the lift on the way out of the venue and sick in the taxi and sick again when I got to Franc's house, where I was staying. He put me to bed in the spare room and wouldn't speak to me. To be honest, I can't say I blame him.

The following night was Franc's office Christmas party – no one could say I didn't have stamina. After a fair amount of grovelling, he seemed to have forgiven my disgraceful behaviour the previous night. His hand, warm and firm on the small of my back, steered me about the room. I was wearing the black backless dress I'd worn on our first date and as we danced a slow dance to Sixpence None the Richer singing 'Kiss Me', Franc did exactly that. It was a very, *very* long kiss. I heard Jeannie's daughter squeal, 'Franc is *kissing* Helen!' And all the pain of the past year was forgotten in an instant. It was a magic trick he performed over and over again in our time together, as though he could put his hand inside my chest and squeeze my heart. I thought if I was struck down right then, right there on the spot, I would die without complaint. It was a public endorsement of our relationship and I was ridiculously happy for a whole five days, right up until Franc went back to France to spend Christmas with his family – and Sophie.

We were shopping in town when he bought her Christmas present. He asked me if I thought she would like it. How the fuck would I know, was what I said. It was a graceless comment and it didn't go down well. What did I expect?

After he left for Stansted I found a letter on my pillow:

21 December

My darling Helen
    I think this is the fourth time I start to write to you and then I stop . . .

He stopped, he said, because he didn't have anything specific to say to me but wanted to tell me that I was always on his mind and he wanted to share *only some* of his thoughts.

    My intention is for you to receive this letter when I am away. I understand that this hurts you. I feel the same. If I think about the time I spend with you I cannot image [sic] being without you.

He wrote that he thought there was 'something really strong and intense between us' and he could tell I felt it too because he could see it in my eyes.

He didn't exactly apologize for being thoughtless over Sophie's present but he did explain that he had done it 'without malice and no intention whatsoever to hurt you', even though he knew it was 'a little bit unfair'.

He was pleased that I would miss him.

    I will miss you too, no doubt about this.
    So Mum, ehm . . . I mean Helen try to enjoy it and do not

drink and smoke too much because that will not do any good neither to you or to me.

He was thinking, he said, of what his Christmas would have been like if he'd stayed.

I would love to spend it with you. Just you and me.
Bye for now
Your gorgeous, irresistible, sensational, scrumptious bastard
PS As usual, you looked stunning yesterday . . .

'Mum'?

I was a little older than Franc and he had begun to pick at it. He'd pull my leg and joke that anyone seeing us out together would think I was his mother. When you're in your forties and perimenopausal with your life apparently in free fall, this kind of teasing isn't helpful. It hurts. It undermines. It's cruel. However, I was becoming very dependent on Franc. Life with him was lovely. Not all the time because that would have been unrealistic but when it was just the two of us what we had really did feel very special. I would have been perfectly content to spend the rest of my life sitting on a sofa with Franc holding me. If I had that I could cope with everything else.

There is a thinly veiled warning in that Christmas letter about my behaviour. I had been assessed and found wanting. I could overlook that for the rest of it . . . for the 'just you and me' part.

I left Franc's house on Christmas Eve and went home to spend it with my girls. We were never to have another. I think it's a good thing not to know when something is the last.

I seemed to have two homes now, but both felt temporary. For a few weeks I had led a peripatetic existence between the two. It was not a good way to live for any of us except, possibly, Franc, who had the best of both worlds. However, it was, as I kept repeating to myself, not for keeps. We were doing what we had to do to survive and this too shall pass. I hauled bags of groceries and presents back with me. We toasted absent friends and the New Year with champagne and stuck two fingers up at the old one – possibly the worst year ever.

At the beginning of January and desperate to sleep in a proper bed again I was back in Franc's house. I felt as though I was waiting for something to fall. I was counting down the days – hours – until the 4th when my diary says, *FRANC BACK!!* But I had to cross it out because he wasn't, not yet. He said he had flu. I cancelled his dentist's appointment and waited, without much patience.

I took the day off on Friday because he said he would be back then, only he wasn't. And then he had to be in Paris on business anyway so Number 2 Daughter came over. We went window-shopping and did nice things together. Number 3 Daughter was with her father. Every couple of days I had a diary note of the time I was to call Franc: *Phone Franc 5-ish, Phone Franc 6-ish, Phone Franc 8 sharp . . .* I went down with flu myself and took a few days off sick. That was when I fell asleep and missed a phone call. When I called back he didn't pick up. I thought, Sophie . . . Sophie . . . Sophie . . .

By the 23rd I was fed up. I shuttled back and forth between houses. It felt strange to be in Franc's house without him, as though I shouldn't be there. Finally – three weeks later than planned – he walked into the kitchen and wrapped me in an enormous hug. I was so happy to see him again that all the waiting seemed trivial. He took me away for our first weekend together to make up for being late. We went to York.

*

I know York quite well. While my brother was a student there I spent a very happy school summer holiday completing a project of my own devising, full of complicated maps and diagrams and overlays on greaseproof paper showing the architectural bones of the city. That's the kind of twelve-year-old I was – forensic, curious, an autodidact. I get the feeling that Franc doesn't like me knowing more about it than him, that I've been there before, that he's not showing me something new. He hasn't said anything specific but I find the unexpected tension between us much easier when I say very little about the city walls, the Shambles, Clifford's Tower or the Minster. Perhaps I'm being a know-all. I hear an echo of my mother's voice whispering, 'Darling, shush. No one's listening to you.' We wander around, hand in hand, in awkward silence. I don't mind really. I am entirely happy just being with Franc, although I think perhaps I might be even happier if we could only chat more about what we are seeing and what we might do next, if I could tell him about learning to play croquet on the university lawns – and if he told me a little about what he'd been up to in the weeks we'd been apart. (Funny he hasn't mentioned Sophie.)

Just before dinner that evening (hair up + black dress = wink of approval) we discuss the menu. The waiter arrives and turns to me, notepad in hand, pencil poised, an 'Is madam ready to order?' look on his face but as I open my mouth to speak Franc gives my order for me. I pretend this is nothing unusual but when the waiter has gone I ask him why he did that. I am perfectly capable of giving my own order. It is, he says, not 'correct' for a beautiful, well-bred woman to give her menu choices, unless she is dining alone, which she shouldn't be. I assume this is a charming French idiosyncrasy – a manners thing. I have always been dimly aware that there is something different about Franc and perhaps that's it, his French-ness. That weekend I also learn that it is not appropriate for an accompanied (beautiful) woman to speak to a strange man at all; or go into a room first unless it is a familiar one. The man should always precede her. No more doors opened for me then.

★

Immediately after the weekend in York, on 1 February, I had a phone call from my landlord with news that the house was sold and we now had four weeks to pack up and vacate. The girls and I discussed Plans A and B in the dentist's waiting room while we waited for our family check-up. Plan A was a myth. There was no Plan A because Franc had taken my eye off the Plan A ball. I had been distracted and I could feel fear rising, caught in a mistake. Usually I had a solution. It was a small consolation that I could excuse my incompetence on the grounds that there were no affordable houses to rent in our small town. I would have to give back my borrowed car too, with no prospect of a replacement. I felt terribly guilty that this time there was only Plan B – to put everything into storage (in Franc's warehouse) and initiate the break-up of our family. It was heartbreaking and it was my fault. And it had happened before, when my marriage ended.

My diary tells me that on 9 February I met my oldest friend, Lizzie, for a drink after work. We've known each other since we were at school together and she is the person I most often turn to in a crisis, but she didn't know what to do either. I was stuck with Plan B – it was too late to do anything else. Apart from the Franc part, I hated it.

In the short weeks before I was due to relinquish my own house and move in with Franc, I spent more and more time with him. He became my respite from the strain and stress of it all. As I recall, he raised not the slightest objection but said over and over how much he liked having me around, which satisfied any misgivings I had about Sophie. Was it a mistake to assume that a man who had been engaged to marry his girlfriend of twelve years would not move his girlfriend of four months into his home if that engagement still existed? Probably, given what I know now, but at the time I was still nurturing a belief in 'us'.

This was when I first wrote a note for Franc in an A4 pad he'd left on the kitchen table. I would write before setting off for work and he would jot down a reply when he got up, usually after I'd left but sometimes he was up first and left a note for me. These notes became a regular part of our daily conversations. They were often simply about the logistics of sharing a house but just as often they were teasing and affectionate. I thought it was sweet. Here is that first exchange:

10 February

Morning Bastard

Heating off again this morning – I put it on for you – not totally useless you see! Don't forget I'm meeting my daughter tonight after work. You didn't even say goodnight – no kiss, nothing. I fell asleep on the sofa and woke up at midnight. Thanks.

Love and kisses anyway xxx

Franc replied in the same spirit with 'Morning Bitch'. He'd gone upstairs to have a shower and was going to watch television with me afterwards but fell asleep on the bed. His words gave off a mild whiff of irritation.

I modified my approach:

11 February

Darling Franc

> *I feel a little better today – still tired (I could sleep for a week I think).*
>
> *How do I love thee, let me count the ways.*
> *I love thee to the length, and depth, and breadth of all*
>   *my soul.*
> *I love thee with the soft rememberings of childhood days*
> *And to the end of all my days.*
>
> *More poetry and words for you – and lots of stars.*
>
> *I don't need anything more than I need you – or anyone, just you.*
>
> *Don't forget – hairdressers tonight so late back (which I don't like) but I want to look my best for you, always.*
>
> *All my love always xxx*

Hand-drawn constellations of stars are strewn across the margins.

'Ellen,' he wrote, 'That's much, much better!!!' My reward was to be told that I looked wonderful 'always'. And a PS:

> *Back at 8.00 – DINNER READY!! ☺*

I was a good student.

St Valentine's Day that year fell on a Sunday and something significant happened – Franc and I had our first row.

I'd been back to the house I was vacating to start packing for the move and I had returned with a couple of boxes of old photographs. Any pictures I have of my children when they were small, pre-divorce, are precious, because practically nothing in that house, my marital home, came back to me. My husband kept almost all the little knick-knacks, souvenirs and mementoes. But I did have those photographs. I read somewhere that if your house catches fire the first thing you grab on your way out of the door is your family photos. I wanted these boxes with me. They could not go into storage. Memories slip away and bury themselves but a photograph catches the truth.

I was sitting at the kitchen table looking through them when Franc came in. He looked down, sniffed, and walked out again. For the rest of the evening he barely spoke but he would often be silent, it was his way. I had learned that rattling on about nothing in particular didn't help when he was brooding.

When we went to bed I couldn't sleep. Flicking through the past and packing up yet another house had left me a bit raw. I was trying not to think in terms of failure but my brain was racing from the pressures and strains of the last few weeks so, not wanting to disturb Franc and needing a little solitude, I went back downstairs. Amongst a few other things I'd brought back with me was a random bottle of Benedictine. I poured myself a nice big glassful and lit a cigarette. Then I stood looking out of the kitchen window at the night-time city sky and let my mind spiral from one troubling thought to another until eventually it began to empty and sleep felt possible.

Franc's arms looped around me and he nuzzled my neck. I hadn't heard him come in. I nuzzled him back. 'Being bears', I called it.

'I missed you, Ellen.'

'I'm sorry. I couldn't sleep.'

'You know you shouldn't be smoking.'

'You do.'

'And I'm going to stop. You should too.'

'But I like smoking. I can't stop now anyway. Right now I need to smoke.'

'Why?'

'Because I do. It's hard at the moment. Life is hard. I'm not going to stop anything I enjoy.' He kisses the top of my head and I add, 'Like you.'

'Who is that man?'

'What man?'

'The man in the photograph.'

Ah . . .

'It's no one. He isn't . . . he wasn't important.' I place a slight emphasis on the past tense.

'But he is standing with you and your children.'

Why did he have to see *that* photograph?

'He was a friend.'

'What sort of friend?'

Silence.

'What sort of friend, Ellen?'

'He was a boyfriend . . . an *ex*-boyfriend. It was a long time ago. I haven't seen him in years.' I make a heavier point of the past tense because he seems to have missed that part.

'He looks like an actor, that one in *The Scarlet Letter*.'[1] (He means Gary Oldman.)

'A little, I suppose. Honestly, it was ages ago.'

'Do you miss him?'

'What? No.'

'Are you sure?'

'Quite sure. I don't want to talk about it anymore.'

---

1. *The Scarlet Letter* (1995) – based on Nathaniel Hawthorne's book of the same name. Directed by Roland Joffé and starring Demi Moore, Gary Oldman and Robert Duvall.

'Why not?'

'Because I don't . . . I'm sad about moving, and about Sally, and the girls.' I still don't mention my ex-husband showing up again. He's been the trigger for so much disaster that I am reluctant to risk it.

'But you're with me. You should be happy.'

'I know and I am, but I can still be sad sometimes. People can be both.'

'You lived with him, I think. What was his name?'

Silence.

'What was his name?'

'. . . Stuart.'

This doesn't feel good. I pour another glass of Benedictine and light a second cigarette. Franc turns me to face him and takes my hand. He's smiling a nice crinkly smile that looks as though it goes all the way up to his eyes, which is how you're supposed to know a smile is sincere.

'I want to know everything about you.'

'Trust me, you don't.'

'Tell me about your husband.'

'Tell me about Sophie.'

'Not yet. Tell me about your husband. Please.'

'Oh, Franc. You really don't want to know about that.'

'Tell me. I want to understand.'

'He was a bastard. That's all you need to know. Not at first and not always but by the time we split up quite a lot.'

'Hah. You call me a bastard too. How was *he* a bastard?'

'Because he was. I don't know.'

He hugs me tightly and I rest my head against him. I can hear his heart beating, steady, soothing and, piece by piece, Franc persuades, cajoles and wrangles until he's dragged the whole lot out of me: the fights, the recriminations, the bad behaviour, the childish petty revenges, the violence. The way he is listening makes me think that he understands, that perhaps he has some experience of these things himself. Sitting on the floor in the corner with my back against the wall as I drink more Benedictine and smoke more cigarettes, I become much more forthcoming. I haven't told anyone the things I'm telling Franc now, not even my closest friends. It's a relief to be able to tell someone at last and I sing like a canary. Because I'm still ashamed of how my marriage ended – I can't look Franc in the eye and instead I stare at the carpet. Perhaps if I had looked at him my mouth wouldn't have run on the way it did but this story had been waiting a long time and on I went.

It seemed to me that he wouldn't understand anything if I didn't first say something about how and why I'd married my husband, about my mother's death and the rest. A little justification to sweeten the pill.

In my teens I terrified my mother and exasperated my father. Desperate to change my life, I was branded ungrateful and met with staunch parental resistance. But I had the good fortune (or misfortune, depending on how you look at it) to grow up pretty and at sixteen, far from being left on the shelf with my wilful disobedience, I had acquired an unsuitable motorbike and Rolling Stones-obsessed boyfriend. His family were glamorously European, highly social and lived in a massive rambling farmhouse with horses, dogs, cats and a goat. They were the polar opposite to my family, enticingly bohemian to the rebellious girl with a respectable county background. I was utterly beguiled. The relationship endured – largely down to my parents' objections – but a couple of years later my mum fell ill and my boyfriend and I got married because the prospect of me being 'settled' seemed to make everyone happier. And God knows we needed a bit of that.

My mother's illness filled me with horrible guilt about having been such a cow, and that in turn had a lot to do with me getting married when I did – although it was a hell of a way to apologize. And my upbringing was too ingrained for anything more than a half-hearted attempt at feminism. When I caught my husband-to-be with one of my bridesmaids a couple of nights before the wedding I told my future mother-in-law, because my own mother was too ill and I didn't think she'd understand anyway. Her reply? 'Oh, *all* men do that, darling. Don't call it off. Whatever would people think?' More guilt. Then my mum died and my dad moved away and at twenty I was on my own with a new husband and his family, who I hadn't understood were part of the deal. I was a very young twenty, if you know what I mean.

The first year of married life had been spent growing accustomed to the fact that my mother was going to die soon. I thought I'd felt all the sorrow there was through the long months of watching cancer eat her up. But once the flicker of relief at the end of her suffering was snuffed out, a fresh wave of grief hit me. I slipped vaguely through the days after the funeral, hardly knowing one from the other, making myself as still and as small as possible.

I told Franc all this. But there was something I left out.

Eventually, with no sign that my grief would ever allow me to live through a less painful day than the one before, I decided I just had to get on with it. I went on an evening out – a drink with my work colleagues. When I woke up in the bed of a lighting engineer with no memory of how I'd got there, I was mortified. There was pain and blood and bruising. I'd never heard of anal sex before then. He laughed at how slowly I got myself up and told me not to be silly when I flinched. Then he called a cab and gave me a fiver for the fare. My husband assumed I was having an affair because I'd been out all night. I couldn't tell him I wasn't, that the thought had never entered my head. I couldn't tell him any of what happened and to begin with I wasn't quite sure myself. Eventually I realized I'd swallowed a spiked drink. I was sure it was my fault, that somehow I was responsible, and felt guilt and shame and humiliation about what had happened to me.

In 1977 the attitude of the (male-dominated) police force to women who'd managed to get themselves assaulted, or raped and murdered, was not what you'd call sympathetic – it was appalling. The author and journalist Joan Smith writes very eloquently on what she witnessed at the time as she covered the mishandled police investigation into the Yorkshire Ripper murders:

> A senior West Yorkshire detective, discussing eighteen-year-old Elena Rytka with one of my colleagues from the *Sunday Times* (where I was then working), gleefully announced: 'Her fanny was as sticky as a paper-hanger's bucket.' It seemed to me that a gloating disgust was a curious emotion to feel on contemplation of the mutilated body of a dead teenage girl.[1]

As far as the police were concerned women were either tarts or madonnas but usually tarts. Their opinion was always that whatever happened to you was your own fault: you were dressed/behaving provocatively, you led him on, you might have said no but you really meant yes, you were drunk, out after dark without your husband/boyfriend, and you were asking for it. I was with friends, I was bewildered by grief and

---

1. Joan Smith, *Misogynies* (republished by the Westbourne Press, 2013): 'There's only one Yorkshire Ripper', p. 175.

someone spiked my drink. In the great game of 'which would you rather', I chose adulterer over victim.

By the time I was twenty-three my husband and I had papered over the early cracks in our marriage. We had moved into a house across the road from my in-laws and had our first baby – and that was more or less that for the next ten years. I accepted my lot. I accepted that shame, guilt and casual misogyny were what it meant to be female.

That shame and guilt were why I didn't tell Franc. I couldn't bring myself to say the words and anyway, when we were watching television once he had carelessly remarked, 'If my wife or girlfriend was raped I would kill her.' I didn't think he was serious but still I thought it best not to say anything about what had happened to me.

I began my story again in the early 1990s – with my divorce – when a wife, whether she was a mother or not, had very few legal rights once she had left the marital home. I was only dimly aware of that when I found myself out on the pavement at 2.30 in the morning with nothing except a couple of bin bags stuffed with whatever I had been able to grab before being bundled out of the door. In the heat of a blistering row, telling a man like my husband that I no longer loved him was a mistake that would prove fatal to our marriage, but it was out before I could stop it. I had nowhere to go. My husband had taken away my car keys along with my child benefit book and my wedding ring. My feet were covered in fading bruises photographed the week before in A&E and I didn't think I would be able to walk far. I had no idea what to do. I couldn't call my own family and in any case, what family? My mother was dead, my father remarried, I hadn't seen either of my two brothers for years and hadn't spent Christmas with anyone but my in-laws since I was seventeen.

Nobody knew the first thing about my marriage. I was isolated and alone but I did have one friend who was, like most
of them, a mate of my husband – his best friend. I knew he
was nearby because about two hours earlier, after I said what
I did, he had been summoned to our house and accused of
having an affair with me. I called him and he came and got
me.

For the next eight weeks I swung violently between
euphoria and despair – euphoria at being away from the rows,
from continuing to work and be a wife and mother, wearing
a stoically brave face pinned on like a mask; despair at being
separated from my three small daughters and discovering step
by painful step that my soon-to-be ex was every bit as ruthless
as he'd promised. He was first off the mark with divorce
papers – about two weeks after he booted me out – and
when I called our family solicitor I found that because he was
acting for my husband (of course) he could not therefore act
for me. I was so innocent. I had no money and no means of
getting any unless I could carry on making dresses with the
equipment in my work room at home – out of reach for the
time being. I had no home, unless you counted the spare
room in the house my rescuer shared with his mother and
brother. And I did not have my children. I can't imagine what
they felt when they got up that horrible morning and found
me gone. I still can't bear to think about it. My youngest was
only five.

Then out of the blue my husband asked to see me. We met
on a country lane miles from anywhere – which was stupid.
Nowadays I know that abused women are most at risk of
being killed when they leave, but back then I knew so little
about it. And anyway, he wasn't someone you could easily say

no to, though I did refuse when he offered me £400 to go back. I hadn't fallen so low that I would allow myself to be bought. I felt safer out of that house and out of that marriage, and I was staying out. The rejection made him absolutely furious. He told me he would break me and that is what he set out to do.

I reasoned that the children would be better off where they were, at least for the time being. With the main irritant removed (me) there would be – and I was certain of this – peace and stability for them within the extended family unit of grandparents, uncles, cousins . . . all his, of course. They were in the home they knew and their lives would more or less carry on as they had before. I was too afraid to take them with me. If I had he would have come after us . . . come after me. He *did* come after me. Was this cowardice on my part? Yes. Did I feel guilty? Ashamed? Of course. I was a mother who had left her own children – I was consumed by guilt and shame.

On a practical level I had nowhere to take them, no security, no income, and no idea whether or how I would survive. No idea what help, if any, might be available to us. I thought they would be safer where they were. I promised myself I would, somehow, get them back but I couldn't tell them that, couldn't get their hopes up, in case I failed. I couldn't bear to fail them again.

First I had to make some money, which meant somehow I had to get into the house and rescue my sewing machines. Aside from what I would be paid on completion of an outstanding commission I felt a huge responsibility to my customers. I could not let them down. I called the local police station and arranged for a uniformed officer to go with me to collect it all. My husband gave us a long hard look when he answered the knock on the door but he agreed to give me my things. As soon as I had it all the door was slammed in my face and on the policeman's foot. He laughed and said, 'I can see why you wanted me along' – no enquiries about what might have gone on before or why I felt I needed him there. I suspect that to him, a brief spectator on our world, it would have been just a 'domestic'.

It was an exquisite joke to be working on a wedding dress order when your own marriage has gone so disastrously wrong. I toiled through the night and I met my commitments. A couple of weeks later I had some cash, which was an enormous relief and solved any immediate problems, but I needed a more regular pay packet.

I found just the thing with a secretarial job at a tiny company in the next village. But one afternoon the door opened and my husband walked in off the street. He looked around, saw me and said, 'Now I know where you are,' and then he left. My colleagues were first astonished and then kind. I was upset and embarrassed. It's hard to look professional in those circumstances. But I didn't cry or run away, which was what he wanted me to do.

I bought an old car, an orange Marina with a brown vinyl roof. It wasn't pretty but it was reliable. I didn't mind that it wasn't sleek and fast like the car I'd left behind because it was mine. I bought it myself with my own money. Then, one evening, I was driving home along a back road when a Land Rover came close up behind me, made contact with my rear bumper and shoved me hard. It was my husband. We were on a twisty, country lane miles from my friend's house. I was terrified he would nudge me off the road, so I had to drive far too fast to make sure I stayed well in front of him. I took a gamble on making it a further two miles to the nearest police station, where I sat outside trembling and crying until I was sure it was safe to go home.

After a couple of months I had enough money for a deposit and I moved into a house-share – a tiny room of my own and a kind of independence. I had visiting rights to see the children but my husband ignored whatever the courts had stipulated. I was allowed to see them only on his terms, one at a time and never together, which set them up against one another, competing for 'Mummy time'. He changed dates and times at a moment's notice. He threatened me when I picked them up and again when I dropped them off. They weren't safer where they were at all. If anything, I'd made things worse for them by trusting him and allowing him to take advantage of me. He piled more guilt and shame on top of what I already felt – what I still feel.

I did all right in those early months, on my own for the first time in my life, but I was knocked flat by what came next. My solicitor refused to understand why I couldn't sit out the divorce proceedings in the marital home. He continued to hold that view even when I'd explained to him, patiently and for the umpteenth time, that I was sure that if I went back there the only way I would leave would be in a body bag. He lost the case and I lost everything: children, house, furniture, car, belongings, self-respect, trust.

Everything except the moral victory: my divorce was granted on the grounds of my husband's 'unreasonable behaviour'. No shit.

For a wretched few weeks I was beaten, lost in grief for my children. Then I picked myself up, dragged hope and courage out from wherever they were hiding and got a new solicitor. This time I did my research and appointed a woman with a good record in handling my sort of case. To release the court papers, and before I could sue the previous solicitor, I had to pay the negligent bastard's bill so I begged and borrowed, going cap in hand to anyone who might be able to help, to raise the money. (God knows where I would have been without Legal Aid.) The fight back had begun.

I was told about a cottage I could afford to rent. I applied and I got it – a proper home at last. A friend's grandmother died (which was sad) and I kitted out my new home with her furniture (which was happy). Small successes lay the foundations for bigger ones and I had achieved this all on my own. But my ex-husband didn't like these small triumphs. When I drove up to drop off a daughter after an afternoon's visit to my fine new house he was waiting for me outside. He sent her indoors and then tried to destroy my car. A balled fist came flying at me as I struggled to stop him wrenching the passenger door off. I leaned back sharply and dodged the blow. The door was held on with bungee straps for weeks until I could afford to get it fixed.

One of the most abiding and painful memories I have of that time is of driving away and in the rear-view mirror seeing three small girls running after me, calling at me to come back. Every time I felt as though my skin had been peeled off. It was a unique sort of pain: eviscerating. I wanted to throw back my head and howl. What must it have been like for them? Unimaginable, cruel and not – definitely not – my choice. But I had none. As a wife and a mother who had left her husband and children I'd given up my right to choose. The means to punish and control me were in my former husband's hands and I had put them there. To this day I cannot bear to hear a child cry, although I no longer cry too.

People kept asking me why he was the way he was. Why, they would ask, does he bear such a grudge? For some people control is so important they cannot forgive anyone who escapes it. He didn't care that I wasn't the only person he was hurting, although I was at least better equipped to deal with it than the children. On Christmas Eve he married again – two months post-decree and not quite eighteen months since I'd told him I didn't love him. When my daughters showed me the photographs – they were bridesmaids – I mistook his second wife for my mother-in-law. 'Perhaps sometimes,' said the social worker, who was helping me with the custody case, 'mothers and sons are a bit too close.'

One morning Number 1 Daughter voted with her feet. Knowing her father wouldn't miss her until late afternoon, she didn't board the school bus but instead walked seven miles down country lanes to my house. She let herself in and called me at work. She was twelve, and she was frightened. I told her to lock the door and draw the curtains – I would be right there. It was my wonderful girl's seven-mile walk that destroyed my ex's legal case and made it possible for me to win custody of all three of my daughters.

It happened very quickly. I remember driving to collect them with U2 singing 'When Love Comes to Town' on the radio, then Erasure and 'Blue Savannah Dawn'. We had shepherd's pie for supper and that night they slept in bedrooms that had been ready for them, more in hope than expectation, ever since I'd moved into the cottage. As punishment for escaping his control, their father sent them away with only what they could carry – as he had with me. But it didn't matter. It was the first time we had all been together for three years.

Just how much he resented this escape became clear over the next few months. In the couple of years I'd been without custody I had made support payments to my husband of £60 a month, despite having had virtually no income until I'd found my secretarial job. But, out of love and duty, somehow I did it. My ex-husband had family money, a family business and a big house so I didn't think I was being unreasonable to expect a practical sum to help support us now the girls were with me. When nothing materialized I turned my fire on my MP and the Child Support Agency (CSA). I remember calling the CSA to ask about the progress of my application.

'I'm afraid your application is a long way down the queue.'

'What does that mean?' I asked.

'Well, we have all the applications in piles, in date order. These piles cover all the desks in the main office and three desks in the outer office. Your application is at the bottom of the first pile in the outer office. You'll be waiting about six months.'

'What do I have to do to get my application to the top of the first pile in the main office?'

Laughter.

'I've spoken to my MP.'

'That'll do it.'

A few weeks later we were awarded £20.92 a month.

There comes a point when you have to cut your losses and move on. We were together and we were happy and somehow I would support us. It didn't seem worth the effort and expense of pursuing him further.

The last time I spoke to my ex-husband was a couple of days after I had collected the girls. We arranged for him to see them at the weekend but he didn't turn up. A year later, without warning, he dumped all their stuff, now outgrown, on the pavement outside my solicitor's office and then we didn't see or hear from him again for eight years. Not directly anyway.

There was still the occasional 'surprise' or a slow drive by our house to remind us that he didn't live far away.

Given all this it was a bit of a shock when he pitched up again the previous year but I still didn't tell Franc about it. I said nothing about my ex-husband scouting my perimeter fences. If he was possessive about me speaking to ordinary men (which, perversely, made me feel a bit cherished), goodness only knew how he'd react to the man I'd been married to. It would have been hard to describe my feelings now so I hinted at distance and tried to make it sound civilized. Above all, I didn't want to rock the boat.

When I finished speaking, there was a very long silence. Then Franc sighed, took the glass from my hand and hurled it across the room. It smashed against the wall, showering the table, the carpet and me with splintered crystal. Straight away I regretted bringing my precious vintage glass here. I regretted flouting the slippers rule. I crouched in my corner, very still, focusing hard and unblinking on a feather on the carpet in front of me because that is what I know about dealing with this kind of thing.

'Clean this up and come to bed, Ellen.'

I stood up shakily.

'That's it. It's over. We're done. I'm leaving.'

That's what I should have said and if I hadn't seen this kind of thing before perhaps I would have. It didn't feel like a row and technically it wasn't. A row is two people arguing whereas this had been me talking while Franc listened. And then when he was angry he was angry on my behalf. I was shocked when he smashed the glass because he was usually so contained, but I wasn't frightened. I interpreted that flash of rage and emotion as caring. I thought he was angry at what had happened to me, that he wished he could have protected me. Yet it slowly became clear that I must have done something wrong, although precisely what proved elusive. I didn't understand how doing exactly as he'd asked had hurt *his* feelings, how he could turn what had happened to me into an offence against him. Eventually, in bed, he hissed at me that I'd ruined everything, which was as good as a slap. Then he turned his back to me and I lay awake, staring at the ceiling.

The abject, distressed, grovelling apology I wrote in our message book the next morning shows very clearly what was happening.

15 February

Darling Franc

 I don't know what I can write and I'm afraid to say anything. Anything I say makes things worse.

 I know you love me – but do you still want me? Is loving you enough? (For you.)

 I hate myself for the hurt I've caused you.

 I want to be with you but I'm afraid of hurting you more, if that's possible. I don't want to wake you this morning because of the hurt I shall see in your eyes – because I know I gave you that pain.

 I don't know whether to come home tonight because I feel that just by being here I hurt you. I don't want to hurt you – I can't bear it.

 If you wanted to punish me for the things I said, and did, you've done it. You've made me realize how much you mean to me. Your pain is my pain and I wish I was dead.

 I'm deeply sorry for the problems I've caused you, the pain and hurt I've given you – perhaps fighting for you would be wrong, selfish of me because I want you.

 I can't stand what I feel inside this morning – I feel as

though my heart is breaking. If I don't wake you it's because
I'm a coward. I loathe myself this morning.
All of my love,
Helen xxx

I meant it when I said, 'I wish I was dead.' I was worn out, depressed, and the love I felt for Franc was keeping me going. It gave me hope. If he'd decided we were over it would have been the final straw. I'd had enough. I didn't understand what he meant when he said I'd ruined everything. How had I done that? It was all too much. I felt too fragile to cope with it.

Franc wrote a reply and faxed it to me at work in the afternoon. It was four pages long and he called it a 'summary'. It did little to clear up any misunderstandings or make me feel better.

He said he appreciated my honesty, even if he 'did not like everything' I told him. He told me that I hadn't said too much, which was a relief because his reaction made me think I had. His defence was:

> *I feel bad just thinking you may be talking to someone else*
> *(male).*

Then he took half a page to explain why he didn't feel I was making much of an effort to understand him. That I had been so fragile when we first met, he'd thought I wouldn't be strong enough to help and support him, which was what he said he needed.

> *I am not going to tell you what to do. I just told you what*
> *I like and what I dislike. And that I am really jealous about*
> *you. I am jealous because I love you. But I can't be because*
> *I have not decided anything [about Sophie]. Then just to*
> *make things easier you refer with some satisfaction on your*

smiling face about your conversation with that man or
whatever . . .

I had told him about a conversation I'd had with a male
teacher at my daughters' school and a further half a page
described how I'd made him feel when I did that. I wasn't
patient with him, he said, I was ungrateful.

I know is hard for you. I took care of you. I take care of
you. I am at your disposal for everything . . . but I haven't
decided yet [about Sophie]. Now I am confused. Everything
I have done for you seems now to turn up against me.

All of a sudden I couldn't seem to do anything right anymore.

As soon as you see I am in a bad mood instead of helping
me you just quit, saying something ununderstandable [sic]. You
want to stay on your own, cigarettes, drinking time. It doesn't
matter how I feel or what I need.
I feel sad. I have got a lot of grieve in my heart. I hope you
understand this and can read between the lines. I hope your
reaction will not be stepping back because this is the last thing
I need.
Bye for now.
Love
Franc

But I didn't understand. I didn't understand at all.

Reading these two letters today, I can see the first appearance of what was to become something of a recurring theme
in our relationship: me making ever more florid and elaborate
confessions of undying love and begging forgiveness, and him
giving endless variations of the line, 'Whenever you see I am
in a bad mood, instead of helping me you just quit.' In other

words, when he was angry I walked away. It was my way of coping. This Franc was not the Franc I had fallen in love with.

I made an enormous apologetic chocolate cake.

Message for Franc from the Chocolate Cake Fairy
    Not the best chocolate cake this fairy has ever made, icing not quite right and no scales to weigh anything but . . .
    This fairy has red hair and made this cake with love and care
    H xxx

His reply listed ten points:

1. *What is a fairy?*
2. *Cake is delicious.*
3. *Let's see if I can thank you later.*

And the rest all say the same thing: *I need you. (Is it clear enough) F*

This was more like it. This was the proper Franc back again. We didn't talk about our past and present relationships with other people in the week that followed, or ever again – at least not in the sense of an ordinary conversation. It was easier just to write things down, although I suspect much got lost in translation. I had a day's annual leave from work, which, with ten days to go before the move, I spent back home, packing.

Then, on 22 February a letter arrived from Franc in the post. Looking back, I can see that this might seem odd, given that we practically shared the same address and saw each other almost every day. I thought it was romantic, writing down what he couldn't say:

My dear Ellen
    It is a long time since I wrote to you . . .

He said he couldn't stop thinking about me and he wanted to know why.

I like thinking about you, but unfortunately quite often (100 times a day?) they are not very pleasant thoughts.

He said I would understand what he was talking about when he said 'the needle is in my heart'.

That's me and I can't do anything about it. Paranoid mind.

He told me not to worry, that our argument had been about nothing and it was just the way his brain worked.

You definitely are a witch. You must be. How can be explained otherwise all this? Never mind you are the most beautiful one: still a witch.

I do not know what I am going to do with you. Killing you is still the best option I have. But then I will miss you, so I have to think of something else. We'll see.

He wanted me to know how much he loved me. I would be surprised, he said, at how big that love was. He signed himself, 'Your toy-boy'.

I didn't take the 'killing' part seriously – after all, he'd never laid a finger on me in anger. It was a peculiar letter but I believed that I was in love with him and he with me. Although I had a growing sense of something closing around me, I pushed the feeling away.

There was another letter in the post the next day:

Darling Helen

Hope you liked yesterday's letter. I keep writing because . . .

He loved me, is what he said. And he still hadn't decided what he was going to do with me. Perhaps, he said, 'a residence for elderly people'.

I hate hindsight. It shows me things I should have seen at the time.

Attn: Franc

Are you going to the gym tonight? If so, will you want to eat when you come back? If not, I have had the most enormous lunch so I won't want to eat much this evening.

Don't worry, I will be careful this evening (or I'll certainly try).

See you later
Love and kisses
H
xxx

Back came a reply to tell me he would be home at 8.30 p.m. and that dinner had to be ready. As for me trying to be careful, 'Try is not good enough, darling (I am serious about this).'

I don't remember what I was supposed to be careful about but I expect he meant with the house move because the next day our little family splintered as we moved out of the tiny house and all our things went into Franc's warehouse. Our cats went to new homes, except for our beloved Byron who was very old and collapsed that morning – I knew how he felt. I took him to the vet and held our magnificent, indestructible boy as he was put to sleep. Byron always had the best timing, and his passing seemed to mark the end of an era. A neighbour adopted our cocker spaniel. Number 2 Daughter moved in with Number 1 Daughter. Number 3 Daughter moved in with her father and I went back to Franc. I've made it sound easier and simpler than it was. In truth it was brutal. It was everything I'd been dreading for the last ten years and it felt like the end of days.

Still, there was Franc waiting for me so I wasn't alone. It was all going to be *fine*, wasn't it?

*

Not only is coercive control the most common context in which [women] are abused, it is also the most dangerous.[1]

Whenever I think back over the men in my life and my relationships with them the first thought to drop is always and inevitably, How could you have been so stupid? That's the principal reason I never spoke about it.

Not long after my marriage broke down my father asked me if my husband had hit me. I can't remember whether I answered or whether I just looked at him, but either way he knew and then we never spoke of it again. And anyway sometimes I hit back and that makes me no better than him. Once I threw a deep-fat fryer at him – an empty one but even so . . . I wouldn't be writing this now if my dad were still alive, on account of the shame and the fact that I am clearly an idiot because I did this not once but twice. He never knew about the second time, about Franc: I would feel the need to apologize. I seem to have spent so much of my life being sorry for one thing or another.

I did once tell my mother-in-law her son had hit me but her response was that if your husband hits you it's just another way of showing that he loves you. I knew *that* wasn't right. It's funny the way I could acknowledge the wrongness and yet not acknowledge it. The difficulty came with admitting it to myself. Even when you see it in black and white, as I do now, it is still easier to deny it because then you don't have

---

1. Evan Stark, *Coercive Control: How Men Entrap Women in Personal Life* (Oxford University Press, 2007).

to explain. And yet it keeps pricking at you. Telling someone, 'This happened to me,' means you know they will never look at you in the same way again. They will see you as that other person saw you – an incompetent, a disaster, a worthless mess – feelings that swell inside you like an incubus until you are choked into silence.

Two things were significant in releasing me from this prison and they both helped me to recognize that I wasn't alone. Although I somehow felt I was. That wasn't a belief I planted myself but one of the common denominators that characterize this type of abuser. I still feel queasy about typing that word. It doesn't matter how many times I write or speak it.

The first thing was, surprisingly, the long-running BBC Radio 4 drama series better known for expounding on the uses of silage and milk yields in dairy herds. I used to listen to *The Archers* with half an ear while I was busy doing something else but it was the way Rob Titchener moved in on Helen Archer that made me sit up and pay attention.

Helen was a single mother to a son conceived by sperm donor. She had a history that included anorexia and a troubled relationship with a man who went on to commit suicide, a relationship that also included an incident of physical assault, possibly accidental or possibly not. Her romantic history was not a happy one – and then she met Rob Titchener. The first sign that he was not what he seemed came at the housewarming party he held with the wife he had failed to mention. She didn't stay long and Rob swiftly moved Helen in to take her place.

Rob began to lay down the law but he did it in such a way that there wasn't anything specific you could really take exception to and quite a lot of it sounded caring: he hated tuna and said he couldn't eat the tuna bake she'd made (fair enough); he suggested she change her New Year's Eve dress because it was too 'revealing' (maybe); he gave her a magnificent engagement ring and rushed her into marriage when they were on holiday (*so* romantic!); he found excuses for them not to spend time with her family and friends and he wanted to know where Helen was whenever she was not with him (he wanted to look after her). Rob seemed always to be mildly critical of Helen and everything she did, but he often told her he loved her and seemed to demonstrate that love all the time. Helen's family were as delighted as *The Archers'* audience that it looked as if she would at last be lucky in love. But we, the listeners, were privy to things her family couldn't see and wouldn't know about until much later – what appeared to be marital rape, for example. This removed all doubt about what kind of man he was and we could only listen in horror. And hearing the story unfold put Rob right there inside our heads, too.

Rob used Helen's subsequent unplanned pregnancy to bring in his appalling mother, at which point we learned that his father was also abusive. Then Rob began to 'gaslight' Helen, tracking her movements before – with awful inevitability – resorting to violence. By the time she woke up to what was going on, Helen was completely trapped and isolated. And even then she couldn't admit it – to herself or to anyone else. As seems to be the way with all of us, she was ashamed. Does any of this sound familiar?

Then came the second thing to help me: at about the same time as events on *The Archers* were reaching crisis point, the Serious Crime Act 2015 brought in laws creating the new offence of controlling or coercive behaviour in an intimate or family relationship. A conviction carried a maximum prison sentence of five years.

For women like me who thought that not being bounced off the furniture twice a week made whatever was happening to them somehow unworthy of the title of domestic abuse, the Statutory Guidance Framework, which is on p. xvii of this book, made interesting reading.

I quickly ticked off ten of the seventeen Types of Behaviour cited in the Home Office guidance and laughed at the added note: *This is not an exhaustive list.* Indeed it is not, because if there is one thing I *do* know it is that the mind of an abuser is endlessly inventive when it comes to discovering new ways and means of controlling someone they see as both inferior and their property.

The other thing I noticed about this Home Office list is how easy it would be to make a sinister interpretation of an innocuous act or phrase. So, if I might play devil's advocate for a moment . . .

How many of us, in the first flush of a new relationship, have promptly dropped our entire social circle in favour of spending every waking moment with our new squeeze?

How many of us have made or received texts, emails or phone calls from our partner asking, 'Where are you?'

How many of us have joked, 'You're rubbish, you'?

How many of us have a shared bank account and have said, aghast, 'You spent *how* much?'

How many of us have chucked a frock out because a partner didn't like it?

And how many of us have laughed and said, 'I'll have to kill you'?

How easy it is to just laugh at all of this, which – of course – is precisely how abusers get away with it.

Here are two more definitions from the Home Office Statutory Guidance:

Controlling behaviour is: a range of acts designed to make a person subordinate and/or dependent by isolating them from sources of support, exploiting their resources and capacities for personal gain, depriving them of the means needed for independence, resistance and escape and regulating their everyday behaviour.

Coercive behaviour is: a continuing act or a pattern of acts of assault, threats, humiliation and intimidation or other abuse that is used to harm, punish, or frighten their victim.

The key things here are continuity and repetition – coercive control is defined by a pattern, an ongoing and habitual type of behaviour that is intended to subdue another individual, depriving them of their independence and making them cleave solely to the abuser.

My ex-husband was a great arguer and most of the time it was fine, falling under the heading of 'reasoned debate' – such as the great 'Does history exist?' discussion we had that ran over an entire summer. But there is a crucial difference between the cut and thrust of intelligent discussion and the argument that I had no money of my own and everything I had came from him.

'What about my child benefit?'

'Mine.'

'How is it yours?'

'Because it's paid out of my taxes.'

'But I pay my taxes too!'

'Yes, but you work for me.' (I was on the books in the family firm.)

I can imagine the March Hare having a similar discussion with Alice.

I had nothing and therefore I was no one. I couldn't win. Unfortunately, he took this to mean that he had carte blanche to spend our money on whatever he wanted, which generally meant cars and motorbikes. Although, to be fair, he would have done that even if I had won the argument. More than once at the supermarket the children and I found we had to walk away from a trolley full of food because our grocery money had gone towards the latest petrol-driven infatuation. A fact we only ever discovered at the checkout. I've never shared a bank account since so I can at least thank him for that.

Having nothing and being no one was what first attracted Franc but what really gave me away was that I was trying very hard to be someone. The little black backless dress trimmed with cock feathers, the seen-better-days shoes, my smoking of cheroots and slightly affected manner were the armour he saw through to the vulnerability underneath.

Franc and my husband had things in common. Both had the foreign thing. Both had money. Both offered rescue from the slightly dull everyday. Both were undeniably good-looking. I threw myself on their mercy in times of crisis: first the illness and death of my mother in the 1970s and second the series of unforeseeable disasters that befell me as a single mother. It is what I had been programmed to do. If you incline towards the view that relationships are a battle of wits you can see how this would place me at a considerable disadvantage. I can see it now too but I never had that moment of clarity – the one that drops on you like a cartoon anvil.

I suppose I'd never learned how to take responsibility for myself because all I knew about was doing as I was told. I was simply a product of my time. But I worry about the increasing numbers of young women who are finding they've stumbled into this kind of relationship. I wonder if we've swapped parental governance for a far more restrictive one – the discipline of style and popular opinion, as perpetuated by every media outlet from here to Timbuktu.

Despite decades of feminism, we seem to be living through an era in which pornography and physical perfection have become the benchmarks for how relationships are measured, whether sexual or those of women with their own bodies. We are assailed by the dictatorial rules of fashion, the tabloid press in which women's bodies are dissected into constituent parts and in humiliating detail, the repeated harking back to the housewives of the 1950s as the industry standard and the almost universal Western failure to recognize that women come in all shapes and sizes. Men are influenced by this, too, becoming convinced that long eyelashes, pouting lips, pert breasts and the genitalia of a twelve-year-old are what they should be looking for in a partner. In fact, it's regressive and it marks a return to the days when an advert could show a woman being spanked by her husband for buying the wrong coffee.[1]

---

1. In 1952 a Chase & Sanborn coffee advertisement ran in the *New York Times* that actually showed a man punishing his wife in this way.

Chapter Four

At the beginning of March I perked up a bit. The accumulating burden of worry, responsibility and stress seemed to have dissipated as soon as I handed over the keys to the house that was never a home. I didn't have to worry about my girls or the pets, and I had Franc all to myself; this perhaps sounds shallow but the reverse also applied and they didn't have to worry about me. As Franc said, everyone was better off for a bit of clarity.

We had the 'money talk' everyone has when they start living together. I wanted to pay my way as I always had but as Franc pointed out, the company paid for his accommodation and living expenses so there was no need for me to concern myself with it. I said, 'All right then but we'll take it in turns to buy food,' and that seemed to satisfy him.

In the kitchen-table notebook there was a flurry of messages.

1 March

Hello darling!

I think you slept well – but the snoring! Can I have some earplugs? No, I like hearing you sleeping well.

I'm very excited about going to the gym tonight – thank you for helping me with that. First day of a new month and a new week – lovely, no house = no stress (or not much anyway)!

Love Helen
xxx
PS It's raining – for a change! And I do love you.

He replied that he would miss me while I was at the gym but that he was glad I was excited about going. It had been his idea so I suppose he would have been.

On the same page there is an arrow pointing to a blank space, next to which I have written, '£20 for food.' It was his turn to shop.

The next day there were more notes. Even when we were apart we had a compulsive need to speak to each other somehow. It felt as though the two of us were an exclusive club and created a powerful bond.

Hope you are not too excited about the gym.
Be back around 8.00 tonight.
Non faire l'oie, je te recommande [Don't be a goose.]

Darling Franc
Maybe a little excited about the gym . . . but not too much!
Worried about not being home when you come back from work.
I will be home to cook your dinner, don't worry.
French instructions duly noted.
Love
H
xxx

I used to go to the gym a lot, so I was fine with getting back into it at Franc's suggestion. He wanted me to look good. I wanted to look good.

When I think back now I see a woman living twenty miles away from her family, throwing all she'd got into an overpowering relationship with a man she had met just four months earlier. The proverb 'marry in haste, repent at leisure' springs to mind, without the marriage part. In that short space of time I had severed all ties to everything I had known and placed myself entirely in the hands of someone mercurial and possessive, whom I barely knew.

2 March

Good morning, darling Franc.
    Proper breakfast, no cigarettes, not stiff!
    I love you more each day and I miss you so much when we're apart. Counting the seconds again today.
    All my love, always and forever
    Helen
    xxx

Eating properly, going to the gym, not drinking, not smoking, having dinner ready when Franc came home from work. Who was this woman and what had she done with Helen?

3 March

Darling Franc
    Gym tonight. Please take care driving to and from Sheffield today. I'll be thinking of you, as usual, all day. Every moment of every day my love for you grows stronger and deeper.
    All my love
    Helen
    xxx

He replied: 'And of course I want to check the [gym attendance] card!!!!'

Who the hell checks anyone's gym attendance card?

*

At work, the consultant I had been working for and had known for some years was about to leave. On the first Friday in March his immediate team, including me, were all going out for lunch, which meant car sharing to get to and from the restaurant. I was placed with the specialist registrar (married with children) who also had the best car – a two-seater sports convertible. I love fast cars, and this was a great treat. I was excited when I told Franc, thinking he would be happy for me. He left me a long letter telling me exactly what he thought about it:

5 March

Dear Helen

I do believe you love me, but could you explain me why, then, out of all the people going to the lunch you are going with a male in a sport car??? Could you please explain me that??? Between all the people and the cars that was the only place available, and it happened you were just talking to that man at that moment. Not with someone else, not another time. Just when it was right to be there. You knew it would have hurted me. You knew that. Don't tell me it was not your intention to arrange for that.

The rest of what he's written is contradictory and hard to follow: he needs me to understand him and I <u>should</u> understand him because I tell him I love him all the time but I keep leaving him on his own, 'biting' his thoughts. I don't say anything to explain myself, and that makes him sad. He told me I arranged that lift with a man to hurt him but he knows I love him so he believes I didn't really do that. He doesn't take me for granted but he thinks there's something wrong. He needs me. He is 'storing' these feelings. I should forget it. He can't wait to see me. He will be back at 7.30 p.m. . . . . 'Love Franc'.

Franc was right. I didn't – and still don't – understand how he could see a lunchtime lift to a restaurant in a party of a dozen people as a betrayal, an infidelity. I had expected to see one of his slightly sarcastic notes but what I got was this rant, with his name underlined several times. His pen had gone right through the paper.

He sent a fax to the office:

Et regardez-moi et pas dire un mot. [Look at me and do not say a word.]

This was different from the night he smashed my glass . . . I'd had five days without worry. Not even a week.

There was change in the air at the hospital too. The departure of my boss and the arrival of a locum consultant was a catalyst that changed the dynamics of the small office where I worked. Doreen Milson was promoted to department head and it was as though she'd been let off the leash.

One day I walked back into the office to find her sitting at my desk. She hadn't seen me come in so she carried on with what she was doing – an impression of someone I quickly grasped was meant to be me. She tossed her hair about, pretended to have long nails, mimicked my accent and my lisp and the way I said, 'Gosh', and 'Crumbs'. Then she pretended to light a cigarette, announcing to the room, '*And* I'm Franc's bird.' No one laughed because they'd seen me but Doreen carried on. She only saw me when she swung the chair round. An appalled silence descended. I did what I normally do with embarrassing things I don't know how to cope with – I ignored it. I went quietly to my desk, sat down in my still-warm, recently vacated chair and got on with my work.

I can take a joke. Living with three strong-minded daughters I'd had the piss ripped out of me on a daily basis. My departing boss sometimes affected not to understand my occasional lisp, but it was all done in good heart with no offence meant or taken. It was part of our daily banter, like calling me the 'bag lady' when I was a freelance because of my preferred method for picking up and dropping off completed work. But Doreen's performance had been spiteful.

Shortly afterwards a large leather bullwhip appeared, mounted prominently on the wall of her office. We all remarked on the interesting choice of decor and the message it sent, which was of course why it was there, despite the offence it might cause. After that whenever Doreen was in the staff common room the conversation swiftly deteriorated to graphic discussions about vibrators, periods, the shape and size of people's genitalia and insinuations about everybody's sex life (except her own). It was so awful I stopped going in there and started having lunch in the cafeteria or at my desk. I didn't tell Franc – but then I'd grown careful about telling him anything I didn't think he'd understand or that might provoke an argument.

In our message book on 10 March:

Morning Franc

> *I feel very out of sorts this morning.*

> *Anyway – gym tonight and I'll try to remember everything we went through on Sunday.*

> *Long day without you – again.*

> *Love and kisses*

> *Helen xxx*

You don't need to be 'out of sorts'.
You are so lovely anyway.

> *Love*

> *Franc*

Darling Franc
  Can you kill me soon please? I can't stand these long lonely days at work without you!
  Drive safely to Derby, and back, and I'll see you this evening.
  All my love
  Helen xxx

Dear Helen
  It will be a pleasure for me to kill you (as soon as possible).

Franc had photocopied a cartoon and left it next to this last note. It shows a woman bending over a sink, washing her hair. With her head down and her hair dripping wet she can't see and is reaching out to a man standing behind her. He holds out a gun by the barrel as she says, 'Pass me the hairdryer.' Franc has drawn on the man's face so that he looks like him. The woman's head is a flurry of red scribbles. I wonder if perhaps he meant to show my red hair . . .

But I was more anxious about something else. Occasionally Franc referred to something he'd written but which I didn't remember having seen. I asked Jeannie if she still got her daily faxes from Dave and she said she did. Other colleagues who regularly received personal faxes were getting theirs too.

Dearest Franc
  No faxes today then? The day is a desert with no water! I'll meet you at the oasis tonight! See you later.
  Love and kisses
  Helen xxx

*

My diary in March tells me that I was going to the gym a minimum of three times a week. I had a gym bag and I needed more kit so I bought some new stuff at one of our office sales. When I got back to my desk I showed it to Sarah, the typist who sat alongside me.

Doreen walked in and delivered her opinion: 'Fuck. You must be a right skinny bitch to fit in that.' She wasn't wrong because, through diligent hard work, cardio and resistance, and following the exercise plan and diet Franc had devised for me, I had gone very quickly from a dress size 12 to a size 8. Doreen was somewhere north of both of those.

'You've got no tits. Are you a lezzer?'

I smiled politely and turned back to my work. The 'Skinny Bitch' handle stuck. 'Oh, hello – here's the Skinny Bitch.' 'I don't know – ask the Skinny Bitch.'

That weekend Franc and I drove to Manchester because he wanted to visit the Trafford Centre. While we were there he bought me a gorgeous grey wool shift dress, sleeveless and trimmed with duck-egg blue at the neck and arms. It was lined with the same colour and came with a matching silk cardigan. I didn't think I'd ever owned anything so beautiful and I know I looked fabulous wearing it. All the way home I sat with the bag on my knee, holding it tight like a surfboard. It had the name of the designer on the front and it fastened with Velcro. This was the bag that would become the receptacle for all the words Franc and I exchanged, the bag that would sit beneath my bed collecting dust, the bag that sits on my work table now. The dress is long gone but the cardigan survives, as do the words and memories.

*

For two weeks there were no notes on the kitchen table but my diary tells me I went to the gym, once with Franc so he could check my progress. I went to the hairdresser and I had a manicure and a pedicure. On 25 March I met Number 2 Daughter and her boyfriend for a quick lunch in the hospital canteen. It was a tense half-hour. She told me that my ex-husband had promised each of my girls a hefty sum of money if they never spoke to me again and that none of them liked Franc very much. It's not surprising the lunch 'did not go well' as I recorded in my diary afterwards. But I can't blame them for taking the money. I would have done.

My eldest daughter didn't speak to me again for many years but I managed to stay (secretly) in touch with the younger two. At the time it felt as though everything that followed my separation from my husband was repeating itself. And, of course, my children's dislike of Franc drove another wedge between us.

Franc was ill immediately after the quarrel with my daughters and lying on the sofa all day gave him time to think, which I had discovered was never a good thing. I began to notice that when he was angry what he wrote didn't always make sense. When I got up for work on Monday morning, three freshly composed pages were waiting for me on the kitchen table:

Dear Helen

I hate being ill. I feel useless. And I have too much time free so my mind wanders around and around. Of course I have a lot to think about but I'm not going to bore you with work problems.

I have tried several times in the last few days to talk with you . . .

But he hadn't because he didn't know what to ask or say and because it seemed to him that I didn't want to talk.

Then came a list of things he was worrying about. He said he thought I didn't do things the way I normally did because I was afraid of upsetting him. He said I had upset him because he wanted me to be myself and not change. On the other hand, he said, he loved having someone in his life 'who lives for me in every respect'.

He demanded to know why I wasn't writing. He wanted me to write and that, he said, was why he kept asking me about it. If he was the love of my life (as I kept saying he was) why didn't I write? Perhaps, he suggested, the reason was him – perhaps 'I am not an inspiration for you at all. So what kind of love is this?' He went on:

> *If this love is so big why don't you feel the need to write?*
> *I feel bad about it because I know you have the talent to write*
> *and it seems I do nothing to inspire you. Your American friend,*
> *he does 'motivate' you.*

He said he thought I must be bored with him because we'd stayed in all weekend, although 'I am not questioning your love'. None of this, he said, was my fault but – and he was sorry to say it – I had done nothing to help him understand . . .

> *Don't say anything about hopes and things like that please.*
> *At the end of the day you are here so . . .*

He said he couldn't spend five minutes of his life without thinking of me but that most of those thoughts were 'the wrong ones'. He wanted to know why I didn't talk to him about this. He said he didn't know me.

> *I feel a lot of the time you would like to say something and you don't do it because you think you will upset me. I can see it in your eyes . . .*

And then, just before the end, he wrote:

> *At the moment I am really struggling to cope with your past. I want to know all about it. I do not want to know it at all. If I don't know I cannot think about it. But I know there is something so I will think and create it anyway.*

And then he stopped, as if in mid-air, which was probably just as well.

Franc didn't encourage my writing – instead, he hectored me. He asked so many questions saying he didn't want answers, but then – almost in the same breath – that he *did*. His reaction when I'd told him about my ex-husband made me careful not to mention my past again. But every now and again he would ask about the photograph he had seen of my ex-boyfriend. Every so often he would take a sharp dig at my American friend, Quinn. They'd met once and when they did Quinn had given Franc's hand a firm shake, keeping hold of it slightly longer than was necessary while he gave him a beady look and said, 'You make sure you take care of this girl.' I don't think Franc liked that. I don't think he liked that I had turned to Quinn when Sally died. I was beginning to discover there was quite a lot that Franc didn't like.

He was barking up the wrong tree with Quinn, though. There was never anything physical between us and our friendship was based on a meeting of minds. We were as thick as thieves, Quinn and I. We joked about it, once.

'Pet lamb, my wife's jealous of you.'

'That's funny. Franc's jealous of you.'

Quinn slapped his leg and roared with laughter. 'Hell, honey . . . if I had any kind of sexual prowess I could understand it but I'm eighty years old, for chrissakes!'

When I lived nearby Quinn and I would often spend an afternoon at the weekend in his studio, smoking cheroots, eating big American pickles straight out of the jar and drinking vodka. He taught me almost everything I know about modern art and quite a lot about life, mostly the bits I'd missed when I was out buying shoes or was shacked up with unsuitable men. He had known Diego Rivera and Frida Kahlo ('he was real mean to her') and in the Second World War he had travelled through North Africa, across to Sicily and up the leg of Italy with General Patton's army. He was a remarkable man, a great storyteller and very good company – a true friend. All three of my girls were immensely fond of him. Quinn once said to me, 'Don't let anyone clip your wings, honey.' I think he must have had a premonition, or perhaps he just recognized the type when he clapped eyes on the man whose sense of ownership was evidenced in the arm draped proprietorially across my shoulders.

Perhaps I failed to see the danger because Franc was so different from my ex. Franc was meticulous about the way things should be done. My husband was laid back to the point of neglect, except when he had a bee in his bonnet about something, and I don't think he really cared all that much about how I dressed or looked, whereas to Franc that was everything. One was a sledgehammer and the other a scalpel. With one, you could rub along quite nicely, having fun and being a family, for months; with the other the brooding could go on for days on end while I tiptoed around him being as quiet and unobtrusive as possible, hardly speaking.

The nicknames these men gave me are revealing: when I first met my husband he called me 'Squeak' – because I was quietly spoken – which later became 'Mouse'. Franc christened me 'Sock' because, he said, I was always under his feet. But then that was where he seemed to want me to be.

In my purse there is a small square of paper I cut out of one of the notebooks. In Franc's writing are four words: 'I love you Sock.' I carried it with me – and still do – as a reminder that I was loved, or believed that I was. While I long to make a bonfire of everything else Franc has ever written to me I would find it hard to part with that. But something has dawned on me as I write this: before Franc, 'I love you' was something I only ever heard from my daughters. A longing to hear the 'three little words' had propelled me into making some strange life choices long before I met Franc.

The letters, the faxes, notes, emails and diaries help me to see the progress of our relationship, and in a way of which Franc would most certainly approve: meticulous detail. Reading Franc's letters now reminds me how I felt when I saw one: would it be nice or nasty, make sense or not? As a general rule, the longer the letter, the nastier it was. They had the same effect on me as that maths teacher at primary school – I wanted to hide. In the month after the rant there were quite a few long ones and when I read them they left me winded. Because his English slipped when he was wound up I would have to read them many times over to try and grasp the sense. But they still confused me. I couldn't understand what it was he wanted, even as I groped desperately for the meaning – and for the love. He kept telling me that I was not showing my love for him when I thought I did that every day in so very many ways: when I trimmed his hair and beard, gave him manicures and pedicures, cooked delicious meals, went to the gym and followed his exercise programme to the letter; when I left him a note signed with kisses or by being there for him and doing things properly, the way he liked them. At first, I had been rewarded with a smile and an 'I love you, Ellen' but before long he seemed to expect me to do these things. They went from being a treat to a duty, and the duties multiplied while the smiles and 'I love you's tailed away.

Then Dave decided to sell his house, the one Franc and I were living in. We had to find somewhere else to live. The question of whether we would be moving together, as a couple, was never asked or, as far as I know, even considered. It was simply assumed.

There were some new-build two-bedroom flats that Franc was interested in. The fact that they were pristine and no one had lived in them appealed to his fastidious side. We arranged to go and look at one together. I had a hair appointment in the city centre after work so Franc was going to meet me at the hairdresser. The timing went slightly adrift and I was thirty minutes late coming out. Obviously it wasn't my fault that the hairdresser was running behind. I could see Franc through the window and waved at him, mouthing, 'Come in.' I don't know why he stayed outside, pacing the pavement, but I began to feel anxious and if I could have left I would but my hair was wet, waiting to be dried. When I finally emerged he smiled and told me my new, slightly shorter style made me look much younger. Then he rolled up the magazine he'd been reading and bounced it up and down on top of my head: 'DO [thump] NOT [thump] EVER [thump] DO [thump] THAT [thump] TO [thump] ME [thump] AGAIN [thump] ELLEN [harder thump for emphasis].' I carried on smiling because I didn't know what else to do. People looked at us curiously and gave us a wide berth, but no one did or said anything. I fixed my smile, transmitting the 'nothing to see here' message, but if you looked – if you *really* looked – you would have seen that it wasn't right. My eyes were spilling over and I had blushed scarlet. Then we went and saw the flat as though nothing had happened. Franc decided to take it and signed the agreement on the spot.

On 2 April, Good Friday, we went away to Bath as we had planned and then on to Salisbury and Stonehenge, returning home via the Cotswolds. We stopped off at Charlecote Park on the way back. It was chilly but sunny and I was relaxed, so relaxed I mentioned that this was one of my favourite places and I had a book about it somewhere. That was all it took for Franc to start picking away at me to find out who I'd been there with before. Eventually he dragged it out of me – I'd been with Stuart – and so we had to leave. On the drive home, every time I looked across at him he had his lips pressed tightly together. He wouldn't take my hand in the car as he usually did so I rested my hand on his knee, in case he changed his mind. That evening I had to explain again about my husband and about Stuart. I didn't want to. I knew it would cause trouble and we'd probably be up half the night going over this tired old ground. The next day I took my precious box of photographs to work and locked them away in my cupboard until I could take them somewhere safe.

The weekend of the 9th, we were away again, this time to London because he wanted to see a brands exhibition at the Business Design Centre in Islington. I'm not sure the fact that this coincided with one of my father's occasional visits to the Midlands was entirely incidental.

We stayed at a hotel on Upper Street and Franc talked

about how he would like to work in London. 'You will come with me,' he said, suggesting a long-term future together. We were standing looking in a shop window when Franc kicked my foot to straighten it and then he kept kicking my feet every time I turned my toes in. He did it all weekend. When we were on an escalator at Angel Tube station he whacked me between the shoulder blades because he said I wasn't standing up straight. He did that all weekend too. I won't say I accepted this from Franc but I could see why he was doing it because I'd grown up being told that I was pigeon-toed and round-shouldered. He bestowed a kiss after each reprimand to show it was for my own good.

On Saturday night, over dinner, we had our second dis-agreement about money. It wasn't exactly a row, more a difference of opinion. He told me I should save money. It was sound advice but as I pointed out, I wasn't yet in a position to do so, having just moved house again. He offered to help me to manage my money better but I, having been fleeced by my ex-husband, thanked him and declined. Predictably, he took offence, wanting to know why I didn't trust him. Managing my own money was my line in the sand. I stuck to my guns. He was a bit frosty for a couple of hours, but it seemed quickly forgotten.

After we got back, Franc sent me a very long fax. It's faded now and quite hard to read except in good light but it contains, if you like, the essence of the man. I've labelled it with a Post-it note. I call it the Shove.

I do not know what has happened to me in the last four months. I do not know why I feel so deeply involved with you. But I do know that I cannot carry on like this. It is not right for me and it is not right for you.

Reading this made my heart contract for fear of what might come next.

> *You keep saying you love me so much and that I am the love of your life and that . . . and that. The problem is I do believe you and therefore I do expect something from you.*

I knew he was complicated. That was very clear and he said so often enough. He was always telling me how he was used to dealing with problems on his own, that he was self-reliant because that way was more straightforward. He wrote (again) about how he was thinking about me all the time and repeated that 'unfortunately' these thoughts were almost always bad ones. He said he was living his life for me alone and wanted to help me.

> *And I am sorry if I talk about money but is just to explain what I think . . .*

By the end of the first page I understood that he expected me to show my feelings all the time and especially when he did something for me. I thought I did that quite naturally but it seemed whatever I did, or had done, was not enough.

> *Yesterday I wrote on the book I bought for you something I thought would have made you very happy. Maybe I am wrong but I thought I would have seen some reaction from you showing me how happy you were. Your reaction . . . well, let's forget it.*

He told me I was an artist, romantic, so in love with him but I never showed him that side of myself and he had expected that from me. He felt cheated, thwarted, as though I should be Cathy to his Heathcliff. That was all he needed, he said, to make him feel better.

*All I ask to someone who keeps saying how much she loves
me is to show me that love when I need it. And in this respect
to say 'I love you' does not count. If I am not even breathing
because of a picture I have seen I cannot believe you not doing
the easiest and simplest thing: get the picture (I did not like
that movie with Demi Moore –* The Scarlet Rose? *– because
one of the actors reminded me about the picture).*

I couldn't get the picture, which was safe under lock and
key at work, and I panicked. I kept telling him there was nothing to hide, that I had told him everything, but he didn't
believe me.

*I knew you took the pictures away. And you did say
nothing. And I felt betrayed and hurt in my feeling, and I
could not understand why you did not want to help me. And
the more you say there is nothing the worse it goes because
I cannot understand why then you do nothing for me.*

What more did he want me to do? I thought we talked so
much. Was it that I said the wrong things? Did not knowing
what to do mean he was right, that I didn't love him? I believed
I did. To think that I was wrong, that I had somehow been
dishonest and hurt him was hurting me, too.

*Is it so bad just talking to me about your love for me? You
say you love me and you do not want to stand in front of me
and say just a few words to feed my needs. How do you expect
me to believe you when you say I am the love of your life if
I can't get support from you?*

Then he turned to my marriage. How, he wanted to know,
had I been able to put up with that for so long and yet I wasn't
able to do 'any simple thing' for him?

*Please do not leave me to destroy what there is between us.
Please help me with your love. I need you to talk with me. And
talk with me. And talk with me.*

The feeling that I was about to lose him began to settle
heavily in my chest, yet I still couldn't understand why. He
said he thought there were things I did not want to tell him,
although he said he did not want to know everything 'for the
sake of knowing it'. But in the next breath he said that if I did
not tell him 'everything' he did not believe we were 'as close
as we claim to be'. He did not think I felt I *could* tell him everything.

*I need to see real love. In the simplest possible way. I know
I am not asking anything impossible if you really love me (as I
know you do). I do need to know you live for me and that you
are prepared to support me.*

Then he said he would have written another hundred
pages about how he felt but that he couldn't go on. The final
sentence told me that when we went out for dinner the night
before, and in spite of everything, he had been struck dumb
by my beauty. I was so confused I didn't know what to think.

When I got back from work, he kept me up half the night
going over and over it. Eventually, at about 4 a.m., shattered,
I went to bed and left him downstairs. Christ. What a mess.

The next morning, as Franc slept soundly, I found another
long note waiting for me on the kitchen table.

*I need to write again. I need to do it because I can't bear
all this anymore. I owe you an apology anyway. Please do not
think I do all this to hurt you. It is for me. I need to get rid of
all these awful feelings and sensations. I know I am selfish in
this respect.*

He knew my past was not my fault but he found it difficult to live with. Every time he saw something that reminded him of my 'previous life', he felt sick. He said when I didn't say anything it meant I wasn't thinking about him. This, he said, made him 'very jealous' and I must therefore always tell him my thoughts.

> *I see you thinking not about me but about a time when you did the same thing with somebody else. And you never say anything. Or all you can say is 'there is nothing I can do about it'. How do you think I feel when you say that?*
>
> *I need to trust you and at the moment I can't because you are hiding things to me. You still are.*

One of the things I'd said during the previous night's interrogation was that I had no experience of a relationship as intense as ours. I asked him to be patient with me because he was so much more experienced than I was and I needed to learn. He said he didn't believe me, and he wrote it again in his letter.

> *And why do you always leave me on my own when I need you? Why?*
>
> *I have to stop now.*

*

Wednesday the 14th is a sunny April morning but I can barely see it. I have read Franc's note over and over and my eyes are swollen and red from crying. My voice is hoarse from the night before, saying the same words repeatedly until I can't say them anymore because they don't work. I cannot make Franc see how much I love him. I drink coffee but I cannot eat because I am brim full of pain for everything that has happened over the last few months – the loss of my home, the loss of my family, our pets, our things all packed into boxes and standing unloved in a cold corner of an anonymous trading estate, the job that I wanted so much but is beginning to look like another misjudgement, the deaths and tragedy, the failure and Franc . . . Every time Franc behaves like this it releases so much agony inside me I find it impossible to carry on doing normal things. I have Talking Heads on the Walkman. David Byrne is singing 'Once in a Lifetime'. I feel as though I am no longer myself, as though the world has cut me loose. I am slipping into something unknown.

I walk out of the house I share with Franc, leaving a note asking him to call me in sick at work but I don't say goodbye and I hope he won't see me or find out where I'm going because I catch a bus out to the countryside village where one of my friends lives. I have called her and she's in. Nina is a good listener, steady and wise, and she doesn't ask difficult questions – a rock in this sea of catastrophe. There will be calm. I need calm because I feel as though I'm going mad.

It doesn't last long though. I don't know how he found me but very soon Franc is at the door and then we are in Nina's back garden and he is standing over me, talking. Franc is always talking at me – except for when he's not, of course, when he's brooding silently over his disappointment in me. In all that talking he never asks how I'm coping with all those recent bad things; he never mentions Sally, or my poor cat, Byron. He has mentioned my children once, to tell me that they are a 'reminder of another man's fuck'. When he said this I say nothing about them being conceived in love and how hard I'd fought for them, how hollow and pointless my life had seemed without them, my adored babies. To add to everything else I am a craven, miserable coward. What is happening to me? I've always been so strong.

Franc thanks Nina and puts me into his car. I will not (he says) take you home because clearly you cannot be trusted. Instead I am to go with him to his meeting in Nottingham where I will sit in the car and wait patiently until he's done, like the badly behaved child I am. Three hours later and we're on our way back again. Franc talks the whole way about what he needs from me, about what I do wrong. Then he talks the entire evening about the same things. He doesn't seem to notice that all the spirit has gone out of me; that I've been hammered flat and thin and that I've folded in on myself. Feeling as insubstantial as smoke I drift upstairs to go to the loo. My overriding wish is that Franc will shut up, press 'pause', leave me alone for a bit. I can think of nothing else so I take a fistful of pills, the antidepressants my doctor had prescribed. I don't suppose this is quite what he had in mind when he said they'd help me and I'm sorry for that, I'm sorry for everything. I'm sorry I'm a disaster, hopeless, helpless, useless . . .

The next thing I know is that Franc has his fingers down my throat and I'm fighting him hard to let me go but what I'm seeing jumps around in fits and starts and clouds over. Then I'm in the back of an ambulance. I can hear an irregular beep, which I recognize as a heart monitor and I know it doesn't sound right. It's frightening until I begin to sink down, fading into warmth and peace. Gratefully I let myself go while I keep repeating my mantra: I'm sorry, I'm so, so sorry . . . I can't do this anymore . . .

It turns out you need quite a lot of antidepressants to finish the job. When I wake up on a hospital trolley my stomach has been pumped and there's a nasty taste in my mouth. I feel like shit and Franc is nowhere to be seen. He's gone home. No one asks me why I did this desperate thing, although statistics estimate that almost thirty women a day attempt suicide and that three women a week kill themselves as a result of experiencing domestic abuse. My bruises are assumed to be a result of Franc's heroic attempts to save me and they are, partly. I did make him do that, although perhaps he didn't need to be quite so rough. Poor Franc. Heroic Franc. I am simply asked if I will do it again. I shake my head, ashamed. I am discharged in the very early morning with a taxi waiting and a follow-up appointment with my GP. I go home too. Where else can I go?

I crawl into bed and Franc brings me a cup of tea – black, with honey – and my Walkman. With one earpiece each we lie wrapped up together and listen to the song he has chosen, REM's 'Everybody Hurts'. For me, this album is forever associated with Sally. 'Nightswimming' was played at her funeral. He knows this. I told him.

The next day Franc goes off to Milan on business and I keep my doctor's appointment. We talk about what I did. Did I really mean to kill myself? No, not really. I just wanted it to stop and I felt desperate for some calm. What did I want to stop? God, I wish I could answer that. How long have you got?

I don't say a thing about Franc. I just talk about how awful the last year has been. The doctor signs me off for a week – the note says 'exhaustion' and 'nervous collapse'. When I get home there is a letter from Doreen at work telling me I will be docked two days' pay because I didn't notify them that I was ill. Franc read my note and didn't bother to make the call. I don't say anything about anything when I go back to the office – only that I wasn't well. I tear up the doctor's note because I'm fearful of Doreen too now. I can't lose my job on top of everything else.

While Franc was away, I wrote a letter for him to read on his return. The language I used makes me cringe – but I knew that it was my best shot at pleasing Franc and not finding myself abandoned and on the street again.

18 April

Darling Franc

I've been thinking all weekend about how to express, or write down for you, the way I feel about you – how to describe for you my 'big love' so you can believe that, in spite of everything, it exists for us.

When I fell in love with you I began to live by a light that shone within me, shining into every corner of my life. This light, the beauty and truth of my feelings for you, became a well-spring bubbling up with affection, tenderness, sweetness, passion, longing, desire, love and an almost impossible yearning. It unites my heart, soul, mind and body in a common cause, to love you.

Thinking of you now, so far away from me, I feel the deep and penetrating pain of separation. The flow of feelings for you, blocked by your absence, could drown me. The misery I feel when I'm not with you could engulf me, suffocate me. This is my love for you; I could and would, die for you. This huge overwhelming big, big love gives me both torment and bliss.

I look the same when you're not here, I do the same things but I'm only half a person, not complete. I am empty without you, part of me is torn away. You are in my thoughts every second of the day and night.

And so on. Reading this now sickens me.

Franc replied, at length, the next day:

Darling Helen
  I have read your letter. I do like it.

Then he immediately picked on what I said about my 'big love'. This, he said, was the crucial point and although he said he believed me . . .

> *If I am with you now is because last Wednesday you showed to me how much you loved me. Despite the fact you loved me so much, despite the fact you knew I need you, despite I told you not to leave me on my own, despite the fact you knew how much I worried about you, despite all this and much more you just run away.*

He wrote about how, when he took me with him to Nottingham, we had talked and I had told him how much I loved him. He said I had promised him everything.

> *And despite that again you did what you did to me. Despite the fact you loved me so much, despite the fact you knew how much I loved you too, you hurt me to death again. We will talk about this again and again.*

The 'again and again' part torpedoed any hope I might have had that we could recover from this and be as we were when we first met. He told me not to use his anger over that photograph of me with my ex-boyfriend as an excuse. Yes, he said, it made him crazy to see me with another man and yes, it made him crazy that I had taken 'that bloody picture' away. He demanded to know why I hadn't brought it back. If I'd told him I was afraid to he would have hit the roof. He would have seen it as further proof that my 'big love' didn't exist.

It was not the picture. It was about lies or half truth as you like to describe it. Forgive me but I cannot forget it. And that is because I 'see' you thinking about someone else while you are telling me you don't remember.

He said he loved me so much that he could not accept 'normal things' about me, like a photograph.

He finished by telling me that my behaviour had made everything much worse – for him.

How could I resolve this obsession with a photograph? I felt battered and hollow. What he wanted was impossible. It's not as though I could un-take it. So I said nothing. There was nothing to say.

★

Why didn't I leave? That's the question women like me are always asked. It was all over my Twitter timeline when Helen Archer was going through hell on the radio, as was the stock reply, 'Why doesn't he stop?' In my experience the right answer is, 'Because he can't.' Men like Franc don't understand what they're doing is wrong so why should they change? They might occasionally ask for help because they know that's what they're expected to do and they might even change their behaviour – for a while. But once an abuser of women, always an abuser of women. Abusers lack empathy; they don't instinctively know that it's wrong to torture another human being. And for many, if not all, it's an addiction.

Like other addictions – once an alcoholic, always an alcoholic – it can lie dormant for a very long time but it's always there, sweaty, volatile and dangerous. And women who are abused have their own addiction – that desperate search for 'true love', the love we were promised since we first read

Sleeping Beauty or *Cinderella*. We want the man we fell in love with back, the one who was so adoring and lovely, who couldn't do enough for us, who made us feel so special and loved and cared for. We know that man is real because we see him often, in between the other stuff. We think we can change him and heal him, return him to his true self and make him a better man. We think we can banish the monster. Unfortunately, I don't think there is a twelve-step programme for that.

Now when I read these letters from Franc, asking me to help him, I still feel a stab of conscience. Whether he meant it or not is another matter but his words triggered a hard-wired instinct in me to help, to do whatever I could to make it all better, to get the grateful smile. Franc knew he was throwing me a bone, something to keep me 'under his feet', his 'Sock'. Women like me know our place.

And it seems to me that as long as misogyny, gender inequality and sexism remain ubiquitous, women will be forced to remember their place. And that is one of the reasons why men who practise coercive control are so successful at it. Take Franc's little 'rules':

1. Dinner ready promptly at a time specified by him.
2. Always keep the house clean and tidy to a specified standard.
3. Provide personal grooming services as and when requested, to include but not limited to: manicures, pedicures, beard trimming, back waxing, hairline trimming.
4. No bare feet.
5. Do not leave the room when he's angry.
6. Do not be late.

7. Answer the phone by the third or fourth ring.
8. Immediately you answer the phone go somewhere quiet where you can hear.
9. Eat only proteins and salad.
10. Stop smoking.
11. Do not drink more than one glass of wine (white).
12. Go to the gym at least three times a week for ninety minutes a visit and following the prescribed exercise schedule.
13. Do not speak to men.
14. Keep nothing back and tell everything about all previous relationships.
15. Do not ask questions about his previous relationships or family.
16. Have a schedule ready for the weekend by Thursday evening.
17. Wear clothes approved by Franc.
18. Always look nice, tidy and well groomed.
19. Smile.
20. Showers, not baths.
21. Shower before sex.
22. Shower after sex.
23. Be passive during sex.
24. Do not go to see, go out with or talk to family or friends.
25. Do nothing that might make him jealous or have 'bad thoughts'.
26. Do not be better at anything than he is.

And that's only part of it. The terrifying thing is that for generations of women it will sound all too familiar. Here's the 'Good Wife's Guide' from a 1950s women's magazine:

1. Have dinner ready. Plan ahead, even the night before, to have a delicious meal ready, on time for his return. This is a way of letting him know that you have been thinking about him and are concerned about his needs.

2. Most men are hungry when they come home and the prospect of a good meal (especially his favourite dish) is part of the warm welcome needed.

3. Prepare yourself. Take 15 minutes to rest so you'll be refreshed when he arrives. Touch up your make-up, put a ribbon in your hair and be fresh-looking. He has just been with a lot of work-weary people.

4. Be a little gay and a little more interesting for him. His boring day may need a lift and one of your duties is to provide it.

5. Clear away the clutter. Make one last trip through the main part of the house just before your husband arrives. Gather up schoolbooks, toys, paper, etc. and then run a dust cloth over the tables.

6. Over the cooler months of the year you should prepare and light a fire for him to unwind by. Your husband will feel he has reached a haven of rest and order, and it will give you a lift too. After all, catering for his comfort will provide you with immense personal satisfaction.

7. Prepare the children. Take a few minutes to wash the children's hands and faces (if they are small), comb their hair and, if necessary, change their clothes.

8. Children are little treasures and he would like to see them playing the part. Minimize all noise. At the time of his arrival, eliminate all noise of the washer, dryer or vacuum. Try to encourage the children to be quiet.

9. Be happy to see him. Greet him with a warm smile and

show sincerity in your desire to please him. Listen to
him.

10. You may have a dozen important things to tell him, but
the moment of his arrival is not the time. Let him talk
first – remember, his topics of conversation are more
important than yours.

11. Make the evening his. Never complain if he comes home
late or goes out to dinner, or other places of
entertainment without you. Instead, try to understand
his world of strain and pressure and his very real need to
be at home and relax.

12. Your goal: Try to make sure your home is a place of
peace, order and tranquillity where your husband can
renew himself in body and spirit.

13. Don't greet him with complaints and problems.

14. Don't complain if he's late home for dinner or even if
he stays out all night. Count this as minor compared to
what he might have gone through that day.

15. Make him comfortable. Have him lean back in a
comfortable chair or have him lie down in the bedroom.
Have a cool or warm drink ready for him.

16. Arrange his pillow and offer to take off his shoes. Speak
in a low, soothing and pleasant voice.

17. Don't ask him questions about his actions or question
his judgement or integrity. Remember, he is the master
of the house and as such will always exercise his will
with fairness and truthfulness. You have no right to
question him.

18. A good wife always knows her place.

I've always found number 17 chilling.

It's easy to laugh at something that seems so quaint and

old-fashioned but sixty-something years later a large number of men will still believe this is how it should be. They might not say so – they believe it nonetheless.

But the real point I'm making is that this is mostly trivial stuff, which you would be doing anyway. So what if you need to make some minor changes because that's the way he likes it done. Women are coached from an early age in the art of making things nice, of pleasing, of making people happy, keeping things running smoothly and taking pride in a home. Women have traditionally taken on, and still do, professional roles that require those same skills, as nurses, secretaries, clerks, receptionists, cooks, cleaners, hairdressers, beauticians – all the service industries. There's nothing wrong with that, providing we can lift our eyes higher and not self-limit. Women in subservient roles are vulnerable to controlling men who merely take advantage of the status quo.

Coercive control is embedded in ordinary humdrum domestic tasks. And it is all too often overlooked by the way we, as a society, measure injury – by what we can see. We measure damage by bruises, black eyes, lost teeth, bald patches where hair has been pulled from a head, broken bones and, a troubling and more recent development, acid burns.

A woman who has been repeatedly shouted at for failing to answer the phone within set time parameters, or who has been the subject of a strict diet and exercise regime, who hasn't seen her family or friends for months on end, who is some-times absent from work with no explanation, is easily ignored if she doesn't bear the outward signs of physical assault. Psy-chological injury is much harder to spot. A woman subjected to either form of abuse haemorrhages clues to what is going on but as a society we are still turning away, uncomfortable about asking questions which might be seen as intrusive.

In Liane Moriarty's book, *Big Little Lies*, recently adapted for television, beautiful, wealthy and abused Celeste hits the nail on the head: 'I was waiting for someone to ask the right question but they never did.'

For most victims of domestic abuse the 'right question' has to be asked not just once but on several occasions over a period of time and not only because abusers spend a long time enforcing their victims' silence: it also takes courage to answer truthfully because to do so means admitting that you *are* a victim, that what you've sold to everyone as your very own fairy tale is nothing of the sort. Admitting to that means losing whatever shreds of pride and comfort you've managed to hold on to because it's the last concession to your condition, the one that comes at the end of the road when you finally admit failure, and failure is so hard to admit because it is what you have been told you are for however long this has been going on. Your confidence, self-esteem, ability to make decisions, your whole sense of self has been lost in a mire of petty domestic tyranny. It's an absurdity, too, that should a woman take the enormous step of asking for help she will probably ask several times before that help is forthcoming. And each time she goes through the same agonizing mental process.

The reference to fairy tales is important. The promotion of love and marriage, romance and motherhood as the most desirable state of womanhood has never gone out of fashion. The moment in 1981 when Lady Diana Spencer walked down the aisle of St Paul's Cathedral to marry Prince Charles seemed to be the beginning of a modern fairy tale, about a beautiful young princess with the world at her feet. Google 'fairy-tale gown' and in a heartbeat 1.5 million results will pop up on your screen, most of them wedding dresses. Weddings are big business. Last year *Harper's Bazaar* reported that the average cost of a UK wedding was £27,000,[1] not including whatever was spent on the honeymoon. When I got married – in 1975 in a registry office with 'only' eighty guests (my husband-to-be would not countenance a church wedding) – I remember a conversation with my grandmother who was concerned I would regret not having had my 'big day'. She needn't have worried.

The problem we have is that we are led to believe we have an entitlement to be 'princess for a day', that we are entitled to our own fairy tale. The wedding has become such a symbol of status that it hardly seems to matter whether you really are marrying the love of your life. A survey carried out by the Office for National Statistics in 2016 appears to bear this out, confirming that 42 per cent of marriages end in divorce and that marriages are most likely to end between the fourth and eighth wedding anniversary.[2]

Coercive control follows the pattern of many fairy tales – a flawed love story lived out through a series of increasingly impossible tasks with the promise of a handsome prince at the end. Only, unlike *Cinderella* – but very like *The Little Mermaid* – the love of the handsome prince is never won, which doesn't mean you stop believing it could be. That's the odd thing about it. If this was about industrial relations and a promised pay rise you'd go on strike but instead you keep doggedly on, trying to meet impossible targets while the person in charge tells you that you're feeble and that you'll never do it.

Fairy tales are not real life.

---

1. Bridebook.co.uk (wedding planning website), December 2017.
2. Office for National Statistics, *Statistical Bulletin: Divorces in England and Wales: 2016: Dissolutions and annulments of marriage by previous marital status, sex, age, fact proven and to whom granted.*

Chapter Five

The note I mentioned a while back, the one that says, *DM – Can't do things for kids anymore*, appears in my diary on 23 April that first year with Franc.

A little bit of digging through another pile of papers turns up a statement I wrote months later for Frances, my union rep, referring to that note: 'Doreen commented that it was probably a good thing that I had been ill because my children needed to understand that I would not be "at their beck and call anymore" and it would get them "off my back".'

The note sits above a reminder that on the same date I also had a meeting with an HR manager where my knuckles were rapped for breaching hospital protocol on data protection. On the day of my thwarted attempt to leave the world, and unknown to me, my second grandson entered it. When I went back to work I checked the hospital system because I knew the baby was due and my daughter wasn't allowed to speak to me. I was desperate for reassurance.

I'm surprised it all turned so complicated so quickly. The period of time over which I became deeply and irrevocably entangled with Franc, experienced the deterioration of my situation at work, and was again separated from my children, felt like an agonizing eternity while I was living it. Who could bear that kind of pressure without cracking? Not me.

There was something else. Doreen had intercepted one of

Franc's faxes, and sent back a reply of her own, pretending to be me. It perhaps explains the two or three faxes I'd never seen – had she taken those, too? She must have thought that replying to one was a huge joke but I was in such trouble when I got home. Doreen hadn't used my deferential tone. When I went home I walked into an ambush.

'Hello, Franc. How was your day?'

'You know how it was – I sent you a fax.'

'Did you?'

'You know I did. You told me to grow up. Not funny, Ellen.'

He reached into his jacket pocket and put a fax in front of me. The handwriting on it looked a lot like mine but it was in capitals. I never used capitals.

'But Franc, I didn't write that. Truly I didn't.'

'Don't lie to me. You did do it.'

'I'm not lying. I didn't send it.'

And so it went on for most of the evening until I cried and Franc decided I was telling the truth.

I took the fax to work next day and asked Jeannie if she knew anything about it. I checked all around the machine to see if anything had slipped behind it. Nothing. It never occurred to me that it might have been Doreen – but when she saw me searching she volunteered the information with a laugh, then handed over a couple more of Franc's faxes. I wonder if she'd have laughed if she'd seen what happened. As it was, she did the finger-eye thing to let me know she was watching me.

*

Franc and I spent May bank holiday in the Lake District and it was lovely but then I'd never been there before, so our time away was, for once, free of his 'paranoids' and 'bad thoughts'.

When we returned home things seemed to be back on an even keel, so much so that I took Franc with me to a family dinner to meet my father and brothers. I don't know what they thought of him, they never said, but he seemed to like them. He was on his best behaviour, which reminded me how much I loved him. We felt like a normal couple again. I was proud of him that night and allowed myself to believe that as long as I could keep things like this I had Franc back.

We'd already filled one notebook with our messages so I got a new one. Over the short week following the bank holiday our notes, letters and faxes flew back and forth. On the face of it, they paint a picture of a loving, caring relationship. Unless, of course, you can read between the lines. In the notebook for Tuesday 4 May:

Morning darling Franc

I know you didn't sleep well – try to stop worrying about the house [and having to move] please! I'm sure it will all be fine.

Anyway, back to being without you for a whole day again – harder after our beautiful weekend away, and it was beautiful wasn't it?

With the tenderest, sweetest, deepest love you can imagine.

Helen xxx

PS No gym tonight so the Sock will be home first.

Franc said he thought that the weekend had been beautiful as well. He said he had enjoyed spending time away on our own, just the two of us.

Home first and a lot of housework to do: very good.

See you later.

Franc

Next came a letter. At least I think it was a letter because it's been folded into three as though it's been put into an envelope and I'd asked him not to send me any more faxes.

The first part contained a mild rebuke that I no longer wrote letters to him. (He underlined 'your letters'.) That puzzled me because it simply wasn't true. Then he asked if perhaps 'the excitement of the first period has gone'. He said he loved my morning notes though so I decided that maybe I didn't need to worry too much.

> *I think you will be reading this letter at work so I will not write anything too . . . dangerous.*
>
> *No bad news, don't worry. I just wanted to say I had a wonderful weekend with you and I hope we will have some more others like this one.*
>
> *Keep smiling*
>
> *Love*
>
> *Franc*

Then the notebook again, Thursday 6 May:

Dearest Franc

> *Why didn't you wake me and I would have gone into the spare room? I hope it wasn't my fault! I panicked when I woke up and you weren't there.*
>
> *I will be home as soon as I can tonight to tidy the house etc. Take care, you must be so tired.*
>
> *Yours, always and forever*
>
> *Sock*
>
> *xxx*

There is an arrow pointing to 'I will be home' and Franc has written:

YOU'D BETTER BE! Dear Sock, it was not your fault
anyway. See u later. Franc.

On the 7th, Doreen had me in her office to point out that
it was inappropriate to send or receive personal faxes in the
office. She was perfectly pleasant about it and I apologized
and told her that I'd explained that to Franc – who perhaps
hadn't understood – so there shouldn't be any more.

Notebook, Tuesday 11 May:

Morning Franc
  Love isn't something that one can measure. I can't say
'I love you xxx much', can I? All I can tell you is that my
feelings for you are strong and true. I love you in an infinite
number of ways and my love for you fills my soul and colours
my days and nights. When we're apart I think of you all the
time and when we're together . . . well!
  Franc + Helen = complete bliss!
  I love you now, always and forever.
  Helen xxx

'Darling Sock', wrote Franc, telling me that although he
didn't have much time to 'waiste' writing notes, he loved
me too, but just a little bit which, as he said, was better than
nothing. Then he added,

MEAT FOR DINNER.

And signed off 'Franc'. No love, no kisses, just 'Franc'.
I was disappointed and hungry for the affection he used to
show.

That week Franc took me to buy a pay-as-you-go mobile
phone by which I mean I bought it because he wanted me to
have one. I'd been wanting one for ages but I no longer
bought things unless Franc was with me. Of course, it also

meant that he could keep tabs on me. But because the phone was usually in my handbag, I didn't always hear it ringing. In any case we were not supposed to take private calls at work.

On 13 May the first fax arrived at 10:24. In it Franc told me he was leaving in fifteen minutes to drive to Nottingham but I knew that; he'd told me over breakfast what time he was leaving. Then he accused me of not listening to him properly and of not understanding him. He finished:

> *Pleased if you do not like my fax. It means that when you want to you do understand!!!*

I didn't know what that meant. Alarmed and anxious I replied ten minutes later, although I knew I was breaking my promise to Doreen.

> *Attn: Franc*
> *Sorry I didn't hear the phone. No sign of the alleged fax.*
> *I'm going to the gym after work so that will keep me busy.*
> *Drive safely and dinner will be ready when you get back.*
> *Love*
> *H xxx*
> *PS Please please don't send any more faxes to the office. You-know-who is about.*

Ten minutes after that, at 10:45, Franc replied. Of course I hadn't heard the phone, he said, I never did – and I never listened either.

> *Do not understand your PS. Do not actually know 'who is about'.*
> *See you some time tonight.*
> *Bye*
> *Franc*

Franc must have gone home before he went to Nottingham because when I went into the kitchen there was a note
waiting for me:

Hi Helen
   Note for you in your 'witches' book.
   Franc
PS Bad mood – very bad.

There was nothing, no matter how small, that Franc
would not put his own spin on, take offence at or find suspi-
cious. And there was no possession of mine he would not
examine in minute detail to find something to feed those sus-
picions. It was also typical that he would hide his accusations
together with his 'evidence', forcing me to find them. I was
guilty before I even knew what I was accused of.

My books were far too precious to store in Franc's warehouse: my mother's copies of John Buchan's *Book of Escapes*,
and of Daphne du Maurier's *Rebecca* and *Jamaica Inn*; my
favourite children's books, the rebound seventeenth-century
copy of City of London import taxes (whale bones for corsets
1/- per bundle) and my treasured first edition of Byron's
Works, Diaries and Letters. There were about ten boxes of
them. Apparently, Franc had gone through every box and each
of the books within. Like every other person I know who
owns books, I have notes and letters, cuttings, pressed flowers
and other mementos between the pages. A personal library is
greater than the sum of its parts.

His excavations had struck a rich vein of information
about my wicked past. I knew the book Franc was referring
to: it was from a collection of research material I had gathered
for a project about local pre-Christian rituals and customs. I

had planned to write it up, perhaps into a book of my own. I had written to the author and she had been kind enough to answer my questions in a long letter, followed by another shorter one. These letters are what Franc found.

I don't have them anymore. I probably destroyed them. It was easier to do that with something Franc fixed on, in an attempt to stop him going back to it over and over again, usually during the night, until I was desperate and aching, crying and exhausted with it, said something I shouldn't and we had a row. It's the same technique used by professional interrogators – hammer you with questions and accusations, deprive you of sleep and rest, food and drink, isolate you, confuse you, wear you down. I don't believe there was anything incriminating in those letters and I still can't think why they made him so angry. Perhaps it was that they mentioned my old house, which had an unusual name and history (and a connection to Stuart, although he couldn't have known that); perhaps it was that the letter was from someone I hadn't mentioned, or that I hadn't talked about the abandoned project. Perhaps he thought he'd found proof that I really was a witch. Who knows?

In the bundle of papers I have in front of me there is a loose page torn from our message book and folded into four. The date is right: 14 May. It is the note Franc left for me the following day.

He began by complaining that I had left for work without saying anything or leaving a note but 'after the argument we had last night' he declared that my behaviour just completed the picture.

He accused me of being 'cold' when we were talking and 'actually', he said, 'you were laughing at me.'

It seems to me you were not so bothered about my pain.
Your face was saying that that was not my business so . . .
   To get just a word from you was very difficult not to
mention that you carefully avoided to talk about the two
'personal references'.

Again he complained that I had not said goodbye, telling
me he had got up when I left to check whether or not I really
had gone. He couldn't believe I would go without speaking
again, that I left him in his misery. But I knew that if I had he
would have carried on where we'd left off and I would have
been late for work or not got there at all.

He said he did not know what to say. He hoped my day
would be better than his. Perhaps, he suggested, I did not
need him anymore. Now that I was 'back on track' perhaps
I did not need to be as close to him as I used to be.

   (And you used to be closer to me I can assure you.) Of
course I am happy about that but it changes a lot of things.
Where is the Helen so worried when I had one of my moods?
Now you are laughing at me.

Again he said he did not know what to say or think, that
my behaviour was incomprehensible to him. How could I
treat him like this?

   Again I think I do not know you. I am living with someone
who I do not know. And every day there is a new discovery.
And this makes me think there are so many (bad) things you
have not disclosed. And this worries me. Because this makes
me unhappy. And I am tired. I am tired of this unhappiness,
of this situation with so many bad thoughts in my head.

He said I did not want to understand him. Why, he wanted

to know, didn't I say anything to make him feel better, why didn't I care?

> *I know it is not true but then why?*
> *Love*
> *Franc*

He was right. I *had* laughed at him because it seemed such a stupid thing to get worked up about. I was shaken, though. I decided it was best to ignore the whole silly business and carried on as though nothing had happened.

One day that week he showed me a photograph. It was of a girl standing barefoot on a beach – one of those European beaches where the sand is cleaned twice a day. I could see the tyre tracks. Her bare arms were thrown up above her head in golden sunlight – she was aflame with it. Her top had ridden up from her cut-off denim shorts as she stretched, showing a tanned flat stomach above the loose waistband. She was very slim, probably a size 6. Her face was hidden in a flurry of wind-blown dark curls. A broad smile, white teeth, clear skin. Laughing. This then, was Sophie.

It was Franc's revenge for me laughing at him.

*

More and more in my diary I see an entry struck through and 'no' written next to it.

Thursday 1 April – Lunch, Claire. [NO]

Friday 9 April – Dad visiting family? Shoulder of Mutton. [NO]

Friday 14 May – 7.00 for 7.30 p.m. Me and Franc. Maria's leaving do. Chiquito's. [NO]

And slowly these entries peter out altogether. My friends stop trying to arrange things with me when I bail so often. Franc doesn't want to share me and I want to be with him as much as I possibly can. I am only reliable as far as he is concerned – to everyone else I'm a flake.

I have stopped writing anything in my diary I wouldn't feel safe showing him. Also, after his ransacking of my books there is a tiny bat squeak of mistrust. I couldn't be sure that he wouldn't go through anything else. While I was busy covering my back I poured out Franc-pleasing *billets doux* into our message book.

*

Towards the end of May he went to Paris on a business trip and every evening he phoned at 8 p.m. sharp to find out what I'd been up to: how was work, had I been to the gym, what did I do there, how many cigarettes, was I eating, what was I eating? These conversations felt entirely normal – with no evidence of his 'bad thoughts'. I was relieved that he made no mention of Sophie and an 'I love you, Ellen' as we ended our phone calls was, if not quite a hug, a great comfort.

He arrived home in the early hours of Thursday morning, slipping into bed beside me. His skin was chilly, the feel of him gave me goosebumps. He smelt the same, though – alert to any change I noticed these things now. He was back and I had missed him, but it had been a funny kind of missing. Mostly I had been afraid to do anything other than sit around at home and wait for him to call.

Notebook, Thursday 27 May:

Good morning my Franc!
    How completely wonderful it is to have you back. How I

*love to be in your arms and to be kissed by you. Perhaps it's
good that sometimes you go away because it shows me just
how much I do love you.*

*Gym tonight? Will you come too? Phone me and let me
know. If you want me to come straight home, I will do that.*

*I cooked the venison on Tuesday evening for tonight. I have
taken the tagliatelle out of the freezer too. Will this be OK?*

See you later

All my love

Helen

xxx

PS *Call me!*

We were moving to our new flat over the weekend and it
felt like a fresh start. I was excited – I felt not an ounce of the
dread that had accompanied the last three. Perhaps I felt that
way because I hadn't had to make any decisions this time;
Franc had taken charge of everything. I spent the day cleaning
Dave's house and packing. The flat would be the first home
we had chosen together. Except Franc chose it and Franc's
name was on the lease. For me, a new city-centre flat in a
block of identical others was out of character. I am a country
girl, born and raised. I'd spent the last ten years living in old
houses, surrounded by open fields and as far away from other
people as was practicably possible. It would be impossible to
avoid other people there. The new flat was a two-bedroom
box, full of anonymous flat-pack furniture chosen by Franc,
assembled by him and Dave.

That said, the flat had its attractions: it was convenient
for work and the gym; more importantly, it would contain
my adored Franc; and finally it represented security after the
recent peripatetic years. With hindsight (again) it was com-

pletely daft to think that – I had no legal right to be in that flat at all, my name didn't appear on any of the paperwork. It was as though I didn't exist. At the time I was so wrapped up in him I don't think it even crossed my mind. I put a positive spin on things I wouldn't normally have considered doing. I told myself that it was good to experience different lifestyles, even though I could see no trees from the windows, or the river, which was only twenty yards away. On one side I could see a car park, on the other a row of modern terraced houses and beyond them the taller buildings of the university. The flat was at the wrong angle for good natural light. What did come in was muted and opaque by day, dull orange by night. The stairwells were concrete and sterile. The front door had a security chain and a spyhole. This was not a home that invited me to love it.

I had taken the day off on Friday and when Franc came back from work there were boxes in every room but he had yet to say anything to confirm that we would definitely be moving the next day. Nor had he mentioned the van he was supposed to hire. We didn't have much and a large Transit was all we needed. We were going to the theatre that night, so I showered and changed into a dress. I wore hold-ups instead of tights but they kept falling down because I'd lost so much weight. In the end I discreetly took them off and popped them into my handbag. I thought Franc might be cross but instead he laughed affectionately. Although he still said nothing about the move.

The subject didn't come up on Saturday morning either. We had breakfast as usual and Franc carried on as though it was a weekend the same as any other, to be spent drinking coffee, going to the gym, watching football. I wasn't sure what, if anything, I was supposed to be doing. Eventually, after lunch I timidly said something, trying not to make it sound like nagging and it turned out he *had* been expecting me to book the van. I was sure he had said he would do it. Had he asked me and I'd forgotten? Did he write it in a note somewhere?

I phoned around frantically and found a van we could hire and collect on Sunday morning – from a garage twenty miles away. I kept apologizing, probably too much. Franc wasn't pleased, more exasperated, and said why don't we take some clothes over now in the car. I hadn't packed our clothes yet. I was worried about creasing his designer suits – his Gaultier, Dior and Armani – the suits I snuggled when he was away so that I could imagine he was still there. I even sprayed his Acqua di Parma on my pillow.

Franc, however, had come up with a plan. I was to sit in the back seat of the car holding the tip of a broom handle. The passenger seat was folded down and the brush end rested on the dashboard. Onto this makeshift clothes rail Franc slid his suits, shirts and ties, still on their hangers. It took an hour to get across town and the broom got heavier and heavier. When we reached the flat Franc whisked his suits and shirts up the stairs and straight into the wardrobe. I sat there with my arms trembling as the weight was lifted. Only when he'd finished was I able to haul the bin bags containing my own clothes inside, shake them out and hang them up in the spare wardrobe in the spare room.

The plan for Sunday morning was that Franc would drive the van and I would take the car back. But he had a French licence and the van place wouldn't let him, so I had to. On my own I'm a perfectly capable driver, but I was always terrified driving with a man in the passenger seat in case I made a mistake, real or imagined. Franc wouldn't be in the van with me but he'd still be there, watching.

Although I'd driven plenty of vans before I felt anxious climbing up into the driver's seat of this one and the weather was atrocious. I was to follow Franc, who would go ahead in his car because I didn't know the way. I wasn't familiar with this bit of the Midlands at all. The van was light with no load and skittish in a strong gusting wind, and the wipers couldn't cope with the downpour. Franc's rear lights winked through the spray, but they seemed to be getting further away. I wasn't keeping up and I already thought I was driving too fast for that van in that weather. I couldn't lose sight of Franc. He'd be angry if I got lost. On the passenger seat, my mobile rang.

'Ellen. You know that pedal on the right?'

'Yes, Franc?'

'Use it.'

'Yes, Franc.'

And the bastard sped off into the rain, taking the middle lane and overtaking two slower cars. Just in time I caught sight of his indicator as he took the slip road. I executed a hasty manoeuvre that was not strictly legal and followed. There was a huge roundabout at the bottom and I went around it twice before I spotted Franc in a lay-by. As I pulled in behind him he drove off again.

The next day was a bank holiday, which gave us – or rather me – time to unpack and settle in. I enjoyed that part – the making-a-home part.

Dearest Franc
  I found the notepad!

A little arrow points to where Franc has written, 'Oh no!'

> *Thank you for my wonderful hug this morning before I got up. I need that, and you, so badly. I love you so very much – please understand how much you mean to me.*
>
> *Always, your Sock*
>
> *xxx*
>
> *PS Imagine the biggest hug and the hugest kiss from me today.*

After my note Franc drew a little heart.

★

We'd been living in the flat for a couple of weeks when Franc decided he was bored and wanted to learn to play golf. There was no suggestion that we could learn together so I went with him to his lesson and sat and watched while he practised his swing on the driving range.

The following weekend we made an exhaustive tour of the local golf shops so that he could decide what he needed to buy. It looked to me as though acquiring the right clothes was more important than a decent set of clubs. That golf comes with considerable sartorial excess was a large part of its appeal for him.

It was also the weekend of yet more royal nuptials. Given that I used to make wedding dresses I wanted to see what this bride wore. We were in a vast sports warehouse when I spotted a television, so I stopped to see the news, hoping to catch a glimpse.

Someone whistled and there was Franc, making a gesture peculiar to him. It meant, 'Come here.'

Dutifully I trotted up, glancing back at the receding screen, which showed the happy couple just emerging from the church.

'Yes, Franc?' (Another glance over my shoulder.)

'I want you here, Ellen. Here. This is where you should be.'

'I just wanted to see . . .'

'Here.' And he pointed at his heel.

★

Any misgivings I might have felt about the flat soon vanished in the weeks that followed. The city centre was only ten minutes' walk away and that meant Franc got far less fed-up and irritable than he used to when a walk around the shops meant a drive in the car. I liked the clean simplicity of it. To begin with it did feel like a home and I was sure we would do well there.

Franc's mellow mood meant that when Nina invited us both over for supper on the last Saturday in June Franc said we could go. Furthermore he suggested spending the afternoon in and around my old stamping ground. I was surprised, but pleased. I didn't think there was any hidden agenda.

We visited Quinn first. It was really good to see him but our conversation did not flow as freely as usual. There was an uncomfortable Franc-shaped elephant in the room and it didn't drink vodka on a Saturday afternoon, smoke cheroots, kick its shoes off or eat pickles out of a jar. Nor did he have the faintest interest in a lively discussion about art, although I could see he wanted to observe our interaction. It felt a little uncomfortable. As we left, Quinn hugged me tighter than usual, and formally shook Franc's hand. 'I see you,' he seemed to say.

Part of my justification for wanting to go to Nina's was that when the girls and I moved from our large old house to the tiny new one, a quantity of our stuff ended up in her garage and attic. There were some things of mine that I wanted to bring back to the flat to make it feel more homey.

Franc and Nina had only met once, when I'd fled to her place in April and he'd followed me. It hadn't been the best start and I thought this was a chance to set the record straight, for her to see how good we were together.

I wanted to show Franc off. I wanted him to be clever and funny, charming and affectionate, just enough to make it clear how much we loved each other, and that our relationship was sound. There had been so much wrong in my life that it was important this new stage looked right, at least on the outside. I wanted to believe that true love existed for me too. Others seemed to have it so why not me?

As the evening progressed Franc adopted a shut-in impassive expression and I knew what that meant. He had a way of letting you know what he wanted without saying a word. We'd only been there an hour and had just finished eating when he suggested it was time for us to leave. But lingering after the meal is usually the best bit of dinner with friends. 'Oh, Franc,' I said, squeezing his hand gently, 'there's no rush.' And I took some dishes into the kitchen where Nina and I laughed and chatted while we made coffee. We didn't leave him alone for long.

An hour or so of stilted conversation later and I was forced to accept defeat – the evening hadn't turned out quite the way I'd imagined it would. It wasn't terrible but I was disappointed.

'That's quite a thing to do,' said Franc as Nina fetched our coats. 'To store all that stuff for Ellen and for how long?'

'A year? Eighteen months? I don't know but it's fine. I have the space. We help each other.'

'I wouldn't have done it.'

'Ah, but I have known and loved Helen for a lot longer than you have.'

(Ouch. But at the same time HURRAH!)

Franc was silent during the drive home. There was only the rhythmic thud and squeak of the wipers, the rattle of rain on the windscreen. I caught intermittent glimpses of his profile, eyes fixed on the road ahead, and I turned to gaze, mute, out of the window at the city sliding greasily past. I wasn't sure what had happened.

There are some moments in life that come at you like one of those flick books, a frame at a time. When you go back over it you can stop at a specific point. I remember Franc unlocking the front door and stepping back to let me in first. I remember walking up the stairs and into the flat, dropping my bag down beside the sofa and shaking my coat before hanging it on the hook. I'd been smoking and drinking and I remember thinking I'd get a glass of water to freshen my mouth in case Franc wanted to kiss me as he often did when we came back from somewhere.

When I pitched unexpectedly towards the wall, I thought at first I'd stumbled. It was so quick I couldn't bring my arms up in time to stop myself falling against it. My shoulder made contact first, then my head. My teeth rattled. My ears rang. I bit my tongue and drew blood. I remember a noise somewhere between a crack and a thump and a burst of coloured lights – I literally saw stars. I was wearing a loose cream jumper and a pale grey skirt with a side vent that Franc had bought me. The carpet was tabby-coloured and soft under my cheek. I remember keeping my eyes closed and lying very still but not tense, never tense. Fight, flight or flop. Experience has taught me to favour the flop. While I lay there I tried to process the fact that Franc had just landed me a wallop. He'd punched me on the side of the head, hard enough to knock me flying. I remember very clearly thinking, 'I've done it again.'

It was quiet for a while and my eyes were still closed but I could feel Franc looking at me. I could only guess at what he was thinking but I hoped he was shocked by what he'd done. When I eventually opened my eyes, he helped me to my feet, stroked my hair, kissed my forehead and sent me off to bed with a little pat on my bottom. A bit later he came in with a couple of aspirin. He wasn't so considerate that he left me in peace to sleep, though – we had to talk about what I'd done wrong.

In the morning there was a note in the book:

As I told you, you are a bad girl!
I should have killed you before.

He said he hoped I would 'be better' later. The first time I read that I thought he meant my headache but now I wonder if he meant my behaviour. Everything he said, or wrote, seemed to have two meanings. I remember I begged him to help so that I wouldn't keep getting it wrong and he wouldn't keep being so cross with me.

Help? Well, I understand you want to be independent and you do not like to be told what to do, do you?
If you don't think asking for anything you might need is so dangerous for you (as we could become too close . . .) please feel free to ask.

We had known each other eight months.

*

There are no stronger or more binding lies than those we tell ourselves. How could I believe I was in love with someone who did this to me? And I did believe it. I believed it so easily. I know it doesn't make sense. I needed him (like a drug – the most common analogy people come up with). This was the love I'd read about ever since I was a little girl – feeling overwhelmed by it, the breathless rapture and longing, the self-sacrifice – exactly how it was described in any book I'd ever read, film I'd ever seen, song I'd ever listened to. I suffered for love exactly like the little mermaid or any other fairy-tale heroine. That is what we're supposed to do. I'd ticked off what I felt against the checklist I'd assimilated and I got 'mostly A's. 'Congratulations! You're in love!'

In March 2016, a documentary was screened on BBC4 looking at the inner workings of the Crown Prosecution Service (CPS), *The Prosecutors: Real Crime and Punishment*. The second episode, 'The Proof', dealt with domestic violence and showed the process for deciding whether a case could be taken to court and the perpetrator put on trial. All the cases covered in the programme were of women who had been victims of violent assault by their partner or ex-partner. The meticulous thoroughness with which each case was handled and the complexity of the process was a revelation.

As interesting to me were the stories of the women brave enough first of all to bring charges against the men who had done this to them, and second to take part in the documentary and go public with their experiences. The courage required should never be underestimated – doing this is a huge step and always deserving of utmost respect. One woman's story in particular stayed with me, not for how she'd got there but for the way she reacted after she had appeared as a witness for the prosecution and learned of the subsequent harsh but richly deserved prison sentence for the man who had been her abuser. When she was interviewed outside the court she broke down in tears. 'I can see in his eyes that he still loves me,' she sobbed. And I knew, I just knew, she was going to take him back when all this was over and the whole thing would play on repeat. I suppose I would know that, wouldn't I?

A couple of months later I mentioned this documentary in a conversation I was having with a recently retired senior police officer. I talked about a study I'd read which estimates that 85 per cent of victims of domestic abuse seek help from professionals at least five times before getting the support they need,[1] adding something along the lines of 'Isn't that shocking?'

'I'll tell you what's shocking,' he replied. 'That sixty per cent of women collapse cases on purpose so they can go back for more.'

Excuse me?

'Women go back because they need to be beaten up.'

He seemed angry. I don't cope well with angry men. 'Can you back that up?' I asked carefully. And he ran through his entire police career, finishing with, 'Never let the facts get in the way of a good story.'

I went home and wrote the exchange down verbatim while it was still fresh in my mind because this is the lie, isn't it? The lie told by abusers to justify what they do. A throwaway lie. A convenient lie. And the result is that the world blames the victim and not the abuser.

We stay because we enjoy it. Of course we do.

The next day, after I'd thought about it a bit, I sent him an email:

I was intrigued by what you said yesterday on the subject of domestic abuse. Specifically, you said there was a statistic on

---

1. Home Office, *Ending Violence Against Women and Girls Strategy: 2016–2020*, March 2016, p. 37 (Making VAWG 'everyone's business').

the number of women who deliberately collapse a case to go back to an abusive partner. Do you know where I might find that? Or perhaps I misheard (slightly deaf in one ear).

He replied promptly, enclosing a link to Home Office Statistical Bulletin HOSB/06/16 [July 2016]: *Crime outcomes in England and Wales: year ending March 2016.*[1]

The point he wanted to make was the 'startling headline' that 60 per cent of reported domestic abuse crimes have evidential difficulties and that 35 per cent of those were down to victims' refusal to cooperate with the police in prosecuting the offender. But reading the report closely I realized that he had almost halved the number of victims who collapse cases. As the report itself explains:

The majority (60%) of domestic abuse flagged offences recorded in the year ending March 2016 had evidential difficulties outcomes . . . This consists of 35 per cent of flagged offences where the victim did not support further action and 26 per cent where the victim supported further action.[2]

Looking at the different categories of outcome shows that Outcome 16 is the most relevant:

Evidential difficulties: suspect identified; victim does not support further action: Evidential difficulties victim based – named suspect identified. The victim does not support (or has withdrawn support from) police action.[3]

---

1. https://www.gov.uk/government/statistics/crime-outcomes-in-england-and-wales-2015-to-2016.
2. Ibid., p. 39.
3. Ibid., p. 55.

The report continues:

In comparison . . . [of] violent offences not flagged as domestic abuse 30 per cent had evidential difficulties where the victim did not support further action.[1]

In other words, there is only a 5 per cent disparity between violence (non-domestic) and violence (domestic) in terms of the number of cases in which a victim 'did not support further action' (or 'collapsed the case on purpose').

But it's surely not beyond the wit of man to see what most of these 'evidential' difficulties might be. Wherever there is a threat of physical violence or death people are afraid. And domestic abuse is not perpetrated by an unknown attacker but by the man with whom you share, or have shared, your life. He knows where you live. He has intimate knowledge of your daily routine, where you work, where your parents live, where your children go to school and who your friends are. His influence is everywhere and he knows what makes you tick.

We shut up because we are terrified of the very real threat of retaliation.

Who can protect someone from a person intent on doing them serious harm? The police don't have the manpower, budget or – at least sometimes – the understanding to protect every woman at risk from domestic violence.

Navigating the shifting sands of data sets, one wonders if they can ever present an accurate picture of anything. In the 2016 report I've just referred to, the figures relating to domestic violence have been collected from just seventeen of the forty-four police forces in England and Wales. In the 2017

---

1. Ibid., p. 40.

report the number of contributing police forces has risen to thirty-four – a considerable improvement. However, it should be borne in mind that it was only in April 2015 that the Home Office began collecting information on whether recorded offences were related to domestic abuse and were only 'flagged' as such if they met the government definition:

> Any incident or pattern of incidents of controlling, coercive or threatening behaviour, violence or abuse between those aged 16 or over who are or have been intimate partners or family members regardless of gender or sexuality.

Until April 2017 the age range had an upper limit of fifty-nine. Why? It is nonsensical to assume that abuse stops at sixty. We know it doesn't. It has now been increased to seventy-four, but why stop there?

★

My dad was a village bobby. We lived in a police house, and a few doors down lived a married couple. Most Saturday nights the husband would go to the pub, get roaring drunk, then come back and knock seven shades of shit out of his wife. After he'd done that he would walk up the road to us, knock on the door and politely offer himself for arrest. He always said the same thing: 'Me name's M—. I live at 33 Main Street and I've hurt me missus.' Sometimes my dad was there but not always. Sometimes he would surrender himself to my mother – this enormous and terrifying man with hands like shovels. My mum was five feet tall in her stockinged feet. Quite like his wife, in fact.

One Saturday night his wife locked herself in the outside lavatory to get away from him, and he shoved a load of straw and paper under the door and set fire to it.

I was only a baby when it happened, safely asleep in my cot upstairs. I only know about it because it was trotted out as a funny story from time to time – the idea that this thumping great wife murderer would come and expect my tiny bird-boned mother to lock him up. And that she would do it.

It's not funny though, really, is it?

It was what the police called 'a domestic'.

Chapter Six

The messages in our notebook don't mention Franc's attack. They skip along blithely. Tuesday 6 July reads:

> *Morning Franc*
>
> *What a long day it will be today. And then, do I go to the gym or iron your shirts? Perhaps I could do both – oh, I don't know! Take care, enjoy your golf and I'll see you later.*
>
> *Love and kisses*
> *Sock*
> *xxx*

> *What do you think I would say??? Franc*

Of course I did both.
On Tuesday 13 July:

> *Morning Franc*
>
> *I'll go straight to the gym tonight – are you coming too? See you later. I do love you – really!*
>
> *Big wet kiss from*
> *Sock*
> *xxx*

Then later the same day:

> *Hi*
>
> *Been home (obviously). Gone to gym. Back 7.30–7.45 ish.*

> *See you later.*
> *Kissy, kissy*
> *Sock*
> *xxx*
> PS *Don't forget that programme I'd like to see on TV tonight?*

We had a date night on the 14th, after I'd been to the hairdresser. He took me to a new restaurant. The note I left for him next morning suggests that I felt a little neglected:

> *Morning Franc*
> *I know you look for your note – I always look for one too.*
> *Look back through this book and see who received the most and what they say.*
> *Love (unrequited)*
> *Sock*
> *xxx*

> *No note. I don't know where you are or what you're doing.*
> *Worried sick of course.*
> *H x*

'And is this the reason you are out and about??' Franc wrote on the next line, when he returned from the golf lesson he had forgotten to mention and found his Sock wasn't at home.

There was a note in my handwriting scrawled on the back of an old letter of mine, which lay discarded on the kitchen table. It said, 'I need some air. I'll be back.' I don't think he can have seen it.

In the notebook for Thursday 22 July:

> *I do appreciate that sometimes is difficult to describe feelings but why can't you say something to me. You asked me to talk*

*and I did it. I know I should not do it because what I have to
say hurts you. And I do not want to make you think about that
[Sophie].*

Why didn't I say anything that would help him, he wanted
to know, when he too was 'in torment'. I wrote back:

*The last thing I want in the world is for you to be in torment
– ask me anything, anything at all, and I will try as hard as
I can to help you. It does hurt me, but (and I mean it) I would
go through anything for you – because I do, truly, love you.*
   Hx

At the end of July it was time for the regular staff rotation
at the hospital, when the team of doctors under a consultant
moved on to further their training. As a rule this happened
without any kind of fanfare but on this occasion, because the
team had been such a good one and we'd weathered a fair few
crises together, it had been decided that we would all go out
together to a restaurant in town.

Franc didn't want me to go. But I liked my colleagues, I
saw them almost every day and I wanted to say thank you
for their hard work, just as they wanted to say thank you for
mine. I was as much a part of the team as any nurse, ward
clerk or doctor. I promised to behave myself, though.

There were about twenty of us seated at a long table down
the middle of the restaurant. I was halfway down, opposite
the consultant and facing a long window that looked out onto
the street. It was a terrific evening. I was going to miss this
bunch of doctors, even Matt, who was so obviously not meant
to be a doctor that he cried every time he had to stick a needle
into someone. His family were all medics, but where *he*
should have been was at art school, where his heart really lay.

He confided this to me over the first course, leaning in so no one would hear. His family had pressured him into a career in medicine and he was thoroughly miserable. Why not give it up and do what you love? I asked, while we waited for the next course. Be happy, I said. Be free. I saw no incongruity in this.

A gust of laughter swept down the table and I looked up. Through the window I saw a tall man, wearing a white shirt collar and a dark suit jacket. He had his phone to his ear and his back to me. The jacket, a shade too tight, pulled slightly over his shoulders. I knew that back. It was Franc.

I rummaged about in my bag for my mobile. There were twenty-two missed calls, thirteen text messages and four voicemails. I began to shake, excused myself, and locked myself in the Ladies. The messages were all on a theme, rapid-fire variations of the same question.

WHERE ARE YOU?

But he knew where I was. And he was there, outside, on the pavement. Whatever I did now would be wrong. It was too soon to leave and it was too complicated to explain, not that I wanted to. If I didn't leave, Franc would be furious. At the back of my mind was a memory of crashing into a white painted wall. How could this man I loved and who said he loved me make me feel so on edge? This man who told me he needed me over and over again?

When I returned to the room the main course had arrived so I decided I would stay for that, then leave. It would be a waste of money not to eat it, as well as rude. Franc hated wasting money. That was something he would understand. It was ridiculous to be afraid of him and yet as I sat down I could feel him watching me. When I looked up he waggled his phone. I hesitated, then shook my head. Suddenly I didn't have anything to say, or, for that matter, much of an appetite.

Half an hour later I was being walked through the town centre with Franc's hand gripping the back of my neck. Some of my hair was caught between his fingers. When I tried to turn and speak to him he wrenched me back to face the front. We were walking so fast that I was practically running. Running in heels. Thinking back, someone must have seen us. There is no way it could have looked right. Come to that, someone must have seen him reach out and grab my throat when I left the restaurant, walking towards him with a smile. I was early leaving, it was summer and it was still light. Someone must have seen.

It took twenty minutes to walk home and I don't think I thought about anything during that time but keeping my feet moving fast enough to stop me from falling. I was shoved through the front door of the flat and lost my balance. Franc snatched a handful of my hair and I put a hand on each wrist, to stop him pulling. It hurt. He dragged me backwards the length of the hallway to the bedroom. My shoes were off and my skirt rucked up, my tights laddered. I kicked frantically, trying to find some purchase on the new carpet, but my feet kept slipping. He hoisted me onto the bed, straddling my hips, using his weight to hold me down while his hands circled my throat, squeezing, thumbs hard under my jaw. I can remember choking, burning pain and – once more – disbelief.

Strangling seems to take an age when you're the one being strangled. I stopped fighting – it was getting me nowhere. If he was going to kill me, he was going to kill me. Then, abruptly, he relaxed his hands, got up and left the room. I don't suppose it lasted for more than a minute.

At work the next day I was standing by the admissions desk, speaking to one of the doctors. I leaned over to get something and when I turned back she was staring at my throat. The scarf I was wearing had slipped.

'You know, you shouldn't put up with that.'

'Put up with what?' I pulled my scarf back up and tucked it into place.

'I just thought you might need help?'

'No. Really, I'm fine. Honestly.'

'Well, you know where I am if you want to talk.'

'I do . . . and thanks.'

When I got back to the flat there was a note for me in the message book:

I'm sorry for what happened. I've already told you it is not easy for me too. Apologies. You do know in your heart I love you. Do not spoil everything as if this was not true . . .

His name at the end had been written 'with love'.

'Do not spoil everything' meant it was my fault.

I stayed up late, long after Franc had gone to bed, and tried to write a reply but I was angry and could only seem to write things that would make him angry too so I tore up my attempts and put them in the bin. I should have known that wouldn't be enough.

The next day there was another letter for me – four tightly written pages.

When I woke up I wanted to read the letter you wanted me to read last night. With regret I noticed it was not on the table.

I did phone you to ask about it because I needed to know what you wrote in it. I needed to 'hear' something from you.

He said he had left work early because he was so preoccupied with me he couldn't do anything. He said he'd come home and,

> . . . *like a child with a new toy I started to put together your letter. I need to talk with you, to know you, and what's the best that you write? And here we are:*
>
> *'You have broken me.' 'This is your fault.' 'Do not ask anything.'*
>
> *I am not sure I believe what I read. I was so keen to read this, to try to calm down reading some love words from you and . . .*

He did everything for me, he said, so much that it 'burned his brain'. Taking me out to restaurants and buying me things were all to build my confidence. I do not have to do this, he said.

> *This is not my mission. I want to live. I have still all my life in front of me. I can do everything. I do not have to use all my energy and all my efforts for someone who as a thank-you says, 'you have broken me'.*

He said everything he did was because he loved me. He didn't expect anything back from me, 'and what: you don't have anything . . .'

He did not know what he had done wrong or what I wanted from him. He said he did not know who I was and he was certain he did not deserve to be treated this way.

> *If this is a punishment from God for my behaviour I think is too much.*
>
> *You say I twist your words. I hear no words. I have been asking for your help for months and you let me [sic] (always) on my own.*

I spend my time thinking about things to do with you and places to go with you. (Of course I have a long list of things and places deleted because . . .)

He said that if I could not find the words in my heart to help him when he needed me then I could not say I loved him.

For a writer saying she cannot find words to describe her love is quite . . . amusing, is it not?

He told me he felt 'the most incredible and unbearable love' and 'the deepest affection' he had ever felt for anyone.

This somebody is you. Whatever happens you will be that somebody.
Yours
Franc

Notebook, 29 July:

[Me:] I don't know what to write except to tell you that I love you from the bottom of my heart and from the very heart of my soul. Please, please, believe me.
Hx
PS I have work to catch up after yesterday so I will be a little late – home just after 6 p.m.?

[Franc:] All I want is you to show me your love.

[Me] . . . and I do love you – really. I need your love, Franc. Pls love me. Sock xxx
PS And I really do think about you all day at work, and I miss you. Every moment spent away from you is a wasted moment.

[Franc:] I KNOW YOU LOVE ME. AND I LOVE YOU TOO.

I'LL TRY MY BEST. PLEASE TRY TO UNDERSTAND ME. CANNOT WAIT TO HOLD YOU AGAIN.

And then he executed a perfect swallow dive into a deep pool of abject self-pity, where he wallowed for a week or so before going to France for a five-day visit to his head office. At first it was a relief having space to breathe and be myself. But after a couple of days, no matter how perverse it sounds, I felt pointless and lost without him. Adrift. Bereft.

But I had something to ward off any possibility of boredom while I waited at home for him to phone. He had asked me to arrange our summer holiday – a week in Scotland.

Notebook, Friday 13 August:

> *Not long now – and a whole week off (with you all to myself)! What bliss!!*
>
> > *Anyway, gym tonight?*
> > *Love and kisses*
> > *Sock*
> > *xxx*

*

I wonder if there is a special pheromone we give off when we're in an abusive relationship, an irresistible lure to other potential abusers.

Clearly there is a pattern – something that, if you don't recognize it, can lead to a second, third or fourth abusive relationship. I've demonstrated that beautifully myself. Somehow I was able to carry two contradictory opinions in my head at the same time, each diametrically opposing the other. I knew that what Franc did and the way he behaved were wrong but at the same time I was able to tolerate the bad times for the good. I fancied Franc something rotten. I was utterly committed to him. I remained ridiculously, stupidly in love. I was a bubbling wellspring of devotion for someone who did awful things and behaved in ways that baffled me. I was so confused and so hopelessly muddled I stopped trying to make sense of it. What I felt for him overrode every grain of doubt I ever experienced. Each time I thought I saw things as they were, that insight, that clarity slipped away again, despite my spending an awful lot of time thinking about it. So I gave up and decided that if this was the way it was then this was the way it would have to be.

Now, of course, I know what was happening to me. It was 'gaslighting'. The term comes from a 1938 stage play, *Gas Light*, but most people know the 1944 film starring Ingrid Bergman and Charles Boyer rather better. The villain (Boyer) is an initially charming man who plays out all manner of psychological mischief on his wife (Bergman) in order to convince her she's mad, leaving him free to follow his natural, murderous inclinations. It's a form of psychological abuse and abuse does not make you more lucid. Its effect is to bring about a state of such anxiety and confusion that the victim no longer trusts their own judgement. They can't see what's in front of them, second-guess everything they do, question their own memory of events and eventually become totally dependent on their abuser as their only anchor to 'reality'. It is the nastiest kind of manipulation. Women who have been abused often say that the violence wasn't the worst part – that was the psychological abuse. The mind takes longer to heal than the body.

*

Understanding the psychology of controlling relationships is the means by which we can avoid them. It should be taught to everyone. Gaslighting is the basis for every kind of bullying, abuse, oppression and subjugation from the school playground right up to absolutist governments, totalitarian regimes and despotic rulers.

Typically it has three stages – idealization, devaluation and discarding.[1]

First, the abuser charms their victim, winning them over. Whenever a victim talks about an abuser the word 'charming' will be heard.

Charm is the bait on the abuser's hook, along with being exciting, fun to be with and super-attentive to you – all the things that you might feel are missing from your life when you meet them. This is when, as I did, you fall so intensely in love that you can hardly breathe. You feel euphoric, overwhelmed, delirious. You can't believe this wonderful thing has happened to you.

If it's in the context of a romantic relationship you will feel that here at last is your soulmate, or if it's a professional one then someone who at last recognizes your potential. They go out of their way to make you feel you have a lot in common, a shared experience or that you are special. For example, Maxim de Winter in *Rebecca*, telling his nameless wife, 'We have something in common you and I,' or the boss who said to me, 'Promise me you'll never leave.' We all want to hear those things but this is a fishing expedition to gain your confidence and trust. They listen to you, encourage you to talk about yourself – fertile ground for discovering any inherent weakness, which can later be used against you – and give away

---

1. Sandy Hotchkiss, *Why is it Always About You?* (Simon & Schuster, 2003).

very little about themselves. They give you the gift of hope. This is the idealization stage.

Once you're hooked your abuser sets out to pull you apart. You feel you can't do anything right, that everything you do is wrong or, as with Franc, that everything you do causes hurt and disappointment to the person you love, whom you love like you've never loved anyone before (or hopefully, since).

I was knocked sideways by the strength of my feelings for Franc and my obsessive need to please him. Not being able to work out just what he wanted from me and repeated failure to do so lowered my already fragile self-esteem. His constant references to my 'bad' past reinforced the message. Franc knew he could keep pushing me harder because every time I said, 'But I love you so much,' I effectively gave him permission to push me harder still. This is devaluation.

It's not surprising that I failed time and time again. Perhaps if Franc had helped me, I might have worked it out, but instead his behaviour only compounded my confusion. I kept trying though. But the more I tried and failed the colder and more distant Franc became and the more depressed, anxious and fearful I became – and the more he despised me. Franc kept telling me that if I truly loved him I would know what he needed, what I had to do to make him happy. My repeated failure was 'proof' that I didn't love him, although I was certain I did. Every so often he would tell me he knew I loved him – it's there in his letters. I'd feel reassured and then round we'd go again. It was profoundly distressing. I was terrified that he would leave me. And of course he did, eventually.

This is where the 'Why doesn't she leave?' question comes in. First, it implies free will when by this point in a coercive relationship we have surrendered it. Second, it looks how it's meant to look, as though we are complicit and willing collaborators, ignoring the reality that such men do not have to be in the same room, same house, same town or even the same country to exert control. That we willingly stay is a pernicious, persistent lie. The truth is that we're trapped, but not quite at the point where we have to chew our own leg off to get free.

And then comes your reward: the end stage when you are discarded. When it happened to me it was as though I was, finally, going mad. You are emotionally battered, confused, anguished and suffering. Nothing you can do brings them back but that doesn't stop you trying again and again, debasing yourself even further. You become, in effect, your own abuser and every day is as painful as walking barefoot over broken glass. Often there's no obvious end to the relationship, no date that you can point to in a diary. Instead, you are left with your life on hold while your abuser occasionally toys with you, tells you he still loves you, gives you a shred of hope and then snatches it away. Franc and I went on for years like that.

The fact that you have been conditioned, groomed, primed over a considerable period of time leaves you with a series of behavioural tics that are easily spotted by other abusers and they do gravitate towards you. Despite outward appearances, when I met Franc I was a vulnerable woman susceptible to a certain type of man. He would have picked up on that, not necessarily consciously. For him my vulnerability was my attraction – you don't have to take my word for it, he wrote it himself:

> *You are right to say that the fact you needed someone to help you in some way attracted me even more.*

And when I first met Doreen at the hospital she seemed to be such a warm and friendly person, one of those people you can't help but like.

These two unstable relationships fed off each other. The more dysfunctional I became as a result of Franc, the more my work suffered and the more Doreen picked on me. When, eventually, I came out the other side, I tried to analyse what I'd done wrong (which was when I embarked on those ill-fated therapy sessions) but I don't think I did anything specific. I was just a victim of circumstance – wrong place, wrong time – a misalignment of the stars, fate or whatever.

Just as I can mark the turning point in my relationship with Franc, so I can with Doreen. One day I found her leafing through the patient notes on my desk.

'Looking for anything in particular?' I asked.

'Well, you know Hazel was a patient on the ward last week? I wondered whether you had her notes.'

'Yes. I do, for the discharge letter.'

'Good. Have you typed it yet? Can I see it?'

'Erm . . . no and no?'

'And why not?'

'Because Hazel is a member of staff.'

'Yes. And I'm her boss.'

'Look, I'm really sorry but patient confidentiality and all that. If you want to see Hazel's notes you can request them from Records?'

'Yes, but you could show me now and save time.'

'I'm sorry, Doreen, you know I can't.'

'I could make things difficult for you . . .'

I gave her a long look. 'It's still a no, I'm afraid.'

Was I brave or stupid to stand up to her? Either way, it wouldn't have mattered a bit if Doreen hadn't been the way she was. I don't like saying no – and I probably thought harder than most people before I said it. At some point in the conversation I also had the unwelcome insight that this might be a test (given what had happened over my daughter's hospital records). Were people really that devious? I knew they could be and I no longer knew whom I could trust. Both Franc and Doreen had a problem with 'no'. My job was to say 'yes' and keep everyone happy. As Franc said in another letter:

> You are clever and you have a 'bad' temper but despite that you used to answer, always, with a lovely 'yes, Franc'.

Keep 'em smiling. That was my job.

Chapter Seven

Our week in Scotland was exactly what we needed. The change of scenery and the time away, just the two of us, was as perfect as possible and I did my best to be the way Franc liked me to be. I didn't ask him whether he had been doing the same thing because if he had it would sound as though I hadn't noticed. And I was curious to know whether he'd seen Sophie while he was in Paris but I didn't ask that either, reasoning that perhaps it was better not to know these things. What the eye doesn't see (or the ear hear) the heart doesn't grieve over.

We stopped off at Bamburgh, then drove up to Dundee, working our way back down to Edinburgh. I obediently hauled the golf clubs he had eventually bought around several different courses, earning one or two mild reprimands for allowing myself to be distracted by a bird, a flower, the scenery and not watching the ball so it was lost. I laughed at his jokes. I soothed him when a shot didn't go right, which was often. I tidied things away in our bed-and-breakfast rooms when he waved a hand and said, 'Make some order, Ellen.' Together we discovered Edinburgh, or rather we discovered the Edinburgh Franc wanted to see. I don't remember having much of a say in anything we did but I do remember the warm content of having him to myself for a week. The Franc I loved. When he was like that it was easy to make him the centre of my world.

I only said no to him twice that week – once when he wanted me to give him my credit card and again when we were going home and he wanted me to drive part of the way. I was again afraid that Franc would find fault if he sat in the passenger seat, afraid of making a mistake. It was as though a barrier came down and I just couldn't do it. He was more or less all right about it but it felt a little as though the best bits of us had been left behind in Scotland. But everyone feels like that at the end of a holiday, don't they?

Not long after we got back, I asked Franc if I might go to my friend Lizzie's house for supper and he said yes. Lizzie and I had half arranged this before the holidays but I'd been cagey about a specific date because . . . well, you know, Franc.

She picked me up in her car from outside the hospital after work and off we went. Her house was close to where I had lived before I started moving house every few months so I knew it was a bit isolated – up a gated cinder track in the middle of fields – but it hadn't occurred to me that there would be no mobile signal at all. That made me a bit apprehensive but on the other hand, there was no reason I could think of why Franc would need to call me.

As we waited to pull out from a T-junction on our way to buy a bottle of wine, a car drove past.

'Oh, Christ.'

'What?'

'That was Franc.'

'Where?'

'In that green car that just drove past. That was Franc.'

Although we'd been together for nearly ten months, Lizzie had never met Franc, which seems extraordinary now but he gave every impression (without actually having to say anything) that he didn't like my friends so I kept them away with fibs and excuses. I was becoming quite the expert at rearranging the truth to fit around Franc. I couldn't think why he would be there, almost an hour's drive from the flat. Actually, that's a lie. Of course I could. He was there looking for me, which meant only one thing and I panicked. Then my phone started to go mad – pinging with message after message after message. When it rang and it was Franc I almost threw it at Lizzie, shaking my head, not wanting to take the call.

'He says he's seen us,' she told me. 'He says he's turning round and coming back.'

'Oh God, Lizzie. Can you just drive?'

I shouldn't have said that but I wanted this evening with my friend and I was afraid he was going to take it away from me. I just wanted a couple of hours to be myself.

Lizzie, bless her, didn't ask any questions, but just set off as quickly as she could. We passed Franc again, driving in the opposite direction, before zipping off down a side road and losing him. It was so utterly bizarre I began to laugh and that set Lizzie off too. A few minutes later my phone started to ring again, stopping after a few seconds when the signal dropped out. The wonderful thing about Lizzie's house was that I knew he wouldn't find me there.

I had some explaining to do: over bangers and mash and a large glass (or three) of red wine I told Lizzie a little about Franc, although not all. I didn't tell her he'd hit me. I didn't feel strong enough to look her in the eye and say that. I could tell her I loved him, though. That was easy.

She drove me home and, anxious about facing Franc, I asked her to come in for coffee. He said hello as though nothing had happened, went into the bedroom, closed the door and stayed there until Lizzie had gone. At which point we had an entirely predictable and nasty row. I remember pounding his chest with my fists in frustration while he gripped my arms; his back, for once, against the wall. And all the time, I was thinking, Don't you dare take us back to this again.

In his office the next day, Franc wrote a long letter and gave it to me in the evening like homework. I remember reading it more with inertia than fear, feeling profoundly weary. I don't think I found it disturbing at the time.

27 August

Dear Helen
Another nice day and evening. What can I say? I do not like it. It is not was used to be.

He said he didn't know what to make of me anymore, was this how I thanked him for spending all his time thinking about what we could do together, where we could go and what he could buy for me?

My bank statement had arrived in the post and he had opened it because, he said, he was worried that I was wasting my money. He couldn't understand why I was so cross about it, not when he gave me everything – as though that gave him the right.

He was angry that I had gone to spend an evening with my friend and that I had not taken him, 'the love of your life'. He had phoned me, he said, because he was upset and needed to hear my voice. Why, he wanted to know, hadn't I called him back to make him feel better when 'I phoned you 200 times leaving 100 messages'? And what did I do? I did nothing. I didn't even offer him 'the courtesy of a reply'.

You saw me on the road but two hundred yards is too much for your love. I did ask this to you yesterday but you did not answer. The love of your life, allegedly, was there looking for

you, and what do you do? You do not give a shit; you keep
going and having fun with your friend and off you go. You
could not stop the car. Can you please answer this to me?

He repeated this again and again. He told me several times
that I 'did not raise a finger', that I did not care about him.
Over and over he asked why I had not asked Lizzie to stop the
car, why I was happy to leave him to suffer and why I didn't
show how much I loved him.

I cannot swallow this Helen. I just can't. I do expect you to
be and to act according to what you say you feel for me.

Reading this now I can feel the heat of him, smell him,
remember avoiding eye contact while he stood over me,
shouting. This is Franc's true voice. It puts flesh and blood on
the memory. The words he wrote were exactly the way he
talked to me. This was what he was like to live with. Reading
it then, my head fizzed, my jaw set, my stomach clenched –
and he hadn't finished.

I gave you everything and you do not trust me enough to
lend for two minutes your credit card. You have got some
money now. The only thing you care about is your job. It does
not matter whether I am at your dinner or not. You have got
your career now to think about. You feel strong, confident and
what the hell, who cares about Franc? Cool, cold lady.

We were back to the work dinner again, the one where he
waited outside the restaurant. You would never accuse Franc
of letting things go. It didn't matter how much or how often
I apologized and asked him to forgive me.

What I have done I have done for LOVE. I am happy of
what I have done for you. I am proud of you. I have just to

push you to achieve this. You are a completely different person now. Better looking body, but you can do the last step and appearance (without being nasty you looked kind of rough in the early days). You are a new woman now or better, you have cleaned the surface. I just pushed you to do it. The pride and self-respect you have gained are used now against me.

The word 'rough' really hurt.

How, he demanded to know, did I 'dare to call this love? I cannot. Once again you left me alone while I needed you and your help to have a drink with your friend. This was the important thing.'

Couldn't I see, he continued, that I didn't love him anymore? If I did, he wrote, I would not have been drinking and laughing with my friend. No, I would have gone to him, put my arms around him and told him I loved him. There was no sign of the 'romantic girl madly in love with me'. He said that the more I did nothing the more 'I fade away from you'. The more I told him I loved him and yet did nothing, the more he didn't believe me.

I want to see that you can stop a car in the middle of the road and run to me – even if is 200 yards distant – I want to see you live for me as I used to do for you. I want to see a romantic beautiful lady looking for me and ready to drop immediately everything to reach me.

He said I had to call him back when he was angry with me, which was usually that I hadn't shown my love for him. (It didn't seem to occur to him that I might be afraid to.)

I want you to phone me back because you do understand that if I use bad words with you is because I feel betrayed by you.

*I want you to drop the glass of your gin and tonic and get
out of any restaurant you are in, for any reason you might be
there, because I am the reason you live.*

He promised me that if I could do these things all the rest
would follow, that he would be as he used to be – gentle,
loving and kind. If I didn't believe what he said then it meant
I had not understood anything – 'you do not have anything in
your heart.'

I took a direct hit to that heart when he said I didn't love
him. And I couldn't bear the thought of him not loving me.

*You feel free to hit me several times (5 and quite heavily)
and if I do it – and was wrong anyway – to calm you down
and stop your crises – because regardless of what you say I did
not do it for the sake of do it I did not do it with the intention
to do it . . .*

Then, 'One day you will tell me the truth about your pictures and other interesting stories.'

He said he still loved me but couldn't see how he could
stay with me when I preferred 'joking with [my] friends'
instead of taking care of him. He said he couldn't describe
how angry he was. I had let him down and I treated him
badly.

*How do you think I am going to commit myself to someone
who leaves me on my own to have a laugh with her friends who
does not care to come to see me on the road. For this I have and
am hurting very much someone else. And this makes me feel
guilty and bad. And then I see that everything I have done for
you, and all the pain I have caused to Sophie is worth nothing
for you and this makes me furious.*

In the last paragraph, on the last of four pages of A4, he returned to the subject of money:

> *Yes, I am insecure. I am insecure of putting my life in your hands. I do not know if it is the right thing to do because you claim such a big love and then I cannot even look after your money – not using it – just manage it for you.*

He could not, he said, pay for my 'wasted time', my 'friend time' and my 'daughter time'.

What could I say to all this? I had to say something but trying to reply to anything Franc wrote was exhausting. I was desperate not to trigger the wrong reaction. I needed time to think.

The next day I was late back from work. My new boss was about to start and I had a backlog of work to clear. When I let myself in our message book was open on the kitchen table:

AS USUAL NOT BOTHERED ABOUT ME. AS USUAL.

I didn't want to read any more of these unforgiving notes. Yet I had to read every word over and over again because he would refer back to them and if I missed something or couldn't answer I'd be in trouble. Each letter became a test of my capacity to remember what he had said and when he had said it. He would check again and again that I had understood and if it looked as though I hadn't we would keep going over it until he was satisfied. Worse, I began to accept his behaviour towards me. It had begun to feel normal. It's unsettling to look back now and recognize that I only registered shock about what was happening when he did something extreme.

So I kept house, went to work, the gym or the hairdresser

and did nothing else because these were the only permitted activities. I performed all the offices of a geisha.

*

I have often wondered about what happened over the next couple of months – that I didn't see any of it coming. I've searched through my notes and diaries, statements, emails, all of it, but there is no clue.

I had stopped asking Franc about what he did – it wasn't worth the trouble. It was always, 'Yes, Franc,' and 'No, Franc,' and never, 'Frankly, Franc, I don't believe you.' I didn't ask him about work. I didn't ask him about Sophie. I didn't ask him about his family. I knew he had a brother and a sister. I knew his mother left his father once the children had grown up. I knew his father had business interests in Russia but nothing about him, other than that they didn't get on. Franc showed me a photograph once – a fuzzy indistinct picture of a tall white-haired man standing alone. It could have been anybody. I would never have been able to pick him out in a crowd. His mother I imagined as a petite, strong woman. Sometimes Franc took a phone call and talked for a long time in French, some of which I understood and some of which I didn't. When I began brushing up my French he started leaving the room to have his telephone conversations. I got used to the idea of him having two lives – his French life and his English life. I belonged to the latter and I assumed Sophie belonged to the former. If she was still around he never said. I assumed he'd told her about me because in his long letter he said he was 'hurting' her, or perhaps he meant another kind of hurting . . .

I don't understand why, when he told me I had to move my furniture from his company's warehouse, not urgently but soon, I didn't work out what was going on. Perhaps it was because Franc kept telling me that when I put two and two together I almost never made four. There didn't seem much point in trying when I never got it right. Bit by bit I fell in with his opinion of me. I *was* hopeless and chaotic. My track record of relationships was terrible; I didn't understand money; I'd contrived to lose all my worldly goods and those I loved not just once but twice. I was a rotten cook, a shambolic house-keeper. I said I wrote stories but I never did. I would never make my target weight of 50 kilos. I would never be thirty again. I would never have the right kind of body. My breasts would always be small. I would never invite another woman into our bed as Franc wanted. I would never call one of those phone-box cards and book an appointment for sex, as Franc wanted. I would never enjoy looking at violent rape-fantasy porn, as Franc wanted. Over the course of almost a year, Franc had succeeded in making me abandon every independent thought and made me completely and utterly reliant on him. When he was around I couldn't take a single decision on my own. I looked to him for everything.

'Ellen. Have a shower.'

'Yes, Franc.'

'Ellen. Make some order.'

'Yes, Franc.'

'Ellen. You are a disaster.'

'Yes, Franc.'

'Ellen. Dinner at six.'

'Yes, Franc.'

Over the next few months, Franc went back and forth to Paris every couple of weeks. The trips seemed to get longer each time. In November, after his return from a ten-day trip, we went to a dinner given by his company. I thought it was an early Christmas party.

My diary doesn't say where it was, not that it matters. I wore the expensive grey wool dress and cardigan Franc had bought for me in Manchester. It was slightly loose on me now. I took great care over my hair and make-up. My nails were glossy with the Chanel Rouge Noir lacquer Franc loved. He told me I looked beautiful and my heart turned a little somersault. Other people said I was too thin.

It was a nice occasion as company dinners go but it wasn't a Christmas party at all. It was Franc's leaving dinner.

Awareness that things were not as I had believed them to be increased as the evening wore on. I began to feel nervy and a bit self-conscious, as though I'd been made a fool of.

By the time we got to speeches and the presentation of a gift to Franc, I thought the sheer weight of my credulity would make my head burst. As soon as everyone stood up I excused myself and went with as much dignity as I could muster to the Ladies, where I locked myself in and cried, quietly and carefully, for a good ten minutes. Then I dried my eyes, freshened my make-up, necked a couple of aspirin and returned to the party.

The next morning, a Saturday, I took a deep breath and asked him what the hell was going on. It turned out that the company Franc worked for was winding up its UK operation and he had been recalled to Paris. In fact, he'd been recalled two months earlier, which explained all the travelling. In a few months' time the workforce would be made redundant and the warehouse closed, which was why I had to move my stuff. It seems it had simply never occurred to Franc to tell me any of this. I was reeling. While he played golf that afternoon I went for a long walk to try to clear my head – and think.

In the notebook, 13 November:

I got home and . . . you are not here. I sent you a message this afternoon; I have been thinking about you all day. I wanted to apologize for what happened and . . . try to explain the . . . situation.

He said I had done it again – gone off and left no message to say where I was. I knew, he said, that he worried about me. I replied:

I think you must be blind – you can't see the pain I'm in. I can only accept things with your help, your love, your support. We should give each other strength. If I am certain my love and my future is with you (for my part I know this but what about you?) I will support you and love you and accept things, knowing I will be with you, my love and my life – H

I think I wept all that night and all day on Sunday. I was bereft, abandoned, stricken with grief. Franc, always hating it when I cried, offered no reassurance or comfort, nor did he say anything about where we would go from here. In fact, all he had to say was that my handwriting showed that I was, in his words, 'mentally unstable'. I didn't defend myself. I believed him.

The last entry in our message book is Franc's and it says:

LOVE
YOU

On the Monday he packed two suitcases and left for Paris. He would be back, he said, for a couple of days at the beginning of December and then for Christmas and the New Year. He left a note giving me his new address. This, I thought, is what you get for being useless and incompetent. I despised myself.

I hated myself so much that I stopped eating, stopped drinking. Ten days after Franc had gone I was in a ward at the hospital where I worked, severely dehydrated, on an intravenous drip.[1] I stayed there for five days.

While I was an inpatient some internal post made its way up to me, including a letter from Doreen. It was marked *Personal & Confidential* – she wanted to reappraise my appraisal, which had happened a few weeks earlier and passed without comment. Now it seemed she wanted 'an objective review'. And when I went back to work, Doreen said she hadn't been informed that I'd been ill and she'd docked my pay. This was copper-bottomed rubbish because Dr Bray, our new consultant, had been to see me twice and someone had obviously known I was there because they forwarded my post to the ward.

This was bad enough, but after ten days away from the office I was also faced with a massive backlog of work to get through. Dr Bray gave me a lot more than his predecessor; only one of the new team of junior doctors dictated letters that fitted onto one page, and I wasn't allowed to work overtime. Or rather I could do overtime but Doreen made it clear that I wouldn't get the time back in lieu, nor would I be paid for it. Even so I fell into the habit of working through my lunch break and doing an hour extra at the end of the day when it was a bit quieter. Inch by inch the piles of work started to go down, a small measure of success that made me feel both a little happier and more in control. What I didn't foresee was that I was being set up to fail.

---

1. 16 per cent of victims report that they have considered or attempted suicide as a result of the abuse, and 13 per cent report self-harming. safelives.org.uk, 'Insights Idva National Dataset 2013–14'. (SafeLives, 2015.)

On 17 December I got a message from Doreen to meet her in Dr Bray's office. There, they confronted me. Doreen had made a thorough search of my office without my knowledge and found:

— a backlog of filing
— a backlog of dictation tapes
— a shortage of blank dictation tapes
— patient notes not requested for clinics
— an untidy work area with 'patients' notes on all working surfaces including on top of filing cabinet'

In addition:

— I took my lunch breaks 'outside the [specified] departmental lunch sessions'
— It was 'highlighted' to me that I was not identifying on the department outboard when I was leaving the department

I was guilty as charged but this is what happens when a PA is out of the office – work becomes overdue, things get untidy and people leave you messages. And although the charge sheet sounded terrible, my office was not substantially different from that of any other of my PA colleagues. We were all overstretched. It wasn't as though I hadn't been pulling my weight. I had been ill, a patient in the same hospital. I was upset but I didn't have any fight left. This broadside from Doreen and Dr Bray merely reinforced Franc's opinion of me that I was useless. I promised to pull my socks up and thanked them for taking time out of their busy schedules to discuss their concerns with me. That's right. I *thanked* them.

There was only one reason I didn't go under completely. In mid-December, just before I was hauled over the coals,

Franc had made his promised visit and asked me to go to Venice with him for a long weekend after Christmas. The only problem was that once Franc went back to France his company stopped paying the rent on the flat, so it became my responsibility together with the bills. Obviously I hadn't budgeted for this and it would be a struggle. Even though my flights were not expensive I couldn't afford them. Perhaps as a reward for losing weight Franc said he would book them and our hotel. I would only have to get myself to the airport. I didn't care that he had told me I had bad breath because now I had something to look forward to. Nor did I care about the note he left me on the back of a shopping list after I said I was worried about my sleepless fidgeting in bed:

'Dear Bitch,' he began and told me not to worry about keeping him awake because, 'I am going to kill you so it will not last longer.' He hoped my day would not be 'so bad', that he would see me later, and he signed off 'The Boss'.

By the time he came back on Christmas Eve, I felt as though I'd been steamrollered.

The first thing he found fault with was the arrangement of flowers on the table. I'd done them myself: white, purple, green and a bit of sparkly glitter on the holly. Tasteful, I thought, and not too blingy. Purple was the colour of death, he said, and so was white. I had just wanted to make the flat look nice for our first Christmas together – our only one together. I gave him a traditional English Christmas dinner, which I cooked myself. He didn't like it.

I hoped Jeannie and Dave's New Year's Eve fancy-dress party would be more successful.

Hanging in the spare room at the flat was a dress I had designed and made myself for an exhibition some time ago, in what felt like another life. It had a boned bodice, a very full skirt with lots of tulle petticoats and wide off-the-shoulder sleeves. The colours in the skirt were like the night sky – gold and grey and midnight-blue, and here and there I had embroidered golden stars trailing shivering strings of twinkling crystal drops – it was a fairy-tale gown. This would be my costume. I knew Franc would think the neckline too low so I tucked and stitched in a chiffon scarf to raise it a bit. When I tried it on it fitted me beautifully. Franc told me he was hiring a blue brocade frock coat, waistcoat and trousers. We would match – a couple.

I don't remember feeling excited about the New Year. I felt flat. Why should the next year be any different from the last? With hindsight, I know I was on a slow descent into depression. In one of the photographs Dave and Jeannie took that night, Franc and I are standing together, smiling for the camera; I'm holding on to Franc's right arm with both hands, as though I'm afraid he might float away. What I wanted was for him to put his arm around me or hold my hand but he didn't. I received a chaste kiss on the stroke of midnight and for that I had to search him out in the front garden where everyone was watching the fireworks. Dave grabbed me, though, planting a smacker on my lips and copping a feel as he veered boozily off towards another of Jeannie's friends. He meant nothing by it. It was just something that some men do when they're drunk and in my experience, par for the course on New Year's Eve.

Franc saw it, though. And he saw Dave point his camera and take a snap of my breasts rising majestically from their corset. I saw the photograph a week or so later and I must say they looked far better than I thought. It was all what you might call harmless fun. But back in the flat at three in the morning, I would be on my knees amidst clouds of billowing tulle because I hadn't earned closeness and intimacy and a blowjob was all he wanted.

On 1 January we had a huge row that lasted all day. Of course we did. Eventually, I walked out of that oppressive flat and into the clean fresh air because I couldn't stand hearing the same pointless things over and over again.

I stayed out for as long as it took to smoke several cigarettes and clear my head. When I let myself back in I expected a hug but instead Franc grabbed a handful of my hair, hauled me backwards into the bedroom, threw me in and slammed the door. I climbed up onto the bed and lay there quietly until I heard him crying a couple of hours later. When I came out he was lying face down on the sitting-room floor, sobbing. I had never seen a man cry like that before and I thought my heart might break. He had written another lengthy note for me, which ended:

> *I just can't reach your heart. I'm sorry. It is my fault, not yours. I thought I explained what I need.*
>
> *Once again I was wrong. I can't make you understand that I need you to come to me if there is something wrong. Once again you run away and look what you made me do. Was it difficult to sit or lay down close to me? Why didn't you say anything? Please come and talk to me.*

I looked at him and hadn't the faintest idea of what I should do so I sat patiently beside him and stroked his back. How did we arrive at *this* place?

He was up early on Sunday morning. He brought me a cup of tea in bed and yet another letter.

He loved and needed me, he said, but it was clearly not enough even though he did so much to show me his love. Perhaps, he offered, he could be a bit more like I wanted him to be but I would have to help him. Everything I said meant nothing and my 'words were just words'. I didn't mean what I said. I didn't help him at all.

You talk about your big love and then you betray me.

On and on he went. I did not care how he felt. I ran away from him whenever we talked. I did not stay with him and tell him 'something nice'. The way I looked at him was defiant, just to show him I was stronger and did not care.

You keep accusing me of not allowing you to see your friends. You do not have a social life anymore because of me.

I am sorry. I thought you wanted to stay with me. Let me know if this is not the case.

I need some kind words from you that will tell me you love me. But do not tell me you love me.

He loved me in his own way, he said. He was there for me. He said he would do anything for me but that he didn't feel I supported him at all.

I have a lot of problems to solve and the only thing you say is that I don't tell you what is going on. I do not know that.

He wanted me to be happy but all his love turned to 'a great anger' when I ran away from him. And then, as if that wasn't enough, I had smoked a cigarette in front of him 'just to put some more petrol on the fire'.

I am very sorry for treating you in that way when we are arguing. But it is not me. It is a demon in me. I have never acted like that before with anyone else. Perhaps it is a reaction when I see all the love I believed in to vanish in to some smoke or going away from me with a smile in your face.

He told me I had just to say the right things to him to 'stop everything, to stop my demons growing in me.'

Everything you ever read about men like Franc has them talking about their demons. I think what they mean is that when jealousy and possessiveness get the better of them they cannot control themselves. And, in that respect, I suppose they're right.

For the rest of the day we were together. Lying next to him on the sofa while he watched football, cooking for him, being kind and gentle, I tried to show him what he would be missing when he went back to Paris. For one day only everything was perfect, which was all I'd wanted from the moment he arrived on Christmas Eve.

On Monday morning I was again weeping quietly into Franc's jumper while we waited for his train. I always felt drained when he'd gone, as though life had suddenly become meaningless. I had tucked a letter from me into his case for him to read when he was far enough away for it not to matter how he chose to interpret it.

My dearest Franc

I want to write to you. I've been reading the letter you wrote to me on Sunday . . . and remembering. I'm a little afraid of the letter you told me you have written today. I hope there are some loving words in it. Perhaps I haven't earned them – or perhaps I don't deserve them.

In your letter you ask me to let you know something: 'I need some kind words from you that will tell me you love me. But do not tell me you love me.'

I will try.

I have mixed up all my feelings. I am afraid. I'm a complicated and confusing person, full of contradictions.

My feelings for you are so strong and so powerful they frighten me. They frighten me because I feel as though I have no control over them . . .

Here you are: kind and strong, clever and supportive and asking me to turn to you for comfort and advice. I'm very much afraid that I wrong you terribly and quite without meaning to . . .

I skip a few lines. There are eight pages of this self-flagellating bollocks.

You said in your postscript that I should learn to come to you when something is wrong but how can I when you are in France? I can't turn it on and off depending upon whether you are here or not. If I do when you're here how can I survive the long, lonely days when you are not?

What I'm trying to say is that if I allow myself to rely on you when you're here I'm terrified I shan't survive when you are not . . .

'Hurt' is a very small and inadequate word and does not do justice to the soul-searing, heart-scorching agony of being separated from you . . .

Jesus Christ.

I would leave everything and come to you in just the clothes I stood up in if you asked me to. I would beg, steal or borrow to be with you if you asked me. If you asked me I would come to you tomorrow and sod the consequences. Nothing matters to me but to be with you . . .

I am afraid you will hurt me and/or leave me . . .

I hate the things you say in anger. I understand I make you angry so perhaps I deserve what I get but that just makes my confusion worse . . .

> *I could not bear to lose you who is best, dearest, most precious and best beloved of all.*

I think I might be sick.

> *You don't understand why I find it hard to look after myself when you're not with me, I know it makes you cross and I'm sorry for that. As you know, I am not in the least practical and organized like you. I do not see things the way you do . . .*

But you ran your own business and started again as a single mum FFS . . .

> *I don't often sleep in the bed when you're not here because it hurts – I miss you more in the wee small hours when the world is quiet and dark. And the doctor gave me sleeping pills. Please don't be angry. There are no other secrets . . .*

I don't think I would have prescribed myself sleeping pills, not given the state I was in.

> *Forgive me if I have wronged you, if I do wrong you, forgive me for the way I love you and forgive me for not having the courage to show you that I love you when I should because of a selfish fear of being hurt.*

I sign myself with *xxx* as I always do and add a PS:

> *My letters often go wrong – I hope this one doesn't.*

By the last page my handwriting was sloping down, away to the right and off the bottom of the page. Perhaps Franc was right – it did show that I was mad.

Until I started writing this book, I hadn't read this letter in over a decade. I can see why. It's humiliating. All that pleading and squirming and grovelling. It shows so plainly what I had become – and it makes me unfathomably sad. It gives so many clues, in my own words, to why I accepted the things I did. It takes a long time to get someone trained to this point, a long time and a lot of patience and hard work, together with a certain amount of detachment, a lack of empathy and a lack of remorse.

I have his next letter too, dated 3 January, the one I was afraid of reading.

'Dear Helen,' he began, and then told me that the fountain pen I had given him for Christmas was very 'sharp and hard'. He had 'thought it would be softer'. He knew this would upset me but that was how it was. He added 'unfortunately' to soften the blow.

> *I am already missing you. I still think I should have stayed, but then I would have been in trouble at work . . .*
>
> *If I wrote some bad things is because I need to talk about them again, again and again and again . . .*
>
> *I think you do not understand this. I need you to talk to me, not to run away from me. I am sure you know me better than this. And that's why I get very angry sometimes.*

It might look as though he was crazy, he said, but he still wondered why, when I said I loved him so much, I could not go to him when I could see he was upset 'for whatever reason'. Clearly I had 'more important things to do'. He wanted me to explain why I had to smoke in front of him when we were arguing, or 'run away'.

> *Can you try to explain all this to me please?*
> *Tomorrow I shall check for Venice and let's hope we can arrange it.*
> *Love*
> *Franc*

A week later I recorded these measurements in my diary:

> *Thigh 20"*
> *Hips 37"*
> *Waist 26.5"*

I had instructions to make these numbers smaller. And I was going to do it too. As penance.

*

Some of Franc's behaviour could be called stalking: the time he came to the restaurant where I was having dinner with my work colleagues and the time he turned up on a country lane near Lizzie's house. Perhaps too, the time he turned up at Nina's house, on the day I had attempted suicide, was also stalking. Taken individually, these three incidents could be explained away as evidence of Franc's concern for me, for my well-being, my mental state. He would certainly have said so, if you asked him. I'd say something different. And these three are not the whole story.

What about all the texts and phone calls? What about all the faxes he sent? What about all the emails, which came later? He didn't have to physically follow me to stalk me. And today's technology is far more advanced than it was when I was with Franc. In *The Archers*, Rob Titchener installed simple GPS spyware on Helen's phone, so that he could monitor her movements at all times and turn up as a 'surprise'. He too explained this away as concern over her mental state. This is not simply a narrative twist to add drama to a radio soap – it is real life for hundreds of women all over the world.

But I wouldn't have been able to report what Franc did, because at the time stalking was not a criminal offence. It only became one in 2012 and even then the law excluded incidences where the stalker was a partner or ex-partner. If you'd had a fling with someone or been married to them it was deemed perfectly fine for him to follow you around everywhere, pitch up out of the blue, walk into your place of work, harass your friends and family, terrify you by sneaking around your house at night or phone you at all hours to beg, plead or make threats.

And, of course, the majority of domestic abuse victims don't tell. The 2016 Crime Survey for England and Wales estimated that around four in five victims did not report their abuse to the police.[1] And victims of stalking tend not to report anything to the police until the hundredth incident.[2] This is not surprising given women have a marked tendency not to want to cause anyone any trouble or be a nuisance. And all forms of abuse generate fear.

The statistics are shocking:

— 80.4 per cent of victims are female and 70.5 per cent of perpetrators are male.[3]
— In 2011 the British Crime Survey stated that at least 120,000 individuals were affected by stalking and harassment. By 2015 that figure had risen to 1.1 million.[4]
— In 2013/14 Crown Prosecution Service figures[5] reveal

1. Office for National Statistics, *Domestic abuse, sexual assault and stalking* (March 2016).
2. 'Stalking and Harassment – The Victim's Voice: A briefing from Protection Against Stalking (PAS) for the independent parliamentary inquiry into stalking law reform', p. 2 (November 2011).
3. National Stalking Helpline 2011.
4. Office for National Statistics, *Intimate personal violence and partner abuse* (February 2016).
5. Crown Prosecution Service, *Violence Against Women and Girls Crime Report*, 2013/14.

that 743 stalking offences were prosecuted whereas 9,792 were prosecuted for harassment out of the 61,175 allegations recorded by police. Therefore only 1 per cent of cases of stalking and 16 per cent of cases of harassment recorded by the police result in a charge and prosecution by the CPS.[1]

— 75 per cent of domestic violence stalkers will turn up at the workplace.[2]

— 79 per cent of domestic violence stalkers will use work resources to target their victims.[3]

— One in two domestic stalkers, if they make a threat, will act on it.[4]

— A six-month study by the University of Gloucestershire found that stalking was present in 94 per cent of the 358 cases of criminal homicides studied.[5]

Furthermore, for a report published in July 2017, HM Crown Prosecution Service Inspectorate and HM Inspectorate of Constabulary examined 112 cases of stalking and harassment. In '95% of the case files reviewed, care for the victim was deemed inadequate and three-quarters of cases

1. Paladin, National Stalking Advocacy Service, 2015.
2. Paladin, National Stalking Advocacy Service, 2017.
3. Ibid.
4. Dr Rachel D. MacKenzie, Dr Troy E. McEwan, Dr Michele T. Pathé, Dr David V. James, Prof James R. P. Ogloff and Prof Paul E. Mullen, *The Stalking Risk Profile: Guidelines for the Assessment and Management of Stalkers* (StalkInc. & the Centre for Forensic Behavioural Science, Monash University, 2009).
5. Jane Monckton-Smith, Karollina Szymanska and Sue Haile, *Exploring the Relationship Between Stalking and Homicide* (Suzy Lamplugh Trust, 2017).

were not even handled by detectives'.[1] More than 60 per cent of cases showed no evidence of a risk management plan being prepared to protect victims.

The report goes on to say:

> We found that if an investigation was started, victims often felt badly let down throughout the criminal justice process. One reason for this was the failure to impose bail conditions on perpetrators, which sometimes left the victim at risk of further offending.

Seven women are killed each month by a current partner or former partner,[2] a devastating statistic that is unlikely to change any time soon, and will in all likelihood rise.

In 2015 when the new offence of controlling or coercive behaviour in intimate or familial relationships became law, the loophole that had left those of us being stalked by men we had been (or were) involved with outside the protection of the law was finally closed. This was a huge advance. Or it would have been, if the police understood what stalking and harassment really mean. But they don't. The National Police Chiefs' Council (male) head of stalking and harassment admitted as much on BBC Radio 4's *Today* programme on the day the report was published. He said that 'in the majority of cases the police do not understand' and that the women who go to them 'must be taken seriously from the first incident'.

The Home Office *Crime Outcomes Report* for July 2017 raises similar questions about how well coercive control is

---

1. Owen Bowcott, Legal Affairs Correspondent, the *Guardian*, 5 July 2017.
2. ONS (2016), March 2015 Crime Survey for England and Wales (CSEW).

understood: 'Just over 10 per cent of coercive control offences were dealt with by a charge or summons . . .'[1]

This lack of understanding was made quite clear in the horrifying murder of Alice Ruggles on 12 October 2016. Her killer was Lance-Corporal Trimaan 'Harry' Dhillon, a soldier who had been serving in Afghanistan when they met over the internet. Alice had seen pictures of him on a mutual friend's Facebook page. They didn't meet properly until January 2016, three months later.

The *Guardian* would later report that:

> During their relationship, he alienated her from her friends, damaged her self-confidence, and demanded her constant attention. He was also serially unfaithful. Friends described her transformation from being bubbly, sociable and a 'ray of sunshine' to being withdrawn and gradually isolated from them.

When Alice ended the relationship in August the same year, he hacked into her Facebook account to monitor her movements, sent her selfies of him crying, and contacted her mother on social media, asking her to intervene. He begged Alice to come back to him.

When he thought she was starting a new relationship he made 'five-hour, 240-mile round trips from Glencorse Barracks in Midlothian to Gateshead to knock on her bedroom window and leave flowers and chocolates on her windowsill.'[2] Terrified, Alice went to the police who issued a Police Information Notice instructing him to stop contacting her. His

---

1. Home Office, *Crime outcomes in England and Wales: year ending March 2017*, 2nd edition. Statistical bulletin HOSB 09/17.
2. The *Guardian*, 26 April 2017.

commanding officer at the barracks was aware of the situation and also told him to leave her alone. Instead he sent her a parcel with a 'pleading note'. The police asked her if she wanted to have him arrested but Alice declined. She told a friend that she felt she had been 'palmed off' and said to her sister, Emma, that the police would 'respond when he stabs me'. At Dhillon's trial, another friend told the court that the stress of being stalked had led to Alice becoming 'introvert[ed], physically shaking, anxiety, skinny, she lost so much weight'.

Dhillon claimed Alice had died after accidentally stabbing herself in the neck when in fact it was he who had used the knife to kill her. He was sentenced to a minimum of twenty-two years in prison. The judge said he had shown 'not a shred of remorse'.

Northumbria police have referred their actions to the Independent Police Complaints Commission but said 'no one at the time knew the threat he posed', although later it emerged that a previous partner had also been stalked and had taken out a restraining order against him. 'We're in a very different position now than we were then,' said DCI Lisa Theaker. 'Alice didn't fully understand his level of behaviour and the stalking and the lengths of behaviour he was going to.' But I think Alice did understand. She went twice to the police, but if a stalker is arrested and then released wouldn't you be afraid of how he would react?

*

In a 2017 study commissioned by Her Majesty's Inspectorate of Constabulary 'the majority of participants did not have an entirely positive experience to their report of stalking and harassment.' Complaints included 'incidents not being deemed "serious enough", victim-blaming attitudes and responses, not being kept informed, missed opportunities to take action against the offender and counter-allegations'. A number of women told the study that 'they would no longer approach the police due to their most recent experience.'[1]

Of course it is easy to misconstrue someone leaving flowers and chocolate as a threat but the key to stalking and harassment is the same as it is for coercive control – the pattern and number of incidents.

Take, for example, another story I heard:

A secretary, let's call her Lisa, was leaving her job with one executive in a company and going to work for another. On her first day in the new job a huge bouquet of flowers arrived from her old boss.

'How lovely!' exclaimed her colleagues and yes, Lisa agreed, they *were* lovely.

Then the next day another bouquet arrived. And the day after that another. And the day after that. He carried on for two whole weeks.

'He was marking me,' Lisa told me. 'He was saying I was his property.'

It was deeply disturbing. She hated it. But how many 'chick flicks' do we see where a man sends bouquet after bouquet after bouquet and we think, 'How romantic'? No wonder people get the wrong idea.

For the avoidance of doubt, here is a list of stalking behaviours, compiled by the Hertfordshire police:

---

1. Dr Holly Taylor-Dunn, Professor Erica Bowen and Professor Liz Gilchrist, *The Victim Journey: A participatory research project seeking the views and experiences of victims of stalking and harassment* (University of Worcester, 2017).

— Frequent unwanted contact such as appearing at
  the victim's home, workplace, telephone calls, text
  messages, letters, notes, emails, faxes, or other contact
  on social networking sites like Facebook
— Driving past the victim's home or workplace
— Following, watching or loitering near the victim
— Sending letters or unwanted 'gifts' (gifts may appear nice
  but could have a sinister meaning)
— Damaging significant property belonging to the victim
— Burglary or robbery of the victim's home, workplace,
  car
— Gathering information on the victim by contacting
  people who know the victim, using public records etc.
— Harassment of others close to the victim
— Threats to the victim or those close, particularly those
  who are seen to be 'protecting the victim' or acting as
  the buffer between the victim and the stalker
— Assault of the victim

This list is not exhaustive . . .

Chapter Eight

On 28 January my diary says, '*VENICE TO MY FRANC –
YAHOO!!!*'

We were lucky with the weather. In sheltered squares
where we stopped for coffee, we could slip off our coats and sit
in our shirtsleeves, faces turned up towards the January sun.
We walked for miles, hand in hand, across a semi-deserted city.
There were almost no other tourists. We went on a gondola –
not the expensive tourist ones but standing up in a proper
Venetian one. I held on tightly to Franc and he kissed me to
take my mind off the possibility of drowning. We stood on
the Rialto Bridge. We climbed to the top of St Mark's basilica
on Sunday morning and then stepped inside to listen to the
service – the saturating beauty of it made me cry (quietly). I
remember waking up in bed, Franc beside me, and listening to
the sound of bells from the campanile, elated by the reckless
abundance of Tintoretto and Titian, Giorgione, Bellini and
Veronese. It is an astounding place and Franc was kind, caring
and lovely – Jekyll rather than Hyde – perhaps because he
knew I'd never been there before whereas he had. And so it
was my turn to wonder who he'd been with then.

Coming home again was a cold hard dose of reality. It was
almost midnight when my flight got in and too late to catch
a train. I hadn't booked a room because I couldn't afford one
so, when I kissed Franc goodbye at the airport, I knew I would

be spending the night on a bench in the Stansted arrivals hall. I fibbed about that and crossed my fingers behind my back. I had put all my efforts into getting to Venice and didn't care about getting back again. I don't know what I thought might happen: perhaps something extraordinary and romantic, as if this was a novel instead of just life.

Waiting for me on the kitchen table when I got home was a letter I'd read the Friday before – a *STRICTLY PRIVATE & CONFIDENTIAL – ADDRESSEE ONLY* letter. I had to face work again and a meeting at 10 a.m. on my first day back, to discuss what Doreen called my 'current level of sickness absence'. The last paragraph raised a flicker of alarm: 'You are entitled to be accompanied, if you wish, at this meeting with a Trade Union Representative, friend or colleague not acting in a legal capacity.'

One of the human resources managers would also be there. I began to feel, for want of a better word, oppressed. I'd never in my life been in trouble at work. I was absolutely certain that she had been talking about me. Believing that others in my office knew what Doreen had said about me was shaming. I had a surfeit of shame already and no room for any more.

Following standard human resources procedure, a further letter from Doreen arrived after the meeting confirming what we had discussed: that before Christmas I had myself arranged a meeting with the occupational health team, told them I was finding my work stressful and that there was no cover when I was on holiday – and I blamed this for my backlog of work. Doreen wrote that we'd talked about this before and she would arrange for me to have 'basic secretarial support' when I was away.

The letter further informed me that in future Doreen

would be managing my sick leave rather than the more sympathetic occupational health team. I'd gone over her head and she didn't like it. I no longer felt I had anyone in whom I was able to confide.

Franc came back that weekend to collect more of his stuff. We went to the gym together so that he could check my progress (those stubborn unyielding thighs). While I was being put through my paces the man at the next bench leaned over and said, quite seriously, 'Is this man bothering you?' I laughed – well, it *was* funny – and said, no, it was absolutely fine; we were together. 'Really?' said my gym neighbour, raising an eyebrow. Franc's gym coaching style was full on and in your face. I can see why someone might construe it differently. On the other hand, this was now the second or third time a complete stranger had questioned the way Franc treated me in public. What I now thought of as acceptable was clearly troubling to others.

When we went to the station to wait for his train on Monday morning Franc had a lot more in his suitcase than he had arrived with. He seemed to be leaving me by degrees. I hated it.

There was something else I hated too. Franc wrote about it in the letter he left for me:

> *I cannot get this phobia about the flat. After all I have done to give you a place where to stay you keep telling me you hate it etc. etc.*

He said he would ask the building manager to see if it could be rented from March, which horrified me, or, he suggested, I could find someone to share the rent with me (female) – '£60 per week all included.' He said he had paid all his outstanding bills and now it was my responsibility.

He reminded me that I had to pay rent and council tax by the end of the week, which came to just over £500.

> *Money makes me nervous and it makes me nervous what you told me last night (never mind throwing at me remote controls) about what I know and what I don't. I am not sure I know you anymore – only complaints. Never a thank-you, never . . .*

What had I done to make him 'nervous'? I'd told him that I wanted to leave my job and find another. I'd told him I was worried about what was going on at work. I thought he would understand. He told me to 'fucking stay' where I was because of the money. That was when I threw the TV remote at him. It missed him by a whisker.

The following weekend Quinn died.

It was a massive heart attack. Dead before he hit the floor, they said. I think he knew. He had written each of my daughters a letter a couple of weeks earlier and sent me a photograph of one of his paintings with a sweet note on the back. But for the first time anyone could remember there was nothing in his studio. No work in progress. Everything was neat and tidy and put away. He knew.

I hadn't seen Quinn since the day of the dinner at Nina's, although we'd spoken on the phone. I felt guilty. I didn't ask for time off to go to the funeral, because I didn't think Doreen would agree to it. I felt guilty about that too.

*

Doreen now began to apply more pressure. I tried not to be out of my office after her secret search before Christmas but it was, of course, impossible. The department outboard that I had to fill in whenever I left the area – to go to medical records, outpatients, another ward or the pathology lab – was located bang outside Doreen's office so she knew when I wasn't there. I learned from the ward sister that every time I left, Sarah – the part-time typist – would be seen hurrying through the ward on her way to have a quick rifle through my desk. The registrar I shared an office with told me the same thing. Sarah had a legitimate reason to be there because of the secretarial help she was giving me but she also worked for Doreen so it was hard to see it as pure coincidence.

Then, early in February, I got a message from Franc that I needed to move the contents of my old house from his warehouse by the weekend or they would be thrown away. I thought I had more time, that Franc wouldn't have left telling me until the last minute. I had to ask Doreen if I could take the day off. The thought of it gave me the shakes. She said no, and it *was* short notice, but still I tried to explain that I hadn't been given any warning myself, that there were things which were important to me and my children that I really needed to reclaim. That brought the response, 'You're insured, aren't you?' Well, no, actually I wasn't and that wasn't the point. These things weren't valuable to anyone but me – walking sticks my father had carved, one for each of us; Mum's tea service . . . the sentimental kind of stuff. She wouldn't budge. 'Who the hell do you think you are?' was the last thing she said on the subject. I stuck up a picture of Miss Trunchbull in the kitchen at home, imagined Doreen's face on it and used it for target practice.

I phoned around and managed to get an auction house to collect the furniture but they wouldn't take anything else so there was no alternative but to try to put it out of my mind.

Franc came back again a week later to sign off the cleared warehouse. When he'd finished doing that he brought back one or two of the bits and pieces belonging to me that hadn't gone into the skip . . . *literally* bits and pieces. My mother's tea service was returned to me in a plastic carrier bag. I put it straight in the bin. I couldn't even look at it. But then we talked about how and when I would move to Paris to live with him and that soothed away some of the hurt.

On the day he went back to France, I had another meeting with Doreen and Dr Bray. This made three meetings in three weeks, each one followed by a lengthy letter outlining what I'd done, what I hadn't done and what I had to do next.

Every one of these meetings left me with the feeling that I'd been caught in a lie. There seemed to be a suggestion that I was letting everyone down. The only thing I'd ever deceived anyone about was what was going on at home, although was that really deception? My unwilling brain took its time to work out that I was being 'got rid of' but there was nothing I had done which merited dismissal. Evidence was therefore being gathered and that was what all these meetings were for.

That made me angry. I located my spine and kicked back:

Dear Doreen

Further to your letter dated 22 February, I wish to clarify a few points . . .

I was *very* thorough in my clarifications and after I'd done that I decided I might as well say the unsayable.

The situation I find myself in at present is extremely unpleasant and stressful. I feel I have been penalized for being off sick (I was in fact an in-patient here for part of that time) and I feel extra pressures have been brought to bear on me with regard to a backlog of work which is not entirely my fault.

As far as I was aware, before I fell ill there were no problems at all with my performance (as evidenced by my appraisal with yourself) but when I returned to work there seemed to be nothing but problems.

I feel it is necessary, given the situation, to set my thoughts down in writing and also to correct the inaccuracies in your letter to me. I do not wish there to be any further misunderstandings.

I copied the letter to HR. I had quite enough shit in my life, thank you, and I wasn't going to put up with this as well.

Doreen was largely responsible for the pressure I was under at work but the root cause of it – of my absences, my lateness, my lack of concentration – was currently out of the country. I was caught between Doreen and Franc, in a peculiar double bind.

Franc came back in the middle of March. I'd been dying to see him and took both Friday and Monday off so that we could have a long weekend together. We walked about the city the way he liked to. We went to the gym and he gave me a new exercise regime. I cooked for him. Then, on the Monday morning while we were lying in bed, his arms around me, my head resting happily on his chest listening to his heartbeat, he dropped a grenade.

'Ellen, I have something to tell you.' There was a warning in his voice.

I stiffened. Oh God, what now . . .

'What?'

His heart beat a little faster.

'It is Sophie. I think . . . I don't know whether I am still in love with her. I am seeing her again.'

I felt icy cold.

All these years later I can still call up the sensation. As though my body has written it on my bones.

My throat felt full, my forehead tender, my arms and legs weak, and my heart? My heart was in pieces.

Without saying a word I got out of bed, pulled on a T-shirt and walked through to the kitchen. When Franc came in I was sitting on the countertop, eyes swimming, smoking a cigarette by the open window. For once he didn't fire recriminations at me for walking away or rage about my smoking. He knew he had done a bad thing.

He spent the rest of the day consoling me, calming me and hugging me. He said he was proud of the way I had taken it, which only confused me more. Was he dumping me? It didn't feel like it. It felt as though I was expected to take this pain and tuck it away somewhere until he had decided which of us he loved best.

In my diary the page for that day has one word on it: *Bombshell*.

As he was getting ready to leave again, Franc threw me a guilty bone: 'Come out on Friday. Stay the weekend.' So I did. It was entirely unremarkable and did nothing whatever to purge my fears. We carried on exactly as always. I remember wondering whether I could finish it myself but for some reason I found that impossible. Instead I condemned myself to months of bearing the knowledge of Sophie like Sisyphus, waking under the crushing weight of it, then rolling it before me all through the day until I fell back beneath it again in the dark hours. It was a daily struggle. I pounded the apparatus at the gym because it gave me something physical to hit and it punished me, too. I hated myself. I hated everything about me.

Walking back into work the next morning I found a jaunty note from Doreen on my desk, summarizing another search she'd made while I was away. It was timed and dated and she had been joined by Dr Bray. I had to ask myself why, given that he was a consultant doctor with far more important things to concern himself with than my week-old filing.

*

I wasn't going to see Franc again until Easter, which fell at the end of April that year. He thought it best. That doesn't mean we didn't speak. He still called most evenings, usually at 8 p.m., 9 p.m. in France. I was not to call him. I thought I knew why. There were a lot of silences in these phone calls. I didn't know what to say other than tell him about my day, which sounded like complaints because it was mostly about my situation at work or what I'd done at the gym, which was never enough. I didn't ask him about Sophie because I didn't want to know. In any case my imagination got to work on it nightly.

I still didn't tell him it was over, though. I wonder why? My sixty-year-old self would have done that, given him the bum's rush out of the door. But then my sixty-year-old self wouldn't have got herself into this situation in the first place – although, given my track record, it's hard to be sure about that. I think as long as he didn't say anything I could convince myself it wasn't true. He hadn't told me he was actually sleeping with Sophie and I didn't want to confront it. I didn't want to know anything that might kill my dream stone dead. Is this what blinded by love means?

If we broke up, people would want to know why and I would have to tell them about how I'd been betrayed, but also that the betrayal had been mine in the first place for sleeping with Franc while he was still engaged to Sophie. My tower of lies about him would come crashing down.

The thought of Doreen's triumphant face if she found out

about what was going on with Franc was more than I could bear. It was bad enough that she knew he was living in France now. It was a gift – another raw nerve to tug at.

'Still together?'

'Of course.' Avoiding eye contact.

'No *mademoiselles* on the scene then?'

'No.'

'I don't know why you don't find yourself a nice English bloke to screw . . .'

Anyone hinting at Franc being unfaithful was painful enough. Talking about it would have been impossible. I'd have broken down. I still couldn't quite bring myself to believe he could do this to me, which I suppose means I ranked infidelity as worse than him knocking seven shades of shit out of me for smoking, or for walking away during an argument or allowing another man to speak to me.

On the other hand, perhaps blind loyalty was the way to show I really did love him, although I can't believe I actually thought that. Perhaps, having weathered everything, I was too invested in Franc to walk away. Before the Sophie bombshell, when he had talked about me relocating to Paris with him, it had been a tiny hopeful light winking in the distance. The idea of living and working in Paris . . . could you imagine Doreen's face? 'I'm off to Paris now because I have a job there and I'm going to live with Franc. Bye!'

Something in me, though, was realistic enough to have filed that thought under 'fantasy'. The flat was a problem, too. I'd never been allowed to put my stamp on it but I'd made my mark in other ways: there was a dent in the wall where my head had hit it, and on another wall where I'd thrown the remote; a small sweaty handprint, left in a struggle by the bathroom door and which stubbornly resisted cleaning sprays.

The dining table was taped together with duct tape where it had collapsed when I'd ended up on top of it. All these things were reminders that this life was a lie.

One night I heard a couple in a flat across the way having a pyrotechnic row and I watched as she threw all his clothes out of a third-floor window. A few minutes later he appeared outside and began scooping them up and shoving them into the back of his car. He was about to drive off when she ran out into the car park, half-dressed, barefooted, and threw herself onto the bonnet to stop him. Everything was glazed barley-sugar orange in the street lights. It was surreal. I could be that woman, I thought, and yet I'm standing here thinking, how ridiculous. Is that me? Am I ridiculous too?

Franc said he was tired at Easter and couldn't spare much time so if I wanted to see him we'd have to meet halfway – he suggested Cambridge. He was going to fly to Stansted on Saturday morning and go back to Paris on Sunday afternoon. Yes, I said, of course. He told me to jump. I asked how high.

It was an awful thirty-six hours. Worse than if he hadn't come back at all. I knew the weekend was doomed when I met him at the airport. He looked strained, tense, heavy-eyed, not as pleased to see me as I was to see him. His hello kiss was dutiful. I had expected him to be like the Franc of a month earlier, kind and thoughtful and apparently understanding how I felt.

We did what we usually did – pub lunch, mooch about. I didn't know Cambridge, which lifted his mood slightly, but on the other hand I should have done some research, apparently, because I had no schedule for our time there. We sat on a bench behind King's College chapel and although he held my hand and was physically there he wasn't present in any other sense. I badly wanted to cry and eventually tears spilled over, dripping off my chin and dotting the front of my white shirt with mascara. I wore white shirts nearly all the time because Franc liked them. My nose began to run. I didn't want to take my hand from the warmth of his to find a tissue.

'Why are you crying, Ellen?'

'Darling, you know why.'

An unfortunate slip of the tongue – he didn't like me to call him 'darling'. He said I called everyone 'darling'.

'You should be happy I am here.'

'I am, Franc. I am. But it's for such a short time and I miss you so much.'

'Get a tissue, Ellen. Dry your eyes.'

At the pub where we had lunch, I rested my hand on the table in case he wanted to hold it but he left it lying there.

'Look at those two,' I said, flicking my eyes in the direction of a really unattractive but obviously loved-up couple in the corner. 'If they can find each other why can't . . .' I stopped when I caught Franc's eye. It was a horrible thing to say. I was a horrible person.

As we resumed our walk around Cambridge a wetly heavy mood settled on me. The sun was shining and it was a lovely day but I felt numb. Out of it. As dusk fell I began to think about the next day and the awfulness of saying goodbye to Franc. I doubted he'd ever come back.

We had supper, then went to bed. I snuggled up to Franc and he put his arm around me but didn't pull me in close the way he usually did. I rested my head in the hollow between his shoulder and his neck. I was aching to be held and I kissed him lightly, hoping for a deeper kiss back. He didn't move, didn't touch me. He doesn't want to be here, I thought. He doesn't want me.

I think he was trying to be 'faithful' to Sophie. Lying in bed naked with the woman he had lived with for over a year was not a betrayal, as long as nothing happened. For me, however, this added a whole new layer of agony. Had he been like that with her when he was seeing me? I felt bad for her, and then, inevitably, guilty.

*

I've shied away from writing about sex with Franc because I haven't quite been able to face it. It's too personal, too intimate and exposing, and for the most part I've skirted the issue. But I have to talk about it because it's such an integral part of how and why this happened to me.

When I met Franc I was both alone and lonely. Yes, I had friends around me but there was none of the close and loving intimacy you get from the right kind of partner, which strengthens and supports you. I craved this and, initially, it's what Franc gave me. He was a little younger than me, sexy, passionate, with a good body; he was gentle and kind, and he took the initiative, which made me believe he loved me. He certainly told me he did, often, and I believed him. I needed to be loved and cared for so badly.

It's a classic example of the triumph of hope over experience. There is nothing that can tell you whether what you think is love is the real deal. No magazine article or book can ever accurately describe it – it defies description. How we feel is unique to each of us. It's also true that men and women have differing views about sex and love. But sex can be an addiction – it certainly was with Franc – and that perhaps explains why it is so often used as a weapon.

So many women of my generation were brought up to see sex as something wrong, but also essential. Marriage was for procreation. Sex was to make babies, a duty not to be enjoyed.

It was explained to us as a mysterious spiritual thing, a communion of souls, sanctified by the Church and marriage. The first time would hurt and we would bleed but that was as it should be and demonstrated our all-important virginity; we might need to stay lying down for thirty minutes or so afterwards. You can imagine the relief we felt when we found out what sex could really be like.

My mother was a religious woman and took me to church and to Sunday school when I was a child. I was taught to take what the Bible said very seriously. Women who enjoyed and were proud of their sexuality were almost unheard of in my neck of the woods but in the cinema we saw Diana Dors, Marilyn Monroe, Jayne Mansfield – all pneumatic of body and radiating sex appeal. Men went mad for them. It was all very confusing.

I was still prepubescent when I thought I'd finally found out what sex actually meant, and I was horrified. At the age of only eleven I watched the prelude to Soames Forsyte raping his wife, Irene, in the BBC adaptation of the Forsyte Saga – which I also found oddly exciting for reasons I could not fathom. A penny dropped. This, I understood, was what my father meant when he talked about being careful when I was out pedalling my bicycle around country lanes and not being out alone after dark because of 'men'. He placed an emphasis on the word.

More of the puzzle fell into place later when my friend Claire, who at fourteen was a year older than me, took me along to a clandestine rendezvous with her new boyfriend. Claire was well brought up, a middle-class grammar-school girl like me, but her boyfriend was an occasional gardener/handyman in the local park, which was where he picked her up. He was very good-looking in a slightly sleazy way. I was there as lookout while they snogged each other in an empty house on the building site up the road. It's only now that I realize he was quite some years older than us, and possibly a paedophile. Nonetheless, it was an education.

My ex-husband was the first man I ever slept with. We met in our final year at school, and it's fair to say that my experience up to that point was both mixed and limited. When, a year after I was married and two months after my mother died, I found myself being put, painfully, into a taxi by the bastard who raped me, no wonder I didn't tell anyone about it. Can you imagine explaining *that* to the 1970s police? When anal sex was playfully suggested as part of our marital lovemaking I recoiled in fear. Just the thought of it made me want to vomit.

Post-divorce and back on the market again, as it were, my experiences fed into my expectations: women are passive, men take control. When a man I went out with (twice) told me that my mouth 'just asked to be fucked', I smiled politely and changed the subject. Sex is never just sex. It's much, much more than that. In the wrong hands it's a weapon for subjugation, torture and control the world over. The 'wrong hands' explain female genital mutilation (FGM), the sexual grooming of young girls, mass abductions and rape, and why women using social media are intimidated with online rape threats.

When Franc came along, with his lovely smile, good manners and crinkly blue eyes, he gave me what he knew I needed. I didn't have to spell it out. And when he was sure I was dementedly, violently in love, he gently started to mould me into what he wanted. By the time he was done he had coached me into believing that he was a generous lover, unselfish, concerned only with giving me pleasure. What he'd done, in fact, was turn me into an automaton. For the most part sex with

Franc was something he did to me. I was not required to participate other than to demonstrate pleasure and have a pulse. He arranged my limbs. He turned me over. He dressed and undressed me. To remember it now makes me feel horrible. It puts me less in mind of the loving intimacy I thought I was enjoying and more in mind of the Ceremony from *The Handmaid's Tale*, only with a smaller cast. But at the time it felt like love.

When Franc turned away from me in that hotel room in Cambridge, he was telling me that he neither needed me nor loved me.

*

I didn't want to be there, in bed with a man who didn't love me. The pain felt unbearable and I wanted to run away. The furthest I could go without causing a scene (Franc would surely come after me and I knew how that ended) was the bathroom. I locked the door, flicked on the extractor fan, sat on the floor and lit a cigarette. I couldn't see properly because my eyes were swimming with tears. I wished the fan were a bit quieter. I wished I could stop crying.

A tap on the door.

'Are you smoking, Ellen?'

'Yes, Franc.'

'Clean your teeth and come out.'

'No, Franc.' A pause . . . and I added, 'Sorry.'

There. I'd said it. I'd said no. It would have been a start if Franc hadn't taken it so badly. I couldn't help it. I got so anxious now when I was with him and I couldn't eat so I smoked. (Perversely my thighs still measured 20 inches and I'd gone back up to 60 kilos – I swear that man could spot 100 grams of misplaced fat.) The night passed distressingly slowly while

I carried on weeping, sometimes noisily and sometimes not. I wanted him to feel my anguish. I went to the bathroom and smoked again and again, while Franc hissed and swore at me through the door, until the first blackbird started to sing in the tree outside the window.

I didn't eat breakfast. As we walked to the station my body felt weighted, each step taking more strength than I felt I had.

'Pick up your feet, Ellen, and breathe properly.'

'I can't. I'm tired.'

'Pick . . . up . . . your . . . feet.' He kicked my ankle, quite gently but on that bone that hurts if you catch it on furniture. Then a sharp tap between my shoulder blades.

'Stand up straight.'

'I can't.'

'You can.'

'Really, Franc. I can't.' Then I added, very quietly, 'I wish I was dead.'

'Well, why aren't you?'

We walked on a bit further, along a busy road. I watched the traffic, waiting for a moment when there was a car coming fast enough, and then took a step to the kerb. One more step and . . .

Franc grabbed my arm and yanked me back.

'I was joking.' But he should have known by now that I would do whatever he asked me to.

At the station he caught his train and I caught mine. A text arrived, which bewilderingly said, *I love you*. I went straight to the gym when I got home and worked for two hours on my thighs.

A few days later a letter arrived, written on his company letterhead. At the end of almost every line I have scribbled the words I couldn't say to his face.

Dear Helen

Just a few notes. THIS BARELY CONSTITUTES ONE NOTE.

He hadn't forgotten me, he said. REALLY? I wrote.

He didn't phone but he thought that was best 'right now'. FOR WHO?

He said he would call me. WHEN, I wrote, NEXT YEAR?

He was going to be away for four days at the weekend, he said, on business. I BELIEVE YOU (NOT).

He said he thought of me. OH YES?

He told me he missed me. NOT FROM WHERE I'M STANDING.

Hold on, he said, and don't let yourself go. NO INTENTION, DARLING.

He would speak to me soon. ANOTHER LIE.

Love AND ANOTHER.

Franc

*

On the day I received Franc's letter, a Friday, Doreen called me in for a meeting that afternoon. To be fair she didn't know what was going on in my private life, that I was a wreck. No one did.

Seven pages of notes duly followed in the internal post. My most recent misdemeanours were itemized and listed in date order under the headings of: *filing backlog, lunch breaks (timing of), lateness and backlog of dictation tapes.* Seven pages.

I was becoming inured to seeing myself described in the formal language of the line manager on a mission. I read that there had been *many occasions where Helen had not adhered to her directive regarding lunch breaks.* It was also noted that I had been late for work seven times in five months. It's only now that I realize these coincided with times when Franc was in the flat. It wasn't so much that he didn't want me to leave him and go to work (although he didn't), it was more that he kept me awake half the night, arguing.

The notes also required me to start keeping a daily log of my *activities* so that Doreen could *identify any tasks or areas of workload impacting on you unnecessarily*. Every single job I did during the working day had to be written down in the log. Phone calls had to be timed and itemized. Conversations had to be recorded. I had to note the number of letters I typed and when I typed them, the number of tapes I cleared, the number and date of the clinics I cleared, the number of referrals made and when I made them, waiting lists updated with whom and when, the amount of filing done, when I took things to out-patient clinics or wards, what I took, why I took it and how long it took me to take it, when I went to the lavatory, when I made coffee, when I arrived, when I left, when I went to lunch and when I came back. Each day's log had to be handed in to Doreen at close of play. I could have typed fifty letters in the time it took to do all this. It was middle management as taught by the Stasi.

The letter accompanying the meeting notes ended with a sinister phrase: *Your failure to follow reasonable instructions from me could be interpreted as insubordination . . .* So that was how she meant to get rid of me.

'Insubordinate'? Fuck me. If there was one thing I knew how to be it was subordinate.

To his credit, Dr Bray excused himself from this meeting and never came to another. It was, he told me some weeks later, not what he had anticipated. No, a witch-hunt never is.

A couple of weeks later there was a further meeting. This

time attended by the human resources manager who we all knew was also Doreen's best friend and who now helpfully provided a further fourteen pages of meeting notes and the suggestion that I was putting patient safety at risk. I was asked to sign these notes to indicate that I accepted them as an accurate record. They weren't, so I gave them four pages of my own amendments and only then did I sign.

Even now, I can admire the ruthless and meticulous way Doreen went about her pursuit of me. She was tireless in exposing even the smallest mistake – a dirty coffee mug left on my desk overnight, handwriting she couldn't read (but everyone else could), stopping to answer a patient's question on my way through the ward, five minutes late going to lunch, half an hour late leaving the office . . . on and on it went. Nothing I did was right. It must have taken her hours. I'm amazed she found time to run the department.

All of this made me long for the absent Franc, desperate for comfort. He'd made himself the entire focus of my world, the only person I could turn to, and then he'd gone away. He was always going away.

Unexpectedly, and just in time to save my sanity, some good news arrived. It turned out that some of the furniture I'd stored in Franc's warehouse was actually quite good, good enough to go into an antiques auction. It was a complete surprise to me when it made a respectable four-figure sum. I kissed the cheque when it arrived and then did something completely impulsive – for the first time in my life I booked a holiday just for me. And for once Doreen didn't argue about my request for annual leave.

I didn't ask Franc, I *told* him I was going. He gave me strict instructions not to speak to strange men, not to drink anything but bottled water and not to go anywhere on my own.

I'm surprised he didn't tell me to sew my valuables into my corsets. He couldn't tell me not to go, though. Perhaps it was a tacit acknowledgement of guilt for what he'd done.

As my flight passed over France on the way to Athens, there was a huge thunderstorm. It felt as though Franc was shaking his fist at me, and it made me laugh. I felt as though I could do anything. I think it was probably the best holiday I've ever had. Seven days on my own in a small self-catering apartment on the tiny green island of Poros and it was heaven. I walked, I basked in the sun, I swam and had picnics, I ate alone every night at the same table in the same restaurant giving my order myself to the (male) waiter, I read and, most important of all, I began to write again. I had to buy a phone card and call Franc as he had insisted but I didn't tell him where I was, even when he said if I did he *might* come and join me. I didn't want him to know so he couldn't spoil it. It felt unfamiliar but strangely redemptive, and exciting. There was a chance my life still held possibilities. There was hope. On the ferry back from Poros to Piraeus, I wept gently all the way. I could have stayed there quite happily and never come back.

*

Vulnerable adj. not proof against wounds, susceptible of or liable to injury, attack, offering an opening to criticism etc. Exposed to the possibility of being attacked or harmed, either physically or emotionally . . .[1]

'Vulnerable' is an awkward word when applied to women. Certain sections of the media (particularly the press) have taken to interpreting it as a defining factor in any case of

---

1. *Cassell's Concise English Dictionary*, New Edition, 1992.

abuse and assault. If a woman – young, old or middle-aged – seems vulnerable she deserves our utmost sympathy and understanding. If not, then she doesn't.

Of more concern is that this interpretation has long been – and it seems still is – one of the criteria by which judges assess the severity of a case of domestic abuse. This has particular relevance for the successful prosecution of cases of coercive control and is perhaps one of the reasons why there have been relatively few convictions.

'Would you mind being described as "vulnerable"?' I asked Number 3 Daughter, who is now in her thirties.

'Yes,' she said, without hesitation. 'You'd be saying I was weak. I don't want to be weak.'

Smart girl. Yet women who are victims of domestic abuse, and especially of coercive control, are expected to fulfil this perceived criteria. Specifically, they are supposed to look and behave as a victim – a submissive woman. A woman in need of protection. A penitent woman.

The word 'vulnerable' crops up all over the place – especially once you're aware of it. It's used in cases of sexual abuse, assault and rape, often bringing with it more than a whiff of blaming the victim. It is applied to middle-aged women in cases of online dating gone wrong – most recently in the case of Jason Lawrance, the Match.com rapist, who specifically targeted older women because he saw them as easy prey. Lawrance is now serving a life sentence for a total of seven convictions (five rapes and two violent sexual assaults) in a career spanning several years. He was first reported quite early on but little action was taken, and was only arrested after his seventh victim went to the police. He rightly assumed that older women who had admitted to themselves (if not to anyone else) that they were lonely and decided to do something about it would be too ashamed of what he did to them to breathe a word. He no doubt also assumed, again correctly, that middle-aged women would appear less outwardly vulnerable and therefore less likely to be believed if they did say anything. The mishandling of the case bears that out.

The same is true of the case of John Warboys, the Black Cab Rapist. Not all the women came forward (rape is another under-reported crime) but he was finally convicted on one count of rape, five sexual assaults, one attempted assault and twelve other charges. His first victim was a nineteen-year-old student passenger who did report him but he was released after telling police she had been drunk and kissed him, a fact apparently confirmed on CCTV footage. In effect the police took his word over hers because she had been drinking before she got into his cab. She had made herself vulnerable and was therefore to blame.

Then there are Judge Richard Mansell QC's remarks as he decided on a suspended sentence rather than imprisonment for Mustafa Bashir, who had forced his wife, Fakhara Karim, to drink bleach, told her to kill herself, throttled her in public and hit her with a cricket bat. He was 'not convinced she was a vulnerable person' as she was 'an intelligent woman with a network of friends' who 'did go on to graduate from university with a 2:1 and a master's'.[1]

I understand that Judge Mansell was acting very much in his legal capacity when he said this. His judgement was based on the hierarchical scale set out in the Domestic Violence Guidelines for Sentencing. Nevertheless, his remarks were crass and insensitive and, worse, implied that domestic vio-

---

1. The *Guardian*, 27 March 2017.

lence and its effects are less or more damaging according to the class, intelligence and perceived strength of the victim, which is to say, their perceived vulnerability. This is just plain wrong. Not only that but the Guidelines themselves were published in 2006 and are now some way behind the curve on the advances made in understanding domestic abuse over the intervening ten years.

Fakhara Karim's degree of vulnerability becomes even more contentious when you consider that Judge Mansell himself seemed to have been drawn in by Bashir's economy with the truth, behaviour all too typical of an abuser. Bashir's lawyer told the court that his client would sign a contract with Leicestershire County Cricket Club if he were spared jail. This has echoes of recent cases involving professional footballers accused of rape.

Leicestershire County Cricket promptly blew the lie out of the water when a spokesman for the club said they were 'bemused' by the claim and that any suggestion Bashir had been offered a contract was 'completely false'. The spokesman added, 'The club have never spoken to Mustafa Bashir or an agent, nor offered a contract to the player.' Once his lie was exposed Bashir was given a hefty prison sentence. I'm sure I'm not the only one to think that he was jailed more for the lie than for the violent abuse of his wife.

The mistaken belief that women who live with abusive men must look cowed, or have visible bruises, is something that has been enshrined in British law for decades. One notorious case illustrates the point better than any other. It is not by any means the only such case but it is the most documented, the subject of films, plays, endless articles and books. It is the case of the last woman to be hanged in the United Kingdom – Ruth Ellis.

In July 1955 Ruth Ellis was executed for the murder of David Blakely. The photographs we see of Ruth show a petite, glamorous woman, immaculately made up and well dressed. What they don't show is a woman the Sentencing Guidelines Council might perceive as vulnerable. If you study her history you quickly come to understand that she was vulnerable to her core.[1] What people saw on the outside was a protective carapace.

By the time she met Blakely in the summer of 1953, Ruth had spent the greater part of her twenty-six years as a victim of one kind of abuse or another. Her father was a bully and a serial adulterer who seemed to regularly lay about with his fists at the women in his family. Ruth left school at fourteen, fell in love with a Canadian serviceman (who she later discovered was married) and became pregnant. Their son was born in 1944 but by that time Ruth had ended the relationship. 'I no longer felt any emotion about men,' she said. 'I was cold and spent.' She worked to support her family while her mother helped care for the baby. She was ahead of her time in that she wanted to work and have a life outside the domestic sphere.

However, Ruth's lack of a proper education meant that the options open to her were pretty limited. She did a little photographic modelling (sometimes nude), factory work, waitressing – anything to help make ends meet. Then one of the photographers she worked with took her out for a drink in Mayfair and she met Morris 'Morrie' Conley. Eighteen years later, the prison doctor at Holloway noted, '[She] came under the "influence" then of Conley . . . and graduated to the type of life she was leading.' He further added, 'Conley is

---

1. *A Fine Day for a Hanging* by Carol Ann Lee (Mainstream Publishing Company, 2012), is meticulously researched.

one of the worst characters in the West End'.[1] The crime reporter Duncan Webb described him as 'the monster with the Mayfair touch'.[2] Ruth herself pinpointed this as the beginning of her downward trajectory.

'The type of life she was leading' was in one of Conley's clubs on Duke Street where she was paid a flat fee of £5 to sit and chat with a customer as long as he bought a £3 bottle of champagne. Part of the deal was that she also occasionally had to have sex with Conley – much older, portly, 'ugly as a toad'.

She had an illegal abortion in 1950, having become pregnant by one of the club's clients, and later that year she married another regular. George Ellis was a chronic alcoholic and violent with it. She gave birth to their daughter the following year but the marriage did not last. She was soon back in one of Conley's clubs.

Ruth had survived a terrible couple of years but by the summer of 1953 she appeared to have turned a corner. Conley gave her a club to manage in Knightsbridge and it was here that she met David Blakely. Two weeks after their first meeting he moved in.

Their relationship was peppered with outbursts of violence and jealousy, abandonment, infidelity and reconciliation. Early in 1954 Ruth became pregnant but lost both her job and David's baby. Her prison case notes state that she had been pregnant three times with David and each pregnancy was terminated. At her trial Ruth gave a different account, saying that David had become 'very very violent . . . I do not know

---

1. Ibid., p. 52.
2. Ibid.

whether that caused the miscarriage or not, but he did thump me in the tummy'.[1]

On Easter Sunday 1954, Ruth Ellis shot David Blakely outside the Magdala Tavern in Hampstead. There is no doubt that she meant to kill him; she said so herself in her first police interview: 'When I put the gun in my bag, I intended to find David and shoot him.' That was the detail that everyone remembered at her trial. The first line of her statement says, 'I understand what has been said. I am guilty. I am rather confused.' But the statement was taken before she had been charged and there was no solicitor present. Today, it would be inadmissible.

Ruth made little mention of the physical and emotional abuse dished out by David before her trial, but there are some telling phrases in the witness statements of their friends:

Ruth: 'You can't walk on me for ever. I'm only human: I can't stand it.'

David: 'You'll stand it because you love me.'[2]

'"If you leave me, Ruth darling, I will kill you." I heard him say it often.'[3]

'He said, "One of these days I will kill you." I said, "You have done that already."'[4]

'I don't know whether I love him or I'm going mad.'[5]

The last evening the couple spent together ended when they were thrown out of the Steering Wheel Club after David punched Ruth full in the face. The manageress of the club,

---

1. Ibid., p. 168.
2. Ibid., p. 171.
3. Ibid., p. 169.
4. Ibid., p. 167.
5. Ibid., p. 161.

who saw this happen, was surprised not to be called as a witness at Ruth's trial, especially given that it had been so close to the shooting.

Nor was much notice taken of another potential witness, Ruth's French teacher, who said, 'I thought that she looked like a person on the verge of a nervous breakdown and had stopped working just in time.'

Of the day she killed Blakely, Ruth said, 'I felt somehow outside of myself. Although I seemed to be registering impressions quite clearly, it did not seem to be me. I was in a sort of daze.'[1] This sounds like the sort of dissociative fugue state that can result from the cumulative effects of domestic and psychological abuse. It's the brain's way of coping when there is too much to cope with and one I have experienced myself.

Ruth's trial lasted one and a half days and the jury (ten men and two women) took just fourteen minutes to find her guilty of murder – whereupon she was sentenced to death. Three weeks later, she was hanged.

There is little doubt that Ruth Ellis was condemned as much for her way of life as for shooting David Blakely. She was a sexually active divorcee. She had an illegitimate child and she was a nightclub hostess. Her peroxide hair, flawless appearance and her calm and measured speech were not the way a woman who had been subjected to two years of physical and psychological abuse was supposed to look and behave. She did not appear vulnerable.

Her defence counsel, Mr Melford Stevenson, showed a fatally poor grasp of what he was dealing with and portrayed Ruth as a jealous woman scorned.

---

1. HO 291/237 National Archive.

The jury was informed that the defence would call an eminent psychiatrist who would tell them that 'the effect of jealousy on the feminine mind, upon all feminine minds, can so work as to unseat the reason and can operate to a degree in which in a male mind it is quite incapable of operating'.[1]

That Ruth Ellis killed David Blakely is not in doubt. But her state of mind when she killed him is. Today she would not have been hanged, but she would almost certainly have been found guilty of manslaughter at the very least. And the tabloid press would probably still have had a field day over her failure to look suitably vulnerable.

I've often asked myself if, when I felt at my most desperate, I could have killed Franc. I don't know the answer. But given that on the two occasions I experienced a similar 'fugue' state, any harm was directed against myself, probably not.

I am struck by a number of similarities between Blakely and Franc – they are of a type. Both upper-middle class, handsome, serially unfaithful, abusive, manipulative, charming, feckless and utterly unreliable. Mind you, you could say that about a lot of men.

---

1. Helena Kennedy, *Eve Was Framed: Women and British Justice* (Vintage, 2005).

Chapter Nine

My solo holiday must have made Franc think because while I was away he wrote to me. The letter was waiting when I got back:

Dear Helen
A lot of things to say and not knowing where to start.
Perhaps there is no start.

I had told him that I was looking very fit and well but he said he would reserve judgement until he could see for himself, 'with particular attention to the fat issue'.

He wanted to know if I was still planning to leave the flat. He had enjoyed working in England. He thought he would be back one day and 'looking at the way things are at the moment . . .' but in the next sentence he speculated that he might be wrong about that because, as he said, he hadn't got 'a clear picture' of his future. Perhaps, he went on, he could open a small shop in the Midlands, a delicatessen with 'good French wines', or perhaps he could go and work in America.

He said that he didn't mention me on purpose, not because he wasn't thinking about me but just not to 'create more confusion in you'. And this, he said,

. . . explains why I keep telling you to be sensible about

> *your job: I am selfish in this case because I want you to stay*
> *put until I decide something.*
>
> *Au revoir*
>
> *Franc*

He called me a couple of days later and said he was planning to come back for a week or so in August. It was his flat so I couldn't really refuse. Actually, that's not strictly true. It was an excuse. I wanted . . . I *needed* him back. Still. Despite my taste of freedom and my diary filling up again with friends and family, despite everything he had done, I wanted him back. Nuts, isn't it?

On Monday, I signed myself 'IN' on Doreen's whiteboard. I looked rested and tanned. On my computer keyboard I found a news cutting, photocopied from the *Times Mirror, Los Angeles*, with the headline, *Dog's name becomes fodder for joke essay* and a rambling story about a dog called Sex. A couple of sentences were underlined: <u>But this is a dog.</u> <u>He said he didn't care what she looked like.</u> <u>My case comes up Friday.</u>

I asked Jeannie if she knew where it had come from. 'Doreen,' she said, without looking up, confirming what I already knew.

I think, in her own unique way, she was telling me that I was a 'dog' (unattractive) and Franc's only interest in me was for sex. I read the part about the 'case' as a warning that her disciplinary pursuit of me was approaching its conclusion.

Inspired by my holiday and thrilled (if a little nervous) at the prospect of spending time with Franc I thought I'd try to outflank Doreen by going to Dr Bray first with my next holiday request (he'd been much nicer to me lately). With his approval in the bag I went to Doreen's office and closed the door behind me.

'Would it be all right if I took a week off in August, from the seventh? It's a month's notice. I've asked Dr Bray and he said it wouldn't be a problem.'

'No.'

'But . . .'

'No. Sarah's off the following week – you won't have any handover.'

'I said I'd call in to check if there was anything urgent and Dr Bray thought that would be fine.'

'It's not up to him, is it?'

'I'm asking because Franc's coming to the UK – I haven't seen him since Easter.'

'You'd better hope you're not "on" then.'

With that she got up and shoved past me into the main office. I had to go through it to reach my own desk and that's when she started:

'Who do you think you are? You think you're so fucking special. It's always special circumstances with you . . . always bloody Franc. You're not having time off.' And she stormed out.

'What was all that about?' asked one of the typists.

I'd had enough. I went back to Dr Bray and asked him to pull rank.

'Blimey,' he said, 'that's way over the top. I'll have a word with her.'

A form with two days' approved leave duly arrived on my desk the following day – not the week I'd asked for but still better than nothing. When I thanked Dr Bray he laughed and said, 'It's probably her hormones, she'll be back to normal tomorrow.' And he winked.

Normal? While I'd been away she'd ransacked my office and left me a smutty newspaper cutting. She seemed to be obsessed with persecuting me. It was weird and I wanted to leave. I would have if Franc hadn't told me not to because he might come back.

'Because he might come back.' If I could slip through time I would gently remind myself how unreliable he was. I could not and would not let Doreen treat me badly too. Funny, how I could fight her unreasonable behaviour but not his.

I suppose I could have predicted it after the row about annual leave but without warning on the last day of my first week back, I was summoned to Doreen's office to go through the daily logs I'd been meticulously completing. I had not, it seemed, followed procedure. And, staggeringly, she'd also compared all my listed telephone calls with the thousands itemized in hospital records.

I carefully replied to the inevitable summary letter, explaining why an urgent addition to a procedures list had necessitated a departure from normal practice and justifying my telephone calls. I copied it to HR to be sure that everything was on record.

*

Doreen retaliated – I want to say 'punished me' – by giving me an extra job organizing a series of departmental lunches. Not even Dr Bray's intervention helped. I was completely up to my oxters and – perhaps inevitably – I scored an own goal, totally forgetting about a sickness review meeting that Doreen had scheduled. Neither she nor the HR officer who was waiting with her phoned when I was late to see if I was on my way. Instead, the next day I got yet another official letter. Fuck.

In the middle of all this Franc arrived for a ten-day visit. I didn't ask him why he'd come back (I didn't want to rock the boat) – but just accepted that he was there. He seemed different, on his best behaviour, caring and kind. He told me I looked amazing. For once I didn't say, 'Really?' because I knew I did. He even agreed to us both attending a staff barbecue at Dr Bray's house the next day. Going on holiday on my own had been unpredictable. I think Franc found that independence of spirit attractive whilst also being unable to tolerate it – he wanted to reassert his control over me.

The day of the barbecue was warm and bright but I sensed an uncomfortable undercurrent.

We all sat around in the garden, drinking wine and making jokes about the potential irony of our boss giving us food poisoning. I smoked and drank, but not as much as usual – mainly because Franc was there, but so was Doreen and I wanted to keep a clear head. I wasn't keen to introduce Franc but she saved me the bother and introduced herself. Franc was unimpressed. 'She is round,' he said, 'a ball,' giving a characteristic curl of the lip. He grinned and I giggled – I loved him for that. It felt so good not to be dealing with this alone. The only cross words to come out of his mouth were when I went to get a fresh bottle of wine. He thought I'd had enough.

He wrote me a letter during those ten days that was the closest thing I'd ever had to a genuine love letter (like the ones found in attics, tied in bundles with ribbon). I carried it around with me, folded in my purse, for years afterwards, telling myself it was a reminder that once I had been loved.

The letter starts:

> It was not love at first sight. Before you had finished to say 'Hello!' your hand in mine, I was already in love with you.

He went on:

*You are right to say that the fact you needed someone to
help you in some way attracted me even more.*

All that he had done for me he had done 'just and only for
love'. He had never before felt what he felt for me and he
couldn't stay away from me.

I had hurt him too, 'don't worry'. I had made him feel 'the
most unbearable pains' in his heart. But I was everything he
wanted.

He had loved the house where we first lived together best.
He described how happy he had been when he would come
home from work to find me cooking in the kitchen, then
running to kiss him 'hello'. He said he waited all day for that
moment.

*I have spent 5 months of my life away from you. If you
can call that away. Every moment of my day I was thinking
of you. Every place I was thinking I wished you were here.
Still thinking to give you the moon if you wish. My all world
if you want.*

He said he was prepared to give up everything in France
and come back to live in England with me, although he wondered if he would have 'the guts to do it' for the Helen he held
in his heart, 'the gentle, loving, caring' me. He was 'prepared
to make sacrifices' even if he wasn't sure I would want him
back after what had happened; it was for me, not him, to say
'past is past'.

Then he spoiled it:

*It is not your fault, even if at the back of my mind, I want
to make you feel guilty for something it is currently killing
me.*

He believed my new-found strength and renewed social life were all his doing: 'I thought I put you in the right way and said, "Go now." Just that.'

It had hurt him to see me with a 'stupid bottle' because it made him think of me, as he put it, 'some time ago'. He had called me at work that morning because he was crying over everything that had happened, because he could not keep his feelings inside.

He said he was sorry to bother me with his feelings. He hoped I understood what I meant to him. He said it was up to me to decide whether or not our relationship was worth discussing. That day he had wanted to leave.

> *The problem is I care so much about you and at the same time I feel betrayed. Hope you understand it. Hope the real Helen takes control.*
>
> *Whatever Helen, and like you write: all my love always and forever.*
>
> *I do. (You cannot even imagine how much.)*
>
> *Franc*
>
> *PS I forgot to tell you how beautiful you are.*

And he still hated me wearing eyeliner.

Several years later I took that letter out of my purse and read it again, without the love goggles. I photocopied it and put the original, tattered and dog-eared, into one of those plastic wallets – this time to remind myself that something that looks like love sometimes isn't. But for years I had only remembered the first sentence, that he had never stopped thinking of me. I blanked the rest.

The letter he sent immediately after his return to Paris seems to suggest that we were back as we had been:

Dear Helen

> *Once you used to start with 'Love letter for you'. I miss those days.*
> *Back to work and already fed up.*
> *Thinking of you.*

He was also thinking about holidays. He said he wanted to go to the Red Sea for the sunshine, beaches, clear seas and 'a lot of sex as well' but if we couldn't go there then perhaps France or London or Dublin. He talked about the Christmas holidays, too, and whether we should stay at home or go away.

> *I think I will be able to manage the money but still worried about your financial situation (you have not mentioned anything about it and that really hurts me).*[1]

Anyway, he said, 'I wish you were here', and then he talked about all the places in Paris we could go to because he knew I would like them.

He told me to think about the flat. If I didn't want to stay there I should find somewhere cheaper to save money and if he decided to come back then we could find another, 'a better one'.

Had he finished with Sophie? I didn't ask. I just assumed he would tell me if he had.

He wrote again a couple of days later with more holiday suggestions, but ending with a brief reference to the horrors I was going through at work:

> *For that time you will have hopefully cleared your situation*

---

1. He was still trying to coerce me into handing over my bank account.

at the hospital, and won, so we can have some lovely tim
together.

   Love
   Franc

On Friday 1 September those horrors became much, *much*
worse when Doreen walked into my office with a big, beaming smile and asked me to confirm my availability a week
later. She told me I should check with my union rep to make
sure she was also available. What was happening on the 7th?
Had I missed something again? It turned out that it was the
date set for my disciplinary hearing.

I suppose that having put in so much work on it she
wanted the pleasure of seeing my face when she told me.
Naturally I also had the pleasure of seeing hers. 'Jubilant'
would be the word, I think.

I didn't start to cry until after she'd left the office. The ward
manager had a cigarette with me out by the ambulance bay.
I was shaking. 'Go home,' he said, 'and rest. You can't work
in this state. I'll let Bray know.' And he gave me a hug. A letter
formally setting out Doreen's allegations had arrived in the
morning post, *after* I'd left for work.

— That Helen Walmsley-Johnson failed to improve
   sufficiently under a performance management
   framework and may thereby be failing to meet the
   standards of performance required of her in her contract
   of employment as a PA to the Consultant, described in
   her job description.
— That Helen Walmsley-Johnson fails to follow reasonable
   instruction from her Manager, Doreen Milson, with
   regard to punctuality, lunch breaks and information

> about her workload, which occur with such frequency
> that they could be considered insubordinate.

Insubordinate? Small comfort that I had predicted this would be her weapon of choice.

I couldn't rest. I spent the whole weekend going through everything. Then I typed up my version of how we got to this point – eighteen pages of it. I needed to have it all written down so I wouldn't forget any of it.

Pride got me back to work on Monday, although I would have loved to hide at home. The first thing I did was go and see Dr Bray. I had to clear the air or it would be impossible to work together. He was very nice about it and told me to try not to worry. 'It's not my intention to get you out of the door.'

*

On the morning of the hearing I dressed in my favourite navy suit and, for luck, a white blouse Franc had bought me. I felt as though I was dressing for my execution.

The meeting began at 9 a.m. and it was quite a revelation.

Doreen arrived, looking important, pushing a wheelchair loaded with paperwork and files. If she wanted to intimidate me with the amount of 'evidence' she'd accumulated then she succeeded. My heart fell into my tan leather, block-heeled Parisian ankle boots.

We were there all day and because I fought hard, with my union rep beside me, we didn't get through all the evidence. We were to reconvene ten days later.

Part Two of the Trial of Helen Walmsley-Johnson saw me dressed in exactly the same clothes. Not that I'm superstitious or anything. We started at 10 a.m. and this time we did get to the end. I went home feeling that I had fought a good fight but without much hope.

I can't remember what prompted it but in a coffee break during the hearing Lisa, my union rep, and I began talking about domestic violence. She told me about the time she'd been knocked unconscious and come round with her hands nailed to the sitting-room floor and her husband on top of her. She showed me the scars – I can't think why I hadn't noticed them before. I didn't identify with it though. What happened with Franc wasn't like that.

I probably threw out a few hints to Lisa – a coded message or two. I found myself doing that sometimes, especially now he was back in my life. I couldn't say the actual words though and when Lisa told me about what had happened to her I parked the thought that he was abusive. A bit of shouting, hair pulling and a loss of freedom seemed trivial by comparison, not worthy of the term 'domestic abuse'. I mean, what did I have to complain about, really? Nothing.

By this stage my doctor had signed me off sick, but now that the process had begun I felt too fragile to show my face in the office anyway. I'd been thoroughly – and for all that the hearing was supposed to be private – publicly shamed. I read something somewhere that says the amount of shame you feel is proportionate to the number of people who know what you've done. I don't think that's quite right. The amount of shame is proportionate to the number of people you *think* know what you've done. And I thought everybody knew about this – right down to the snack-trolley man. I felt that very acutely.

My diary shows that Number 3 Daughter came over and stayed with me for a couple of days. I had lunch with Lizzie and Nina. I had my hair done. It also shows that Franc came back on the 21st and again on 29 September. And during one of these trips he told me that he and Sophie were over. There are clues in an undated letter of mine proving I wrote it in this couple of weeks. It shows how much I had changed over the summer but also how much I still needed him, still stubbornly holding out for a hero:

Dearest Franc

I am so, so sorry to have said the things I said to you last night. Please try to understand just exactly what you did to me in March. I know you say that for you it's finished but I still have the fall-out to deal with and you (we both) have the damage to deal with. Until that day I trusted you completely and I felt utterly, totally, entirely betrayed. That 5 months felt like 5 or 500 years. It took me months of struggling to get over it and I thought I had . . . until you came back in August. I had placed myself entirely in your hands – and until that day I felt safe. If it had been anyone but her I think I could have handled it better. She will always represent a threat to me and that's something I'll have to get over myself. But you, you can help heal my wounded heart and help rebuild the trust that was destroyed . . . that you destroyed (sorry, but you did).

What's happening now [the disciplinary hearing] just feels like the end of the world to me, and I'm looking to you for help. I thought I was coping with that and then my body lets me down. I'm not as strong as you or anyone else thinks I am but when I fall apart I try to do it in private. I've spent today falling apart and thinking, allowing myself to grieve for everything that's happened and for the people I've lost and not allowed myself the time to grieve for. I've been spring-cleaning my soul. Probably it was a bad time to speak to you on the phone. Can you understand that every time I have to say

*goodbye to you at an airport, in the flat or on a station
platform a part of me dies? I put on such a brave act when you
were here at the weekend and I could actually sleep when you
were here in bed with me. The reason it feels so bad now is
because I feel so insecure because of what's happened and the
lifeline I need is something that demonstrates real, strong
commitment on your part. My commitment to you is there but
I dare not give it and risk that pain again. It's partly pride
with me as well I suppose because I felt totally humiliated after
what happened. I couldn't go through that again – it would kill
me. You say you could have a job that would involve you
travelling a lot, that's fine if there are two things back in our
relationship – trust and commitment.*

*I think, after what you said last of all on the phone tonight
that you're going to give me an indication of your commitment
and that's all I need. It's not so difficult. If what I hope for is
coming from you then I thank you with all my heart. It means
everything to me and is something I can cling to and cherish.*

The letter doesn't end with my customary *H xxx*. Maybe
there was another page and it has been lost.

On 10 October a letter arrived informing me that a decision had been reached and I should attend a meeting the next
day at the hospital to learn what that was. They really liked to
drag things out. The panel concluded that I was not stupid
(thank you) and I was therefore insubordinate.

So they sacked me. It was the first – and the last – time I
have ever been sacked.

*

In January 2016, the *Guardian* published a feature on 'pernicious' workplace bullying in the health service, which included

the results of an online survey carried out by the paper's Healthcare Professionals Network. More than 1,500 doctors, nurses and other health workers in hospital, primary care and community settings took part. The results showed that:

— 81 per cent of those completing the survey had experienced bullying
— Of those, 44 per cent continued to experience bullying
— A third of victims said they had been pushed out of their jobs
— 41 per cent of victims said they needed counselling or treatment after being bullied
— 87 per cent of respondents think bullying is a big problem within the NHS
— Of those, three-quarters said they did not feel the health service took bullying seriously
— 55 per cent of victims said raising a concern prompted the abuse
— Just over a third of victims said they were persecuted through fear or threats, saying their career was deliberately sabotaged
— One in ten bullying victims was subjected to violent behaviour and aggression
— Fear of reprisals was the reason given by 54 per cent of those who had experienced bullying and did not report it
— Of those who did report bullying 44 per cent said it persisted afterwards
— Only 17 per cent of those who reported bullying said they received pastoral support from their organization[1]

1. All statistics taken from *Guardian* article, 'NHS staff lay bare a bullying culture', Sarah Johnson, 26 October 2016.

Fifteen hundred is perhaps quite a small sampling. However, the *Guardian* survey confirms the findings of the 2015 annual NHS staff survey of 300,000 healthcare professionals across England, which found that a quarter of staff in NHS trusts had experienced bullying, harassment or abuse in the previous twelve months.

Some of the personal statements from the *Guardian* survey resonate painfully with my own workplace experiences.

'The culture is driven by exerting undue pressure on others to get things done. If you don't, you are targeted and eventually you end up with stress and depression.'

'You are [then] managed out of your job through contrived actions designed to make you leave. All this leaves you broken and with no strength to fight.'

'Following a reshuffle, our ward manager was replaced by someone who was known for being a bully. She frequently made comments and used language inappropriate for the role.'

'I was constantly ridiculed and told that medical staff had criticized me even though, when questioned, they quite clearly had not.'

'I was having panic attacks and suicidal thoughts.'

'I believed that I had been targeted as I had previously raised concerns about patient care.'

'The bullying was incessant – my line manager would call me in the evening at home telling me to take time off work and encouraging me to see my GP as, in her opinion, I was unwell – I wasn't. She insisted that I had to contact her every morning to tell her where I was, even at work.'

Now that both Doreen and Franc are well behind me and I can look at what happened more objectively, what strikes me most is how similar their methods were. The winning me over, the slow escalation, the isolation, the sheer craziness of what was going on. In addition, the two separate lines of abuse converged and crossed over. As Franc stepped down, Doreen stepped up and when Doreen stepped down, Franc stepped up again. They only met once, yet you'd swear they were working together.

This convergence compounded the low opinion I had of myself, increased the stress and fed the crushing depression. The strain was immense. God knows how I survived.

But as significant as the 'Doreen period' was in my life it was also relatively brief and mostly, I now believe, a consequence of my relationship with Franc. Without his interference I might not have been such an easy target.

One thing in particular stands out in all the morass of accusations Doreen threw at me.

By the time her campaign reached its logical conclusion, she claimed I had been late on no fewer than sixty-six occasions. I have no idea whether that's true or not (I have my doubts) but I was certainly late more often than I should have been. One of the reasons, as I've said before, was Franc. I wouldn't have made the connection at the time. And to be fair to Doreen, I don't expect she would have done either.

It is estimated that domestic violence costs UK businesses in excess of – drum roll – £2.7 billion each year due to decreased productivity, poor performance, absenteeism and employee turnover.

There are other costs, too:

— £1.6 billion for physical and mental health costs
— £1.2 billion in criminal justice costs
— £268 million in social services costs
— £185.7 million in housing and refuge costs

— £366.7 million in civil legal costs

— £1.8 billion in lost economic output

— The human and emotional costs are estimated at £26 million per day[1]

Violent men don't come cheap.

When you consider that when they are not at home most women are at work, it doesn't require a great mental leap to think that employers and colleagues might pick up signs of abuse in their team members. Yet it's only fairly recently that employers have been urged to be aware of this aspect of their duty of care.

The Trades Union Congress's 2014 survey on domestic violence and the workplace reported that 'one of the striking findings from the survey was how rarely those experiencing domestic violence disclosed it to anyone at work.'[2]

There are the inevitable statistics to back that up: 'fewer than one in three (29 per cent) of those experiencing domestic violence discussed the violence with anyone at work . . . The main reason for not disclosing were "shame" and "privacy".' The survey adds, 'The same proportion (29 per cent) of those who did not discuss the violence they were experiencing believed that people were aware of the violence anyway even though they hadn't been told and they never mentioned it.' The report further adds, 'it is surprising and worrying how few people felt that disclosing had led to anything positive happening.'

Had anyone taken the trouble to look closely at what Doreen was accusing me of, perhaps they would have

---

1. Sylvia Walby, *The Cost of Domestic Violence* (Department of Trade and Industry, 2004).

2. *Domestic Violence and the Workplace* (TUC, 2014).

wondered why a woman who had worked for them for eight years with great efficiency, punctuality and motivation seemed to have changed out of all recognition.

The opening statement of that TUC report makes it abundantly clear how domestic violence affects women in employment:

> A Home Office report in 2009 found that 20 per cent of victims of domestic abuse had to take a month or more off work in the previous year due to the abuse. Other research found that 56 per cent of abused women arrive late for work at least five times a month and 53 per cent miss at least three days' work a month. Nearly all respondents (99.4 per cent) said they thought that domestic violence can have an impact on the work lives of employees.

When I read that I thought, that was me.

The survey also tells us that 'domestic violence may prevent employees from getting to work'. The reasons for that are terrifying:

— Nearly three-quarters of respondents who had experienced difficulty in getting to work reported that this was due to physical injury or restraint.
— For over two-thirds of respondents threats caused difficulty in getting to work.
— Over a quarter of those who experienced difficulty in getting to work said this was due to car keys or money for public transport being hidden or stolen by their abuser.
— Refusal or failure to look after children created problems getting to work for over a quarter of those who reported that abuse had prevented them from getting to work.

Another red flag is that 'over one in ten (12.6 per cent) of those who experienced domestic violence reported that the violence continued in the workplace. In 81 per cent of instances this was through harassing and abusive emails or phone calls.'

Remember all Franc's faxes and phone calls?

And, even worse: 'For nearly half . . . the abuse took the form of their partner turning up at their workplace or stalking them outside their workplace.'

And if the way you're treated at home is mirrored in the way you're treated at work, there's no respite.

As part of the preparation for defending myself at the hearing, I had been asked to write down my feelings. This is what I wrote:

ISOLATED. UNDERMINED. DEMORALIZED. LOSING CONFIDENCE AND FAITH IN MY OWN JUDGEMENT. CONFUSED. VERY, VERY UNHAPPY. INSECURE. MISTRUSTFUL. DEPRESSED. TOTAL DISBELIEF.

The irony is, of course, that all those words could equally apply to my relationship with Franc. The difference being that Franc wasn't difficult all the time. Or, rather, Franc wasn't *very* difficult all the time. He fed me just enough affection to keep me hoping. Now, after I'd been sacked, he was back to spend a couple of days with me every fortnight. He even took me to Italy for a few days of sunshine to help me recover. It was lovely.

Chapter Ten

The work nightmare was over but with no financial reserves I had to pick myself up and find another job – fast. I was terrified that the disgrace would stalk me for life. What would I do about references?

I decided the best thing was to sign on with an agency and towards the end of November I got a long-term temping role at the university just up the road. It was only a ten-minute walk from the flat – a good way to ease my way back into things. It cheered me up no end that they welcomed me with open arms. I'd also seen a solicitor about making a case for unfair dismissal. He quoted good odds so I hired him.

It felt as though I was getting a little of my fight back and I remember that it began to colour my conversations with Franc, especially when he talked about his break-up with Sophie. He wouldn't shut up about it and the implication was that he'd made this huge sacrifice for me so the very least I could do was be grateful, and as often as possible. When the phone rang after midnight and he started again, I said something unkind and it ignited a row. Feeling I needed to explain, I wrote him a long letter:

27 November

> *It [the pressure] has been steady and unrelenting. There was no escape from it because away from work and running parallel*

to it was the stress brought about by the situation with you which I did not feel able to discuss with anyone. I kept it to myself. Even my closest friends had no idea what was going on. That's me – I keep things to myself.

'The situation with you . . .' Let's not go there.

> Now it's Monday night. I was all right today – I have to take each day as it comes and today was OK. I was making plans and getting things straight and then you phoned and woke me. Because I was sleepy I said just 3 words that for some reason made you angry . . .

I don't say what those three words were but I did want him to recognize my strength, to understand that I was rebuilding my life. I wanted him to know that I didn't just give up when things got difficult but I kept trying until I got through it.

> Now you've told me that you've given up your marriage and your chance for children for me. If that's what you feel I can never make you happy and you will always hold it against me. You have refused to acknowledge responsibility for your part in the destruction of my life this year and you appear to feel no remorse or sorrow for what you did . . .

He'd never said anything about wanting children before, or getting married. What a thing to say to me now.

I told him 'the only love I need to get me through this is yours', and now, when I needed him, 'you tell me that it is all my doing and it is my fault that you are the way you are'.

> I cannot think what motivates you. It surely can't be love, to be so cruel and heartless when faced with such pain . . .
>
> It is beyond comprehension the way you speak to me on the

phone, and don't say it is because of the way I have behaved
towards you – remember, you got in first in the bad behaviour
stakes in March . . .

I hadn't been able to forgive or forget the morning he'd
told me he was still in love with Sophie.

Don't tell me that I have destroyed what we had because I
didn't take the first step down that road – you did.

*

Hurrah for this woman who has – finally – begun to demand
that Franc take some responsibility. Of course she was angry.

On 30 November, one after another, three emails dropped
into my inbox. The first a two-page furious reply to my letter,
the second and third expanding on his theme:

> 14:22
> *The only things you say are:*
>> *I am responsible for the destruction of your life*
>> *I am not sorry for what I did*
>> *I have no remorse*
>> *I am cruel*
>> *Good.*
>> *I came back to you giving up everything for you and what*
> *do I get?*

I had told him I loved him and yet I kept 'doing this'. He
wanted to trust me but I kept being 'unreliable'. My new job
was next in the firing line. He told me I could do 'hundreds
of jobs' and yet I was working as a secretarial temp. That, he
said, was not acceptable. It wasn't good enough.

He could not understand why I did the opposite of what I
should do to keep him and yet I 'did it right' for my husband.

I see you do not like money unless is someone else's.

And finally:

Do not lie to me.

14:29
I know now you were 16 when you started to fuck him, getting pregnant every other year . . .
It is even clear how much you are thinking about all that.
Stop lying. Stop telling me lies . . .

I had accused him of being horrible to me. He gave me love and yet I pushed him away, so far away he could barely see me.

I do not call this love. I left everything for you and look what you are giving me back . . .

He told me that when he came back in August, as soon as he saw me, he had known what he felt was love, 'big big love'.

I know I always fancied you and make love to you (some kilos too much now but . . .)

14:37
. . . You keep referring to the hurt I gave you 8 months ago.
If you cannot forget that for now is fine by me but tell me this so I know where you stay. Tell me that you have to be rude, unkind and all the rest. If this is not the case then behave accordingly and let the old Ellen to be back.

That night I sent a carefully worded reply:

Dearest Franc
I suppose what I write about is me but so much of what

you feel is a closed book to me and I really do try to understand you. So much of what you say is oblique. What I can't understand is how you cannot seem to grasp the devastation you caused in my life this year. Why do I still have to do penance for this? Why should I still suffer for this? Why should I suffer at all? All I've done, and do, is love you – even when you don't want me to and even when you turn that love away.

I knew as soon as I saw you again in August that those feelings were still true and strong and that the love was still there for you. I waited for you, loyally and faithfully. When you came back it felt so strange to have you in my arms again . . . I realized I'd got used to being alone and doing things alone and I would have to change that.

I feel very vulnerable . . .

I want the fairy tale now with its happy ending . . .

I still couldn't bring myself to confront the fact that he was an arrogant, manipulative, angry man. I still believed I loved him.

My stomach turns over when I read these letters now. I had forgotten how nasty he could be and remembering that I marvel that I kept trying.

I hadn't known what to give him that Christmas, our second together, so I had some good pictures taken and put them in an album for him, one of those small ones you can take around with you. He laughed when he saw them. I found it left behind in the flat when I came back from walking with him to the station. That hurt.

His letter on 5 January enclosed his present to me – a diary:

Darling Helen

Here it is your 'agenda' (from Latin = things to do).

He said he was recovering from ten days with me now that his mum was cooking for him again, and he was going skiing.

Miss you and hope to see you soon.
   Love
   Franc

Formal, but it contained the magic word 'love' and he sounded happy.

I had a new exercise programme so on Saturday I was back in the gym.

7 January

Thigh 22"
Hips 38"
Waist 28"
Bust 36"
65 kilos

Shit. I was putting weight on when I was supposed to be taking it off.

Franc responded to this crisis with ever more complex instructions. I tried to eat the things he said I should and I measured and weighed myself constantly but my progress wasn't fast enough.

An authoritarian fitness regime was one way of controlling me. Another was money. Except that I still stubbornly resisted his interference and it exasperated him.

As a gesture towards a New Year's resolution I emailed Franc a reply to yet another money question he'd asked on the phone the night before. To encourage me he'd listed what he thought I was earning and spending. It was detailed, thorough and entirely wrong. I took the bait and emailed him back:

9 January 12:23:51

Darling Franc

> *I appreciate you doing my sums for me but:*
> *£680 minus £360 rent = 320*
> *minus £50 council tax = 270*
> *minus £30 electricity = 240*
> *minus £50 hair = 190 (but every 5 to 6 weeks)*
> *minus £42 gym = 148*
> *Water rates were £30 for this year so not too bad.*

> *Telephone is cut down to bare minimum and so is everything else. Christmas came mostly on the credit card and I suppose I shall have to use some of my savings for the next bill.*

> *So you see, things are not quite as bad as you think but then they are not too good either. I'm surviving but I have barely enough money . . . I don't need any emergencies. Thank goodness I DO have some savings . . .*

> *Yes, I worry about it too but I can't spend all my life worrying because I'll make myself ill and miserable so I'm just trying to do something about it . . .*

> *I don't know if you feel any better re the above. Have I helped? It's hard being without money and without my Franc too.*

> *Hugs and kisses*
> *H*
> *xxx*

I sounded glib and pleased with myself. Why, why, WHY, did I do that? I'd spent two years with Franc – I should have known what I was starting.

Over the course of the next two days, eleven emails hurtled into and out of my inbox – on the 9th at 14:13, 14:43, 16:23, 17:18 and 17:59, and on the 10th at 11:35, 14:03 and 14:09.

He *did* know I'd started a new job, didn't he? That I couldn't answer straight away?

When he was like this he left me no space to think about anything else but him. I blamed myself, of course, although I could never quite see what I'd done. I had answered his questions, and instead of being pleased he was angry . . .

Rent is at 370 (increased).
>*What do you mean 'Xmas came on credit card . . .'?*
>*If you use your credit card you spend money.*
>*Cut the credit card in two and use only cash.*
>*You want to upset me.*
>*You are playing with words and figures.*
>*I put down figures and expenses, xmas, holiday – no*
answer.

A list of instructions for managing my budget followed in the next email:

I am getting very upset.
>*1. You keep notes of everything you spend*
>*2. You reduce your expenses*
>*3. You increase your earnings*
>*4. You do not use your savings*
>*It looks like you don't understand me.*

He thought about it for a bit and then sent more commands:

>*Telephone reduced to minimum: how much is it? Have you*
>*planned how much you can afford in telephone every month?*
>*No! Then do it and stay with it.*
>*If you cannot meet ends [sic] this month find a job for a*
>*couple of weekends.*

> *You have got a computer – put the figures down to the penny.*
>
> *Have you received the job [information] I sent to you?*
>
> *You do not have to worry about money all your life as long as you get it right and you are not doing it.*
>
> *I repeat: if you are not bothered I shall not be bothered.*
>
> *You tell me.*

When I read all these rage-stuffed pages it was so unexpected I felt my cheeks go hot and red, as though I'd been slapped. *Love, Franc* at the end wasn't enough this time.

He badgered me for a reply for the rest of the day, until I was forced into it.

I tried first to soothe him, then to atone, for what I'm not really sure. For making him angry?

He called me that night and we spoke for about two hours. I sat cross-legged on the floor and chain-smoked (quietly, so he wouldn't hear). When he was in France the only way he could hurt me was with words. I just had to let it wash over me. I didn't dare hang up. At the very end he said he wanted us to go on holiday together. Stunned, I said I wanted that too but I didn't think I'd be able to afford it – not on a temp's wages.

He hit the roof. His next email began 'Darling Helen' but then screamed at me from the page.

> PROBLEMS ARE RELATED TO YOU BECAUSE I CAN
> LIVE WITH MY SALARY, I CAN HAVE MY HOLIDAYS.
> BUT I DO NOT FUCKING KNOW HOW MUCH I
> SHALL USE TO SUPPORT YOU OR TO PAY RENT IN
> FRANCE OR WHATEVER . . .

He was frustrated with me because I didn't tell him what

he said he needed to know. I didn't understand because I thought I had, on 9 January when I wrote to him explaining my budget.

> *SO DO YOU UNDERSTAND THAT ALL IS RELATED TO YOU AND TO THE FACT THAT I DO NOT KNOW WHAT IS THE FUCKING SITUATION.*
> *NOW ARE YOU GOING TO COLLABORATE OR WHAT???????*
> *Love*
> *Franc*

This is exactly how these arguments went – great blazing rows that ran over two, three, four days and sometimes longer.

In the middle of yet another ranting email, he played a new card, one he hadn't used before, and won the game:

15 January, 10:28

Hello
> *Perhaps it is difficult to understand (but I thought it was not) if I ask information about your financial situation to plan things to be together I do expect you to do it immediately. But not because it is an order but because you love me and knowing I am doing this should make you happy and therefore you would do anything. If you do not do it I start to think that . . .*

He had another complaint: if he phoned me and I was in town he expected me to 'run towards a [quiet] space' to talk to him, not because it was him on the phone but because I loved him and would do anything for him.

He said he wasn't upset because I didn't do the things he asked me to do but he was 'disappointed' because he thought

I loved him. He hoped that 'explained the difference'. And then:

> *I did not want to tell you this but I am not feeling very well.*

His blood pressure was always high, 'like yourself', he said. His head hurt constantly and he woke in the night sweating, with his heart pumping, convinced he was about to have a heart attack. He was 'upset and unhappy' at work.

> *So, when I look for some love from you and I do not get it I start being nasty.*
> *Love*
> *Franc*

He was ill. I had made him ill because I hadn't done what he wanted. Immediately, I capitulated and sent him a list of everything I spent on myself, right down to tampons and vitamin tablets. I told him what was in my bank account, my savings account and on my credit card. But I did not give him control of any of it. I hung on to that.

Put it down to experience.

My reward for compliance was a punishing new exercise regime. There were long pages of detailed instructions. I printed them off, put them into a plastic wallet and headed for the gym.

18 January, 12:28

New workout
> *It is important to do them <u>perfectly</u>.*
> *It is a 4 week programme and it is quite hard so your food intake and your rest is very important.*

He listed my meals – all six, together with the times I should eat them – and the ratio of proteins to carbohydrates was meticulously itemized. Each day was listed separately as Day 1, Day 2, Day 3, Day 4 and Day 5 and concentrated on a different muscle group. Each set of exercises for each day was divided into sets of repetitions. For example:

3 × 10–12 dumbell press inclined bench (max 30 degrees)
*   pyramidal*
3 × 10–12 bench press pyramidal
4 × 10–12 pec deck same weight

I could rest between repetitions for no more than ninety seconds and each action had to be timed to two or three seconds.

He told me how to check my heart rate as I exercised and what it should be:

45 minutes at 75% max heartbeat (220 − age = max = for
*   you = 175; 70% = 122 80% = 140 so you have to stay at*
*   around 130)*
You can bike, treadmill and step 15 [minutes] each or one at a
*   time*

By the time I was at Day 3 the numbers of repetitions were steadily increasing but after Day 5 I could take a rest day.

At the end was one final instruction: *Enjoy it.*

This, for the avoidance of doubt (as Franc would say) is what coercive control and body shaming look like.

One consequence of following this regime was that it took me at least two hours on each visit to the gym and the strict diet left me no time (or inclination) for a social life. After all, Franc would call every evening to make sure I was at home and cooking the right food at the right time. I had to answer by four rings.

When he came back a week later, it was primarily to check

that I was doing what he'd told me to. We spent a *lot* of time in the gym. Was this what my life had been like when we had lived together full time, before he went back to Paris? I couldn't remember – it felt worse. When he was here he seemed to fill the flat, seeping into every corner and choking out the air.

One night, when it all got too much, I sneaked out while he was watching television, sprinted round the corner to get out of sight and walked around the city in the dark. I wasn't running away, I was trying to shake off the feeling of claustrophobia. I didn't take my phone. When I came back, the instant my key was in the door, he was there and ready for me. A handful of hair, the same backwards scramble down the hall, the same trajectory from the door onto the bed, the same slamming wallop to the back of my head.

The next day – a Saturday – I did it again. This time it was two in the morning and once more we'd been arguing about my money. I walked briskly (plugged into my Walkman) across the river, planning to circle the city centre in a big loop. On a tree-lined avenue a flasher appeared out of the bushes. He startled me but I laughed because it was such a cliché. The filthy suggestion he made wasn't funny, though, so I punched him in the face and ran away. All that time in the gym had some benefits.

I had nowhere else to go so I had to go back to the flat. I didn't believe Franc would do what he had done again. But he did. I should have asked myself why I preferred to risk being attacked walking around the city centre on my own in the wee small hours than stay in the home I shared with my French lover.

By the end of February I weighed less than 50 kilos.

*

In May 2016 Mohammed Anwaar was jailed for twenty-eight months at Sheffield Crown Court, for crimes against his girlfriend, Gemma Doherty, including controlling and coercive behaviour.[1]

In a victim statement, read out in court, Gemma said, 'The relationship had started out perfect but everything changed in May 2015 . . . I knew how quickly his mood could change over the smallest thing . . . His favourite model was Graceyanne Barbosa and he would make me look at her fitness routines and practise them. If I didn't he would beat me . . . I was wasting away when I was forced to lose all these calories every day. I felt like a zombie on autopilot and was at his beck and call – whatever and whenever.'

Anwaar forced her to eat only tins of tuna (a shocking fifty a week) and run on a treadmill to burn 500 calories each day. He also told her who she could see and what she was allowed to wear, and he was in charge of her mobile phone.

The report also tells how this controlling behaviour was punctuated with violent attacks and that 'after an argument over money he first smashed her mobile phone before attacking her with slaps and kicks, choking her and causing her to fall unconscious'.

Gemma Doherty was also mother to a young son. That she took an overdose when the abuse became unbearable shows the level of her desperation. Anwaar hit her for trying to take her own life.

In a television interview Gemma explained that when she first met him Anwaar was 'the nicest person' and she thought

---

1. James Dunn, *Mail* Online, 'He wanted me to have abs and a huge a**e like Kim Kardashian', 19 May 2016.

his attentiveness showed how much he cared. It was months before he hit her for the first time and she said it was so out of character and he apologized so much, that although she knew it was wrong she was able to forgive him. She loved and feared him at the same time.

Eventually, she was able to escape his supervision for long enough to report him to the police and he was arrested and charged.

Superintendent Natalie Shaw said:

'This is the first successful conviction we have had under the new legislation regarding coercive control, and I am pleased that Anwaar is now behind bars for his actions.

'Domestic abuse is wide ranging and isn't always clear to see upon first examination. Just because physical signs of abuse might not be present, it doesn't mean that someone isn't a victim of domestic abuse, and coercive control is extremely damaging to a person.'

*

There is an Excel spreadsheet in my folder of emails and letters. Franc said it showed his own expenses, although no item is dated. Perhaps it was his projected expenses for the coming year. It could be *War and Peace* for all I know. It means nothing. Perhaps he thought I was too stupid to read it properly and I wouldn't see that it lacks some crucial information. He added a note that all he wanted was some enthusiasm but instead I told him that my finances were my business, not his. 'Do you call this love?' he asked. 'Think about your behaviour.'

And then he was off again. Every day brought a fresh cascade of emails, phone calls and texts – twenty-nine emails in five days. Pages and pages of them, full of the usual stuff:

You have not answered my questions and sentences. They were important for me and your answers even more important. Never mind.

Let me understand, Helen: you do not have money, you are not going to tell me anything about your financial situation . . .

I have asked you some questions and you do not answer. OK. I wanted to discuss with you what would be the financial situation and you do not want to do it. I still expect you should have just given me anything you had. Just like that. And you are still holding your position on this issue.

I have to accept your way of loving me, you cannot accept my way.

I wrote back:

Franc, you are my beautiful man.

But I also wrote:

Something has to change, Franc – I really cannot go on like this.

He changed tack and started asking about the solicitor acting for me in the case against the hospital. I had only ever been alone with this man in his office but Franc was convinced I was having an affair with him, as shown in his email:

7 February, 12:58

How many phone calls (lovely ones) have you agreed in writing, fees etc? We'll see when it is finished (the professional bit I mean).
By the way, how old is he? Handsome? Gentle and kind?

*Has he already stroked your hair or held your hand? Do not tell
me he is another toy-boy!*

*I will book the holiday anyway, and as I clearly wrote I will
pay for it.*

I was angry and emailed straight back. I told him not to
book the holiday. I wasn't going anywhere with him while he
was behaving like this.

Within half an hour, my phone rang. Franc. I was at work
and told him I couldn't speak to him. That night, there was
another long, ranting email.

*We had already a couple of fights when I phone and you are
with someone else. What do you do when I phone? You treat
me as if it was a call from your bank, a telesales or whatever.*
*YOU PRETEND YOU LOVE ME BUT YOU CANNOT
BE LOVELY ON THE PHONE WITH ME. WHAT A
LOVE . . .*

I changed the subject and told him I was trying to write a
short story. Show me, he said. I suppose he wanted to see
proof that I was spending my spare time in the way I said I
was. Still, I was proud of what I'd written and I sent it to him.
His response?

*You have not told me who is the man you are talking [sic]
in your book. The one you liked so much to hold you and have
his warm body against yours.*

It was about *him*. I had been very clear about that. I
thought he'd be pleased. I wrote back:

*If you mean the story I am writing that you read. That is
about you and only you. The man I am talking about is you.*
The holiday would be wonderful – to spend time with you

in the mountains. Just not now, not the way we are at the
moment. Time is too precious and rare with you to spend it
arguing.

I thought it had done the trick, because he calmed down. But then he found out how much I'd spent on my new phone. I wasn't going to tell him but he'd seen the phone and then it was easier to tell him than not. It was pointless to add that when I'd bought it I hadn't expected to lose my job.

16 February, 09:57

I have asked you many many times to speak with your bank
manager etc etc etc and what do you do? You dash £230 on a
fucking mobile phone . . . I spend every single fibre of myself
trying to help you in terms of organizing your finances . . .
   Who cares if we are in this situation because you do not
have money. You have to spend £230 for a mobile. I say it
again: two hundred and thirty pound plus phone calls.
   And now I understand other things.

One thing he said he understood was that all the 'problems' about not showing him my bank statements and accounts were because I had 'things' I didn't want him to know about.

   You spend a fortune for a mobile and all this behind my
back, telling me lies.
   I could smash all the windows in my office.
   You lied to me.

Get a second job, he said, put your loose change in a jar and save money 'for us'. Why, instead of doing that, had I spent '£230 or more on a bloody fucking fancy phone?' His demons were 'painful enough', he said, without my 'betrayals'.

I have not been hard and bad in this letter for two reasons:

   1. I love you and I care for you more than anything in the world.

   2. I know you are not 'bad' and do not do things like this on purpose.

Yes, Franc.

Then, to my relief, the emails stopped, although we still spoke on the phone – my 'bloody fucking fancy phone' – and a week later Franc sent me details of flights for the holiday I had told him not to book.

On St Patrick's Day, I flew out of Stansted to spend a week in the Alps with Franc. I'm astonished that I went at all. But that's how abusers operate. They make you do what they want you to do.

And, actually, it was fine. It so often was – as long as I 'behaved'.

He met me at the airport and we drove up into the mountains towards the snow. It was bitterly cold, but beautiful.

The only time we almost had a row was when we joined a group for a midnight walk along a mountain trail. I made Franc laugh because I was so stupidly excited about wearing snowshoes but we had to take them off to get down a steep slope to the cabin where supper was waiting. I watched the woman in front of me slip and fall and decided the safest thing was to sit and slide down on my bum. Franc was angry. It was 'undignified'. Perhaps he would have preferred me to go arse over tit. He was even crosser when the mountain guide held out his hand to help me up onto my feet again.

Working, I expect, on the same principle he had applied to me playing golf – that I might turn out to be better than him – Franc refused to let me ski. Consequently, I found myself hanging around a lot either watching Franc to offer praise and encouragement or drinking hot chocolate and smoking cigarettes (both forbidden) while I waited for him to come back. I didn't tell him I'd been skiing once before and was actually rubbish because that would have opened up a whole other can of worms about who I'd gone with and all the rest.

There's a story I read recently about Donald Trump. Once, on a winter holiday in Colorado, Ivana – his first wife and an Olympic-standard skier – whipped past him on the slope. He promptly took his skis off and stomped back up the piste.[1] He couldn't stand anyone being better at anything than him, not even his wife. A spoiled toddler who didn't want to play anymore.

That story really reminds me of Franc.

At the end of the holiday we parted company at the airport. Franc went his way and I went mine.

Three weeks later he was back in the flat for the weekend. He said he had missed me.

---

1. Marcy Kreiter, *International Business Times*, 'Donald Trump a Cry-Baby?', 26 October 2016.

Chapter Eleven

Where do you start when you decide to change your life? Anywhere. You start anywhere. But you need the will to do it.

At the beginning of April, Numbers 2 and 3 Daughters visited me in the flat for Sunday lunch and between us we decided that Number 3 Daughter would move in with me, which would mean help with the bills and rent. By then my youngest was eighteen, pierced and tattooed, with shocking pink hair – I couldn't wait to spend more time with her. I was so proud of all my girls. They had grown into spirited, smart, mouthy and motivated young women. I had a hand in that.

Franc wasn't overjoyed – of course he wasn't – but what could he say, apart from:

I'm glad your children love you and are proud of you, as they should be, but please try not to speak too much, with me, about them because . . . you know . . . 'reminder of a fuck' they say.

On the other hand, I'd done as he'd suggested and found someone to share the bills. Franc arrived on Friday the 13th, prophetically, to spend part of the Easter holiday with me before my new flatmate moved in.

Things started off all right but deteriorated the next day, as they generally did. There was a kind of weary inevitability to it all.

I remember shouting. (I wonder why nobody in the flats around us ever complained about the yelling, let alone the occasional screams and crashes, or came to see if either of us was still alive.) Unusually, it was Franc who stormed out, right out of the flat. Like me, he'd have to come back when he calmed down.

Unlike him, I wasn't waiting by the door to beat him up when he did. I was sitting on the floor in my pyjamas, reading. I looked up and smiled. Perhaps I shouldn't have. I don't know why I did – reflex, I think. Oh, look, here's Franc, smile for Franc. He wrenched the big black bookcase from the wall. It missed me by inches. Then he went into the bedroom. Creeping into the hall I peered through a gap in the door. I could see his feet twitching on the carpet, one shoe off. He'd thrown himself face down onto the floor, in the narrow gap beside the bed, and was sobbing convulsively. It's quite something to see a big man, all six feet plus of him, lying on the floor crying like a child. But he'd done it before so this time I just sat beside him and held his hand until he stopped.

He had to help me lift the bookcase because it was too heavy to manage on my own. The books were fine, a bit bumped and battered – oddly that improves books – but a bowl of white porcelain roses, a teacup from my grandmother's house, a pretty jade-green vase . . .

'Oh, Franc . . .'

They were all smashed to pieces. Beyond repair.

'You did this, Ellen. You did this.' And he held me while this time I sobbed.

Franc left early the next morning, Easter Sunday, before I got up. For the first time he didn't insist I went with him to the station.

I was tired, bruised and sore when I went into the kitchen to make coffee. I lit a cigarette and opened the kitchen window.

Something caught my eye. On the sill was a packet of butter, open at one end, smudged and smeared where a hand had held it. That's funny, I thought. Butter was kept in the fridge. I looked at it for a minute, confused. There was something I didn't want to remember . . . the night before and Franc leaving me on the sofa for a couple of minutes . . . coming back with something . . . I hadn't been able to do what he wanted . . . I was frightened of it hurting . . . a memory of the summer of 1976 when that pig spiked my drink . . . and Franc, considerate enough to grease me up first. I was violently sick in the sink. When the retching subsided I didn't hate myself, I hated Franc. It didn't last long but it was a start. Of all the things he could have done to me he had to do that. The word I hadn't been able to say in twenty-five years. The *Last Tango in Paris* word.

If this had been the Franc I first met we wouldn't have lasted a fortnight. Instead he convinced me that he was the right man for me, at a time when that was what I wanted more than anything. How lucky that he should be that man at precisely that moment. He had led me right up to the door of my cage but he needed me to walk into it of my own accord. And because I did, I could only remain there and perhaps dream small dreams of flight.

'You'll stand it,' David Blakely said to Ruth Ellis, 'because you love me.' That's how well they know their game.

So, for me, for the time being things stayed as they were, more or less. On Easter Monday, Number 3 Daughter moved in and we got on with what I increasingly recognized was a normal life. Having her with me was grounding, supportive and fun. I saw my middle daughter too, much more than I had. And I laughed a lot. At the end of May I bought a washing

machine – no more hours spent in the launderette. And I we
to work.

I had managed to get myself a permanent job. It was only
as a receptionist but the pay wasn't bad and at least there
would be a bit of security with it. It was a foot on the bottom
rung (again) of the employment ladder. I was terribly bored,
but I had expected that. There was nothing for me to do apart
from answering phones and typing a few letters. I built an
enormous elastic-band ball. Day after day it was the same
and it made my brain itch with lack of exercise. To counter
the frustration I went to the gym four, five, six times a week
and followed Franc's diet plan to the last full stop. My diary
for 31 May reads:

> Thigh 19"
> Waist 24"
> Hips 35"

There are no emails from Franc in my folder for May or
June. He didn't come to see me either. No need to ask why,
not when I was sharing with the 'reminder of another man's
fuck'. We spoke a lot on the phone, though, and that's how
he kept his hold on me. So, don't answer the phone? It's no
use saying that to a woman in my situation. You haven't
understood a thing if you think I was capable of doing that.
My mind remained obstinately opposed to the concept of free
will. All Franc had to do was click his fingers, tell me he loved
me or raise his voice.

He knew I'd do whatever he asked, which is why on 9 June
I flew out to spend a weekend by the sea with him. A bit jit-
tery, but sure in the knowledge that he had never hurt me
when we were on holiday together.

That first evening we met some of Franc's friends at a beachside restaurant – none had brought girlfriends. It was a bit intimidating, sitting with all these men, but it was the first time I'd met any of his friends apart from Dave so it felt like a kind of recognition of my status in his life. No one spoke English except to say hello. To begin with I only caught snippets of the conversation but as is often the way I understood far more French than I would have been able to speak and by the time a huge platter of buttery langoustines arrived I was following most of what was being said. I didn't let on, though. I remember that evening for three things: eating langoustines with my fingers; feeling deeply happy and content; and picking up a phrase that stuck, 'I can see you've been dressing her'. 'Her', as though I wasn't there.

We spent Sunday on the beach, just the two of us. Then on Monday Franc had to work. I had a whole day to myself so I sat in the sun, read my book, and listened to music. I waited for Franc to come back. Half my life was spent waiting for Franc to come back but this time I didn't really want him to. I was feeling a bit strange. After nearly two months of 'normal' I was finding it hard to slot back into Franc's way of doing things. It felt restrictive. I couldn't understand because regardless of what he'd done I'd looked forward to seeing him again.

We walked around the town after dinner and then we went back to our hotel room.

I'm not quite sure what happened next, how it started, but something provoked him. It was me, I expect. I probably had a little Pavlovian cry about going home the next day. Franc hated me crying. The more he told me to stop, the more it made me cry. He shouted at me and I slightly lost control. I began to sob – proper snotty sobs that made me gasp and shake.

The next thing I was on my back on the bed and Franc was choking me. I wriggled and tried to get my knees between us to push him away. His left hand let go but he kept hold with his right. Then a pillow came down over my face and I couldn't breathe at all. This time I honestly believed he might really kill me. I bucked and twisted and got free. Somehow we ended up kneeling left side to left side, and my right arm was free so I swung as hard as I could into his back and winded him. He certainly hadn't expected it. I didn't want to hit him – I didn't enjoy seeing him doubled up and wheezing – and I was horrified. I thought I'd seriously hurt him. In that moment of hesitation he caught hold of me again.

I pulled away and tried to get to the bathroom and lock the door but he punched my shoulder, shoving me forwards into the wall. It was tiled in shades of blue, those tiny tiles about half an inch square, like a mosaic. I saw it a few times as my head slammed against it. And then I went limp. It had worked before. I remember briefly wondering if that was why he wanted me to lose so much weight, because I'd be easier to pick up and throw around. And then it was morning.

I felt sick and dizzy, my eyes were bloodshot, my neck hurt and I could barely speak, not that I wanted to. There was an enormous lump on my head under my hair and I had the mother of all headaches. Franc took me to the airport, kissed me on the cheek, waved goodbye as though everything was normal. I was completely dazed – on autopilot.

Two days later the lump was still there and so was the headache so I went to A&E to get it checked out. I said I'd slipped in the shower, which seemed an obvious lie. There was no permanent damage, just mild concussion and extensive bruising in the shape of those pretty mosaic tiles.

I realized then that sooner or later he would make himself angry enough to kill me.

*

I would never have a job I loved as much as the one I'd lost. Or so I'd thought after I was sacked. But I'd been able to get a job when I thought I couldn't so I asked myself, why not? It was the obvious place to start. Casting about the agencies and Sits Vac in this Midlands city was pointless. There was nothing. If I did find anything I liked the look of and bothered to ask why I was being turned down for an interview, more often than not I was told, 'You're over-qualified.' As time went on I reinterpreted this as, 'You're too old.' So I started looking further afield. I could, in theory, go anywhere. That was a good thought. What had I got to lose?

Once I'd decided that, things started to happen. I had three interviews arranged – London liked me! On 26 June, for the first time ever, I went on my own with a first-class ticket to be kind to myself. I arrived at St Pancras – the old St Pancras before it got gentrified for Eurostar – choked with dust, dirt, fumes and people. I was so sick with nerves my legs shook and there was a real possibility I might fall down the steps to the Underground. Gripping the handrail and my *A to Z*, I headed off for agencies in Mayfair, Knightsbridge and the City. I needed a minimum salary of £30,000 to cover my basic London living expenses and I asked for it. It was the upper end of average for a PA in London but I wasn't squeamish about discussing money now. Having nothing to lose makes you bold. I bought myself a glass of champagne on the train back to celebrate crossing my Rubicon. Then I went home and waited.

While I did that I asked myself how serious I was about

moving, now it looked as though I might actually make it happen. Two weeks later I was offered a job with the money I had asked for – in fact, *more* money. It made me confident and glad. All those months feeling miserable, kicking my heels in a town where no one gave a toss about my years of experience, and all I had to do was go somewhere else and ask.

My daughters' response, when I asked them what they thought about me moving to London to work, was unanimous: 'It's your turn now, Mum. And, y'know . . . shopping.' Stuff like that makes your heart sing.

After the last time I'd seen Franc, after what he did, I didn't phone or email. I left him to stew. He phoned me eventually, at the beginning of July, which prompted an email from me. I didn't begin with *Dearest Franc*. The capitals are his:

6 July, 12:36

I'm feeling a little better – thank you for asking . . .
     I go to the gym for me – because I'm proud of the shape I'm in and I want to stay that way.
     GOOD.
     I have more than one job opportunity in London and I'm working on it. The whole point is that I want to be out of [this town], I'm sick of it. I want a career.
     GET THE JOB YOU LIKE. AND GO TO LONDON. THEN WE'LL SEE.
     I wasn't aware you wanted a budget from me all the time. I do check my finances but it is difficult, as I keep telling you. Perhaps it's more expensive to be a woman than a man but it is hard to make ends meet, although I usually do – just.
     I ASKED YOU FOR YOUR BUDGET FOR YOUR HELP. STILL YOU SAY YOU DID NOT THINK I ASKED . . . THE

*BUDGET IS FOR YOU TO MONITOR YOUR EXPENSES
NOT FOR ME TO CHECK.*

  *I'm finding it harder to relate to you at the moment because
you don't tell me anything. I don't feel safe or secure in our
'relationship'. I am a reliable person, whatever you might
think. Perhaps your instructions are not always as clear as they
might be.*

I added a paragraph at the end:

  *As for the bit about Benoit, I can do that if you send me
some dates and is he coming alone or with someone, i.e. how
many for? Edinburgh could be difficult because of the festival
but I would do my best.*

He had asked me to arrange a trip to Scotland in August
for one of his friends and I just couldn't make myself say a
simple no.

I'd had room to think and to breathe. I was making things
happen I hadn't thought possible. I was better than anyone
said I was. And yet, somehow – and I'm well aware of how
stupid, and paradoxical, this seems – I still believed I had to
prove that to him, make him see I was worth something,
make him want me. I don't *think* I still believed I loved him.
I'm sure I didn't believe he really meant for us to be together,
or that I would be going to live with him in Paris. I no longer
believed in us. That was the difference.

  6 July, 14:20

Dear Helen

  *Everything I have done is wrong and I am doing nothing at
the moment.*

  *Everything you have done is perfect and the things you do
now are all perfect, all for me, etc.*

I have caused all this because . . . let me think, last time I
spoke to you on the phone I asked you to do something.

Never, he said, had he ever done anything to wrong me, he
just didn't give me what I wanted and I didn't like that. I didn't
understand him, he said (again), and I hurt him. He told me
to think about what I was 'doing and saying'.

Franc was playing his usual games. And what he said was
baffling, given our history. He was making himself the victim.
He still signed off with love though, and it had been six
months since he'd done that. Occasionally an email would
arrive which told me simply that he had called because he was
worried about me and that he loved me.

How are you? Please let me know.
    Love
    Franc

I might not have believed in us, but I still thirsted for love,
so the little love-light flickered on.

The next time he called he told me he had decided to join
his friend for the motorbike tour of Scotland and that Benoit's
fiancée, Marianne, would be coming too 'so that makes four
of us'. He gave me the dates and a list of things I would need
for the trip. 'You have got all the information you need, if you
want to do it of course.' Did I say I was going? I don't remember doing that. This was a typical Franc manoeuvre. I had
somehow allowed myself to be manipulated into being a tour
guide.

I didn't particularly want to – I was so busy with plans for
my new start – but I did as he asked. That he was coming with
friends meant if I refused I'd be letting them down too. He
knew I couldn't do that, that I would go along with it, that the

good opinion of these people I had never met was too important to me to refuse.

The day before they arrived, I went to London for another
interview. I had accepted one job offer but I wanted to keep
my options open and this one interested me enough to make
it worth investigating.

On 7 August, the French contingent pitched up and parked
their bikes outside the flat. I made dinner for everyone, the
first time I'd ever done anything for and with Franc's friends
on my own turf. Cooking food for friends was something I
used to love to do. This time it made me anxious, nervous that
Franc would criticize me in front of them, but he was fine –
on his best behaviour.

The next day we travelled, in one go, up to Glasgow. The
pillion on Franc's motorbike positioned me higher up than
him, which meant a ferocious buffeting from the wind. By the
time we reached Speyside I had a massive headache and was
very, *very* stiff. I love motorbikes but it was a really long haul
to be wedged between two panniers. And as Franc continually
pointed out I wasn't getting any younger.

The following morning, walking up Sauchiehall Street, my
phone rang. 'Sorry, I have to take this,' I said, and Franc threw
me a beady look. It was the agency with another job offer, so
now I had two (so much for being useless and past it). I had
told Franc a bit more about what I was up to but I gave him
a version that was a week or so behind actual events. I told
him the call was about an interview, which was half true.

'What will you do if someone offers you a job?' he sneered.

'Take it, of course!'

I didn't tell him I already had.

I wonder if Benoit and Marianne picked up any of the
tension or if they thought this was just Franc being Franc.

(Afterwards I could never understand why 'Franc being Franc' was considered a valid excuse by everyone I ever met who knew him.) I gambled that with his friends there he wouldn't do anything; and it turned out that I knew him better than I thought. Benoit and Marianne were indeed a security blanket. They shifted his focus away from me, diluted the scrutiny.

From Glasgow we travelled across to Stirling, then on to Inverness. We ran into bad weather as we went through the Cairngorms National Park. Franc produced bright orange waterproofs for me when rain began to come down in stair rods. They were old and left little orange specks all over the seat and panniers. This was my fault (apparently) because I wasn't lifting my leg high enough when I climbed onto the pillion, and was fidgeting while there. I was tired of this. Never mind that I was stiff and cold and soaked and walked like John Wayne for about two hours after we arrived in Pitlochry. I cheered up a bit when we visited a whisky distillery. Marianne didn't like her whisky taster so I had that too, while Franc wasn't looking. The next day we went on to St Andrews and from there to Edinburgh where we left Benoit and Marianne to spend a few days on their own.

On the way home, somewhere dark, late at night, I realized we'd gone round the same roundabout three times. Franc pulled over and admitted he was lost.

'I just want to go home,' he said.

'I know you do, darling.'

It seemed like an admission. There were a lot more than six words in that sentence.

On the day that Franc and the others went back to France, I got a call from my solicitor. There had been an offer to settle my claim for unfair dismissal out of court. It wasn't much but it was never really about that. The tacit admission that they had got it wrong was far more important. Doreen was wrong, so was Dr Bray. They were *all* wrong. I felt vindicated. Ecstatic.

Before he left I had asked Franc for his key to the flat. As I said, quite truthfully, Number 3 Daughter and I were managing with just mine – and then I told him about London, although not in any detail. I did both those things when Benoit and Marianne were there. He couldn't go off on one because there were witnesses. Grudgingly, he handed over the key and I let go a mental sigh of relief.

He seemed more sad than angry when he left. I still felt a familiar tug under my ribs as their bikes nosed out into the city traffic. I feel it now. It was when he was like that – thoughtful, quiet and a little sad – that I wanted him most. I needed him when he needed me but not when he was yelling his need at me down the phone or typing it into his emails in angry capitals. I needed him when he was serious and gentle and kind. But so often – so very often – he was anything but.

I don't know what he thought would happen to us once I was in London, but I cared more about how I was going to build a new life. The concrete plans that I'd made (for once) were more meaningful than any tentative, vague promises from Franc about what might or might not happen. I had finally acknowledged that I couldn't trust him with my future. Somewhere inside me I must have known that this was a kind of ending.

On August bank holiday Monday I packed up my things and Number 3 Daughter drove me to London and a new life. The first night in my tiny room in Stratford felt weird and unfamiliar. It gave me flashbacks to the early days post-divorce when I'd found a room to rent and been a lodger. It felt like a backwards slide and the thought elicited a few tears. Sometimes, I told myself, you have to go backwards to go forwards. Be brave, Helen.

I made my first commute along the Central line to Bank on Tuesday and joined my new colleagues in a friendly office on Gresham Street. In that first couple of weeks, not really knowing what to do with myself at lunchtime but wanting to get out, I would walk to St Paul's and sit there for a bit, under the great dome, absorbing the calm. There was a lot to do, finding out about things, but my main aim was getting to grips with London: the size of it, working out the geography and how long it took to get from A to B. For the first month or so every day started with a minor battle to get my fear of fucking up under control. When I didn't fuck up I began to relax and enjoy myself.

I grew up a lot in those first few weeks, rediscovering a lot of things I'd mislaid during my time with Franc: self-reliance, determination, assertiveness. I realized how quickly I could pick things up if I persisted, and that I could solve most problems if left to work things out for myself without being nagged every two minutes.

Franc said he was going to be in London at the end of September, but the entry in my diary is crossed out. He decided not to come and only told me the day before, when I asked what time I might expect him. I was disappointed to be denied the opportunity of showing off a bit to him. Perhaps that was the real reason he cancelled and his email on 28 September was just an excuse:

> *I had my trip planned there then my boss got upset with me so he has deleted it. Then I get the flu and I stay at home so I do not reply to your email.*

As for not answering my calls, his phone did not work

when he was at home. Why did I keep complaining about everything when he was so disappointed? I should be kind to him. His boss, he said, was stupid.

> *And I have got the flu and next week I could be with the flu again.*
>
> *Will be glad if I die.*

Was it revenge for my new-found independence?

Instead, he came over a couple of weeks later, flying in on Friday and back again on Sunday afternoon. We stayed in a hotel in Islington. He hardly spoke to me over the weekend. He didn't talk about what was happening in his life in France, he didn't ask me much about my new job. I have a vague memory of us going for something to eat in a pub and him being so cold and distant that all I wanted to do was cry. (Why did I always want to cry when I was with him?) I remember we argued but not what about. I remember smoking in a hotel bathroom again. The weekend was not a success but neither of us could quite let the other go.

I thought about it a lot over the following week and then sent him a short email:

> *Franc, it's all too painful and unless something changes, I simply haven't the strength to go on with it. There is no doubt (and you know this) about my love for you but I cannot keep putting myself through this. You would say that I do this to myself and in some way you are right. I'm sorry, I cannot accept things as they are and I'm sorry for not being strong enough to deal with it. I have tried, really tried. Friday and the weekend were the last straw (no communication). I cannot think or believe that you care. I'm so sorry.*
>
> *Speak to me, call me, do something please.*
>
> *H*

That was the most sensible thing I'd said to him in three years. It was hard to get used to being on my own, I mean properly on my own, without anyone – not even my children – but I was learning to enjoy it. I liked the freedom but especially I liked the peace. I had possibilities and hope. I could do something.

You might think that would have been it for Franc and me. The implication of my email was that we were over. But under Franc's rules it wasn't over until he said it was. He was still in control and just now and again, when I felt a bit lonely, I found myself missing him – which meant I was still vulnerable. At one of those times I wrote, 'I saw your email, which touched my heart, and I thought, well, maybe . . .'

For the six weeks before Christmas, emails flew back and forth. He was coming over for the holidays, then he wasn't, then he decided he was and then he wasn't sure . . .

He told me it was easier to 'start again from zero' as I had, that:

> . . . *it is not easy when you start from a well above average standing position. Do you understand this . . . ? I keep asking you about the flat but I have no idea what's going on despite your assurance that you would tell me before doing anything.*

He didn't see the contradiction in telling me that *he* had no idea what was going on.

I had decided I wasn't going to tell him about the flat until I'd given up the lease and back up in the Midlands Number 3 Daughter was preparing to move out. Without her living there I couldn't afford to keep it on. Franc would insist that I did but doing so might ruin my new life and drag me back into the old one. I wouldn't take that risk.

He tried what he always tried.

> *If you want to know if I love you the answer is yes (and for me it takes a lot after your behaviour in recent months).*

The thing is, I was moving beyond that now. My life no longer revolved around him. I did – I think – still love him on some level but I couldn't be with him. I knew that. He wasn't good for me. I hadn't a clue where we went from here.

Franc, clearly frustrated with my lack of cooperation but unable to shout at me in person, could always be relied upon to do it in print.

> *THE PROBLEM IS THAT I HAVE BEEN TOO MUCH OF A GENTLEMAN WITH TOO MUCH HONOUR WITH YOU. THAT'S WHY WE ARE IN THIS SITUATION.*
> *I SHOULD HAVE TOLD YOU LIES.*

> *YOU NEEDED SOMEONE TO TAKE CARE OF YOU. I DID IT. NOW I KNOW I SHOULD HAVE LEFT YOU WHERE YOU WERE.*

> *I HAVE SPENT THOUSANDS OF POUNDS FOR YOU.*
> *YOU GAVE ME A VERY GOOD JOB – NO.*
> *YOU GAVE ME A PLACE WHERE TO STAY IN UK – NO. IT WAS MINE ANYWAY.*
> *A CAR? NO.*
> *WHAT DID YOU GIVE ME?*

He called me a 'siren', accused me of 'bewitching' him, of giving him nothing apart from 'meaningless words'.

He wrote that he had done nothing but love me and now I turned this against him, and when he needed me I abandoned him.

> *One thing that makes you crazy is when I say you are not*

*right or balanced, not able to control yourself. I do not know
why, perhaps it has something to do with your past . . .*

It was what he always said, that I was mad, unstable. I had
half-believed him before but if I had been, would I have been
living and working in London now?

And he could still play me:

> *I am in the office and I am not feeling very well. On one
> side I would like to spend Xmas with you, on the other, given
> the circumstances and that now I have realized what you think
> of me, it seems not a good idea.*
>
> *Love Franc*

He was ill; he signed with love. He knew I would respond
– and of course I did.

> *Sorry you are not well. Whatever you have 'realized' – does
> that mean that you do not want to try to put things right? It
> shouldn't put you off. I would like to spend Christmas with you
> but I too have misgivings re your coldness and distance. That,
> however, does not stop me from wanting to try with you. It
> hurts to think of what you told me about spending 3 months
> trying to talk someone else [he meant Sophie] into trying again.
> Apparently I am not worth that. I do love you Franc – more
> than you can imagine – but I cannot be hurt again, or
> anymore, by all this. I am sorry if I sounded distant on the
> phone on Sunday evening – I was really glad that you phoned
> but all I was doing was mirroring your own manner towards
> me. It doesn't feel good, does it?*
>
> *Love H*

At the beginning of December he was still going. And
when I told him about giving up the lease on the flat, he was
livid. A barrage of emails mauled my self-confidence.

> *You have got this need to state you are good but you feel insecure anyway.*
>
> *I hope you are capable of keeping peace at work and not changing mood every two minutes.*
>
> *As far as the flat is concerned:*
>
> *1. You have told me it was in your name. I have asked to see some paperwork. Nothing. So I understand the flat was in my name.*
>
> *2. We agreed you would have told me when you decided to do something with it.*
>
> *3. Furniture, various belongings and a £360 deposit was mine. That was my home, heart and soul. MY HOME and you have stolen it behind my back, just to do something against me.*
>
> *4. I did trust you. That's why I let you stay there. Should I go back to [the Midlands] I will have a nice thought about you and my flat.*

On and on he went. I hadn't 'stolen' anything. I had told him that his furniture and everything else was perfectly safe, waiting for him to tell me what to do with it.

I wrote again:

> *Franc – If it's 'no' for Christmas please just tell me. I would be unhappy, naturally, but I would rather know.*
>
> *I love you.*
>
> *H*

Another long email still didn't give me an answer one way or the other:

> *I do not have a place where to go (my place with my furniture) in the UK because someone got rid of it without telling me. I will be alone with nowhere to go.*

Xmas was nice because I was with you in MY house.

Had you said, 'Sorry, Franc, should have told you before (about the flat)' we would not be here now. But here we are because you like playing with words and instead of saying just what is needed you keep flying all over. You are just not able to focus on the subject and I thought you were nearly a businessman.

Finally, on 10 December:

I do not want to know anything about Christmas . . .

BUT I would like you to accept accountability for your behaviour towards me. I have been abandoned by you at the very moment I told you I was unhappy but hey, who cares about me?

He didn't come for Christmas. I went to stay with my father in Suffolk for the first time since I was sixteen and had started to see my ex-husband. On Christmas morning, to my utter horror, I started to cry while I was washing up. It wasn't being with my dad and step-mum. But with no car and no trains I felt trapped. When I felt trapped I felt frightened and when I felt frightened I cried. No need to waste much time wondering why that might be.

*

In January Franc was still talking about coming over to spend time with me, or move back to the UK: 'Perhaps I should come and see you and try to talk. Anyway . . . we'll see.'

Sudden flurries of emails would burst like thunderstorms. He would write or I would write – not quite able to let my 'great love' go. We would reply to each other with our own comments woven through the original so each email became so many tangled strands of claim and counter-claim that the conversation was almost impossible to follow. Although I do know which words are his; they are typed in capital letters or in lower case without a shift key. These email Gordian knots would grow and grow until one or other of us stopped replying, usually as the result of a bitter argument over the phone or because I'd missed something he'd inserted into an earlier email. He still called me at least once a week but all he seemed to have left was his anger.

In April I found myself a flat I could afford to rent – I spotted it in an estate agent's window when I was on a recce south of the river one Saturday morning. The agent took me straight round and by the afternoon it was mine – small, with one bedroom, on the top floor, full of sunlight. It was on the edge of Blackheath but not the fashionable side, the Lewisham side, although that made it better for rail links into the centre – only ten minutes to London Bridge. It was slightly shabby, furnished with a mixture of junk-shop furniture, frayed curtains and on-its-last-legs kitchen equipment. There were holes in the sofa seat cushions. But there were trees, green open spaces, Greenwich Park and the river and, most importantly, no one in my face all the time.

I hired a van (no nerves this time) and drove back up to the Midlands. I was spending the weekend with Nina and collecting all the things she had stored for me for so long, which by this point included things from the flat, too. The van was crammed and I had to move everything up the six flights of stairs in a system of relays. It was exhausting, back-breaking, filthy work but the delight of rediscovering all my belongings – whether personal and precious or mundane and functional – was more than glorious. I played Handel's 'Hallelujah' chorus on my (no longer tape but CD) Walkman. At last, I had my own place with my own things in it. My renaissance had really begun to take shape.

> *I am still thinking to come over and talk. Perhaps I will come over to talk and then stay. (By the way, is there anything I could rent/buy from you?) – Franc*

This time I ignored him. He kept trying.

> *I could have kept you until . . . or maybe forever. I keep begging for some help and I do not get it. I have received no words from you. I thought you loved me enough to keep your anger against me on one side and help me nevertheless.*
>
> *I could carry on as a lovely person in love with you (because after all that is still in place, believe it or not).*

Finally, a glimpse of lovely Franc. I gave in and wrote back:

> *Should you come to the UK I cannot promise anything as far as I am concerned – we would have to see and that would depend on you. There may be too much damage to repair. I feel great tenderness towards you but I am absolutely terrified of being hurt again.*

I could kick myself. I had made things perfectly plain and yet again I allowed him to keep his foot in the door instead of slamming it shut.

Every time I pulled away he wrenched me back, challenging me to prove that I still loved him.

> *You don't understand me or you would not have treated me so badly. I have phoned you, I have asked for your help, I have tried and all I had back has been total no-care about my situation from you. Just remember you have never phoned me in the last months. I have always done it.*

> *If there is someone cold it is you.*

You'd think that the fact that I hadn't phoned would have told him something.

So, of course, because I have spent my life trying to please people and make everything nice and because Franc had trained me to do so, too, I sent back an open-hearted email full of love that I'm really, *really* not sure I felt anymore.

After this he did come over, in May, and he spent a weekend with me in my new flat. I don't think he was impressed with it. He was very quiet. We had sex once, on Friday night when he arrived. On Saturday we wandered about the South Bank and then over the river to the West End. He 'joked' that he hoped I had arranged for a woman to join us that evening for a threesome. It was strange and tense and after all those emails about wanting to talk he didn't say much at all. On Saturday evening he lay stretched out on my sofa (cushion holes hidden under a throw) while I sat at on the floor at his feet and waited for him to initiate sex again. He didn't. On Sunday he went back to France and I was left wondering what any of it meant, or if it meant anything at all.

Monday brought an email:

> *If you are upset for the escort thing I apologize. I think that I have not done anything wrong but if you feel upset etc etc I am really sorry for that. Being brain led the connection 'you get upset for this then you do not love me' is quite straightforward.*
>
> *Yes, I could have been more nice with you. The point is I still love you.*

He said he felt as though he was in love with some of the women he saw 'around but not going out'. He wasn't seeing

Sophie, or talking to her. He said she had a new boyfriend, one with the same 'name and surname' as him. He didn't know if he wanted either of us back, or perhaps, he wondered, he should find someone else.

> *What will happen when I am back in UK? Shall I see you again? Will you want?*
> *Totally unhappy and bored to death.*
> *Missing sex* ☺

Jesus Christ. Could he hear himself?

I tried again to put a stop to it all. But the goading emails kept coming.

> *I am very hurt because I thought that you loved me as I loved you but I see now that I have given away for you my life and in exchange I get nothing.*

There are pages and pages of this stuff in the folder where I kept our correspondence. It's always the same thing – I gave you everything, you gave me nothing, you owe me. My stomach would revolt in response to the trigger of an email from him arriving in my inbox and I would try to resist the phone calls which inevitably followed, but always I gave in. The brainwashing – it's hard to think of it as anything else – had been so thorough: do this; do that; no, not that – *this*. I was so bored with the way he behaved, but I was still afraid of him, sick of being afraid of him and loathing myself for being too weak to shut him down for good.

And then, something happened.

We used to get a lot of overseas visitors at work and one day an attractive and very polite French lawyer came through the doors. Because I spoke French I was included in the meeting and afterwards (in French) he invited me to join him for dinner that evening. I said (in French) that I would be charmed. We arranged to meet in Knightsbridge. I felt terrifically pleased with myself.

We had a lovely dinner in a very smart restaurant and went back to his flat for coffee. I did get the coffee but it went cold. I also got sex. Unprotected sex. Sex I hadn't wanted. Afterwards he gave me a kiss on the cheek, said thank you very nicely (in French) – I said nothing in either French or English. Then he called me a cab and put me in it with £50 for the fare. At least I think that's what it was for. When I got home I sat in a very hot bath and soaped myself thoroughly all over – inside and out – but I couldn't get rid of the smell of him. I could smell him on me for days afterwards. I threw away the clothes I'd been wearing.

It doesn't take Sigmund Freud to work out what happened there and why I failed to resist. I didn't consent, but I didn't say no either. I hadn't wanted to have sex with a man I'd only met a few hours earlier – having no doubt learned my lesson with Franc. He wasn't violent but for all I knew he might have become so and because I was so afraid of that it seemed safer just to let him get on with it. I did what I'd been conditioned to do.

I felt sick and ashamed. And all of a sudden, I could see through Franc. I mean, *properly* see through him.

> *Have you read my fucking email or not?*

No reply.

> *I told you I was coming to see you and what I got back from you was, 'I don't know if I want to see you'. It's not me then, it's you.*

No reply, so he claimed to be at death's door:

I am not blackmailing you. But my health problems are
why I have delayed my coming back to England. I am not very
happy thinking about me dying in bed, alone, with a brain
haemorrhage and yes, I wish I could die . . .

I did reply to that. I told him to pull himself together,
which was more or less what he'd told me when I'd said a
similar thing to him.

More to the point, I had a health problem of my own. A
smear test showed abnormalities and I was referred quickly
down the line to a consultant surgeon. A short while after that
I was booked in for a total abdominal hysterectomy for early
stage cervical cancer. I didn't tell anyone about the cancer bit,
only about the surgery because I had to take three months off
to recover – and maybe more depending on what they found.
I told my daughters and my father which hospital I would be
in. I also told Lizzie and Nina.

I certainly didn't tell Franc about the cancer either, only
that I would be in St Thomas's for about a week. It seemed to
go in one ear and out of the other.

Can you be straight for once?

Why, he demanded, did I change my attitude to complaining, insulting and accusing him when I'd been fine a couple of
hours earlier? He said I kept overlooking the fact that everything was my fault. He would, he said, just like an explanation.
Then:

Please remember that you tried to 'kill' yourself and you
did it against me; a slap is nothing compared to what you did
to me.

There. Right there. He had admitted he hit me. Never

mind that he called it a 'slap', as though I was a naughty child – he had said it. I replied.

> *No comment, deleted emails, not going down this road*
> *again. Sort yourself out – with me if you need to – but I will*
> *not have you shouting at me down the phone again, ever. This*
> *is not love and it is most certainly not the way to rekindle my*
> *feelings for you.*
> H

As Offred in *The Handmaid's Tale* would say, '*Nolite te bastardes carborundorum,*[1] bitches.' When this is all over, I thought, I might have that tattooed on my arse.

But it wasn't quite over – very nearly but not quite. It was easier to get rid of my uterus than it was to get rid of Franc.

He came to see me in hospital the week after my surgery, saying he was in the UK visiting Dave and Jeannie. I knew I looked like shit and that he hated sick people. I couldn't work out why he was there at all until he started talking about himself again; then I realized he was there to dump me – in person. Not for reasons of decency, but because, like Doreen, he needed to see my face when he told me. They were so similar in so many ways.

He told me, gently, that he had decided not to see me anymore. (*He* had?) And that was because he had decided that he definitely wanted to have children (the lack of them was breaking his heart, apparently) and obviously now I lacked the necessary equipment. I think he actually said that, 'the necessary equipment'. It was ruthlessly, incomprehensibly cruel.

---

1. '*Don't let the bastards grind you down*'. Margaret Atwood, *The Handmaid's Tale* (Jonathan Cape, 1986).

But I was still high on morphine so he might as well have been reciting *The Ancient Mariner*.

What he said didn't really sink in until I was out of hospital, at home, off the drugs – and then it punched me right in the 8-inch scar across my belly. I struggled with it for a few weeks and then pitched up unannounced in my GP's surgery, distraught and sobbing, asking for help before I did something terrible. It wasn't just what Franc had said but also the hormonal after-effects of the surgery. My emotions were rioting in protest. Taken together, Franc (the full unexpurgated Franc), the predatory French lawyer and cancer felt a lot like punishment. Punishment for failing Franc, for sex, for failing my children, for getting myself raped, for trying to be something better than I was, for being irrational. But mostly for being a woman. It had a catastrophic psychological effect on me and it took months to get over it but I did, eventually, with the help of my very patient doctor and some little blue pills.

While I was recovering, I did once relapse – in November – and sent Franc a long email about how much I still loved him:

> . . . you are woven into everything I do, see or say. You are around me everywhere and in everything. If a plane flies over I think of you being on it – either going away from me or coming back to me, so much of our life together was spent in such a way. If I'm at a railway station I think of meeting you or saying goodbye to you (the sound of a train brings tears). A friend took me to dinner last week and in the restaurant they played 'New York, New York' (the karaoke song you sang at Dave and Jeannie's New Year's Eve party – you didn't know the tune but you tried anyway. You and me in blue and

gold – I don't have that photograph either). I just sat there in tears at the memory of it . . .

I don't think you can forgive me for the way I have treated you. Perhaps it wouldn't have made any difference if my illness had been diagnosed earlier – but perhaps it would. I wish I knew. Feeling as I do now, I could never treat you with such unkindness . . .

Franc's reply was inappropriately jolly. Perhaps because he thought he'd had the last word and I was destroyed and again a woman he could dominate. My email would have helped him believe that.

Hi

Can't reply properly because I ain't got time.

Not upset when you cry over the phone. I do understand what you feel, believe me.

Yes, at the moment it is quite difficult because I have a friendship. She always asks me if I have heard from you . . . but let's wait and see.

Of course I have to think if I was in the opposite situation.

You have to get back in shape and be strong and go on with all the things you have to do.

I might use you as a freelance when I go back.

Sorry, can't say all I want.

You know I care for/about you.

Please try to be good.

Love

Franc

He just couldn't resist turning the screw.

'She' was his new girlfriend, a young widow with an eight-year-old daughter who, he told me in a phone call, had seen him kissing her mother behind the kitchen door. It hurt so much when he told me that. All I could see whenever I closed my eyes was 'my' Franc kissing another woman.

When I went back to the doctor, he remarked drily, 'You can tell him from me, his timing stinks.'

Franc and I had been together, in some form or another, for four years.

But we weren't quite done yet.

Chapter Twelve

Franc still kept in touch, although we never got together again. He even moved back to the UK for a short time and reclaimed the few things left from the flat, which I think he felt made a point – or scored one. The business he set up with Dave 'didn't work out' (he said; I say 'failed') so he returned to France. He would phone me on birthdays and at Christmas and we would have a short, stilted conversation. Occasionally he pitched up at places where I worked – just to see what I was up to. These visits made me uneasy, but I didn't feel threatened. It was as though he was checking me out, casing my lifestyle to see if it would suit him better than the one he'd got. Bearing in mind that whenever we'd visited London he'd talked about how he'd like to live there I wonder if he was even a bit envious that I'd made this dream happen. Knowing (finally) the type of man he was, I think that's probably exactly what he was doing. But had he decided to move to London, I wouldn't have trusted myself to keep him at arm's length. I was afraid Franc's programming would override my common sense.

Whenever I asked him about his own life he was evasive. One thing was consistent, though. He always told me, without fail, that he was miserable in whatever job he was doing at the time. This was partly, I suspect, to push my 'oh, poor Franc – I must help him' button. On the other hand, he was convinced that his full potential went unrecognized; that everyone he worked for was an idiot and that if only they'd let him get on with it he would be brilliant. I'd never seen him at work and the only colleague I'd ever met was Dave but from the little I knew of it, he was wrong. Scratch beneath the surface and Franc was full of resentment at never being handed the Big Opportunity but he failed to see that few of us ever are. He didn't recognize that most big opportunities are the result of sustained effort and hard work. He was unwilling to take a risk to see where it might lead and if he did, like his start-up with Dave, his own negativity killed the enterprise stone dead. I think he was afraid of being found out and of failing. I recognize those feelings in myself and I felt sorry for him. There was a palpable twinge in the region of my heart.

For all he told me about his qualifications and his general cleverness, I suspect Franc was a profoundly average man. He knew as much, too, but didn't want anyone else to know so he hid it behind charm and arrogance.

Looking back, I realize that in truth I knew very little about him. In the four years we spent together I met his friends only a couple of times and I never met his family at all.

Once, when we were in France, he said he was taking me to his home so that I could meet his mother. I was so pleased he was making us 'official'. Up until then I'd felt like a guilty secret. I was older, had children and was divorced – reasons, he said, for his mother not to like me and reasons I now think had more to do with him than her. I remember a big house with lots of beams and an enormous fireplace which I found quite intimidating. I sat alone on a sofa in a huge dark room for three hours while Franc watched TV from an armchair and never said a word. No one came so we left. I never did meet his mother. I still don't understand why we went or why, if he had arranged this visit, he didn't phone his mother to find out where she was. But he had also told me she had moved out of the family home and into a flat so I wonder whether he ever intended us to meet and if it was just another one of his games. I didn't ask questions at the time (because it was safer not to) but I remember feeling slighted – although no slight had taken place. I felt scabbed with shame for being soiled goods.

Four years later, when I was working in Bedford Square, he rang to say that he was in London and wondered if I was free for lunch. He knew I'd say yes – I always did then. I came out of my office, caught a crisp breeze and folded my arms across my chest, hugging myself to keep warm. 'Why so defensive?' he asked before I'd said a word and kissed me lightly on each cheek. He just had to get me on the back foot. At lunch he produced a photograph and told me it was his wife and that she was my age (so much for the hoped-for babies then). The picture was of a woman I would never, in a million years, have thought was his type. Franc liked tidy, clean, chic, but this woman's hair was a massive unkempt mop. Perhaps she was another *Pygmalion* project for him – a woman to take in hand and 'educate'. I felt sorry for her.

A couple of weeks later he called and said he wanted to get married in London and could I help him arrange it. He said I must have misheard when I told him I thought they were already married. I didn't bother to argue, but sent him some Home Office information and left him to it. He could have looked it up himself. The sheer brass neck of the man for even asking. Putting myself in her shoes I wondered how I'd feel if I found out that my fiancé had asked his ex-girlfriend to help organize our wedding.

He got married, allegedly, in France but I don't know whether he remains so, or ever was. He never says. Four or five years ago he was still talking about coming back to the UK – to work in London. 'What does your wife think about that?' I asked. He changed the subject.

*

I buried my relationship with Franc, and the memories, putting all the letters and emails into that grey bag under my bed, together with the disciplinary correspondence. I kept them there, perversely, to remind me of things I didn't want to be reminded of. Occasionally I would pull them out when I was looking for a pair of shoes or something and push them back in again, thinking, not yet. Over time Franc's letters and emails became a memorial to having once been passionately loved, and the work letters a prompt to hold fast to what I believed in.

Occasionally I'd embark on a bit of humble bragging about my French former lover but I never told other people what he was like. If anyone asked I said he was 'not very nice', a convenient phrase to shut down any potentially awkward conversation and stop the feelings that inevitably bubbled to the surface whenever I was on the point of discussing or thinking about him.

The truth came out quite by accident. I needed treatment for a shoulder I'd damaged hauling too many archive boxes about. Work-wise it was a stressful (but exciting) time and when the consultant who was giving me steroid injections noticed my blood pressure was up I mentioned in passing that I'd had several ferocious headaches. It was probably nothing, he said, but sent me for a CT scan anyway, just to be on the safe side.

'Well now, what have you been up to?' he asked when we met to talk about the results.

'How do you mean?'

He explained the good news: that there was nothing sinister about the headaches – just stress and raised blood pressure – but went on to tell me that my brain showed signs of the same kinds of injury seen in boxers, from repeated blows to the head. He went through my scans with me – all very clinical and matter-of-fact. Then I burst into tears. It was such a shock – a hot gust of forgotten humiliation. I was appalled. Angry.

I told him what I'd never told anyone before. Until then I'd taken the easy route: as long as I didn't say the words it wasn't real and I didn't have to live with the shame and guilt of having allowed this to happen. To speak of it, even briefly, felt alien, as though the truth didn't fit my mouth. On the way home I was so lost in thought and horrified astonishment I went three stops beyond where I should have got off my train.

Once I'd confronted this secret truth, I began to see things everywhere. The way I would sometimes duck on the Tube when a man reached for the overhead rail. The way I immediately backed down if anyone questioned anything I'd done – placating, smoothing things over, 'No . . . no . . . yes . . . you're right.' The way I always did the same thing two ways, reversing the first action, usually back-to-back, because one way would be the right way. Write 'e', write 'ɛ'; write '11.07.17', write '11/07/17'. Always covering my back.

There were things that triggered sharp memories, more than I remember after the end of any other love affair – not being able to listen to certain songs or go to certain places. It was years before I could walk past the corner at the bottom of my road without thinking, this is where Franc threw up because he ate his lunch too quickly and got jiggled about on the DLR. The solitary crystal glass, the one bone-china teacup without its saucer, are reminders of their partners, the ones he smashed.

Every so often I came across something of him amongst my belongings – any stray notes I'd push into the carrier bag with all the others but I occasionally turned up a filthy comment scrawled on the back of a pack of tights, or a key-ring that was his, or a tester bottle of his cologne. These I destroyed. I did, however, sleep in his pyjamas for years, right up until they fell apart. I found them comforting.

There are photographs from our trip to Venice but only of me, in St Mark's Square, wrapped warmly in cashmere and laughing. The photographs I gave him for Christmas turned up when I moved house, still in their grey suede wallet. I see an attractive redhead, laughing, always laughing. It was my way of saying, nothing to see here.

There are books in my bookcases bearing inscriptions from him: in the front of one on Casanova, *I hope you don't think I am a 'Casanova'. (I do)*. In a battered and stained copy of *Angela's Ashes* (it was in the bookcase he'd knocked over), *Will you be the next writer to win the Pulitzer Prize? I am sure you will improve your chances if you write something about . . . me!* They sit uncomfortably beside the books marking the progress of my life since he left it, including the first one I wrote myself.

But all these things are memorabilia, ephemera. More lasting are the physical signs of two destructive relationships, the ones I contrived not to notice or dismissed as relics of domestic accidents and evidence of my own clumsiness: scars on my hands, a burst blood vessel in my leg, toes that were stamped on and jump out of joint every so often to make walking painful, the jaw that does the same, my brain, my throat and neck, the slight deafness in one ear . . . It never occurred to me that what he, they, had done would leave lasting damage that at some future point would require an explanation from me. An honest one.

Any psychological kinks left over from Doreen's prolonged campaign against me were ironed out over time in my newly adopted city. In many ways she did me a favour; I doubt I would have gone to London if it weren't for her. But she changed me, gave me something to prove and the tools to spot others like her. Righteous anger can get you a long way in life. I suppose Franc did the same.

A couple of times I left a job because I witnessed behaviour that reminded me of Doreen. I knew where it could lead and I wasn't prepared to tolerate it.

I climbed the career ladder to the very top, using my experience and skills to become impervious to panic. I might go into the lav for a few minutes from time to time and take deep breaths, or get a cup of coffee, sit in a corner and think about things for a bit, but I learned that there is a solution to almost every situation. Mistakes are all right as long as you own them. Occasionally people, even you, fuck up but it's not the end of the world and it's definitely not unforgivable. I learned to trust my own judgement and that if I didn't agree with something it was OK to say so. Despite all my many imperfections and general mouthiness I never came close to being sacked – the hospital was unique in that respect. The best bit was looking out from the pinnacle of my long and distinguished career as a PA, smiling and saying to myself, See? You're quite good at this lark after all. Fuck you, Doreen Milson. I'm not a PA anymore but I still do it from time to time because it feels good. I never did get rid of my wretched drive to please everyone, though. It sits oddly with a newly acquired ability to see through the crap.

If anyone calls and asks me to do something I still struggle not to say yes just because they will like me if I do. Who *cares* whether they like me or not? I have been infuriated with myself for writing long and elaborate emails giving good reasons for not doing something but jumping through an assortment of hoops to avoid giving offence. I press 'send' and immediately think, You idiot, all you had to do was say no.

It's been much worse since I started writing this book – but then a lot of things have been worse since I started writing this book.

There were – as I expected there would be – flashbacks. The more I poked about inside my memories the faster they came at me. There was a point where it was like standing in the middle of a meteor shower as bright recollections of anger, catastrophe and violence whizzed past. At first, these memories were all unconnected to each other. I only joined the dots later as I traced the narrative emerging from my letters and diaries. With the exception of Franc's 'love letter' when he came back that August, I hadn't read them in over a decade.

As the story unfolded, I began to understand what had happened to me. With understanding and acknowledgement came the shakes. I'd sit at my laptop and tremble convulsively for about ten minutes before I could start. Once I was writing I calmed down, stoical and determined because I felt it was important, but often I'd go outside and walk up and down for a bit, jiggling my hands and talking to myself to try and get whatever it was back under control. I'd end a working day with my jaw set so tight my head would be throbbing. And once I had a full-blown panic attack because that was the day

I was going to write about the *Last Tango in Paris* word. The one I still don't want to say.

Before the idea of this book had become a reality, as a result of writing that *New Statesman* article about coercive control, I was invited to take part in a panel discussion on domestic abuse at the Women of the World festival in London. I didn't stop to think about whether it would cause me any personal difficulty and said yes, without hesitation.

But I discovered that day that remnants of what you've gone through hang around inside your head and that speaking about your experiences to a roomful of people is quite different from writing about it at the kitchen table. I began to shiver and spilt coffee down my frock. The microphone – slap bang in front of my face – was big and round and looked like a fist. I felt very exposed. Then I noticed someone at the back of the room, filming me on a mobile phone. That's nothing unusual but I became convinced it was someone who meant me harm. I stared hard and tried to focus on the face but it remained blurred. I began to think I was going to be punished for going public, for saying what must not be said. I was sitting in front of a window and began planning an escape route in case someone tried to rush me and throw me out of it. It felt as though my brain had short-circuited.

Somehow I got through it and I managed to tell the audience about my experience of domestic abuse. The response was tremendous. There were so many questions from people who had experienced something similar. The atmosphere was warm and supportive. I had no need to be terrified.

Afterwards I apologized to one of my fellow panellists for having been so nervy. She said, 'Have you heard of PTSD?'

Wasn't that something that happened to military personnel returning from war zones, to members of the emergency services who've dealt with terrible accidents? It wasn't something I had ever considered applying to survivors of domestic abuse – or myself.

When I got home I looked it up.

The classic precondition for PTSD is exposure to an event that 'involves actual or threatened death or serious injury' and that induces 'intense fear, helplessness or horror'.[1]

Yes, I did (eventually) believe I would be killed and yes, I did feel intense fear and helplessness. Two ticks.

I learned that the memory of traumatic events can resurface from time to time so you feel as though you're reliving it all over again; a flood of remembered feelings can overwhelm you when you're least expecting it and destroy your composure. Two more ticks.

Additional reactions included under a PTSD framework include anger, inability to concentrate, re-enactment of the trauma in disguised form, sleep disturbances, a feeling of indifference, emotional detachment or attachment disorders, and profound passivity in which the person relinquishes all initiative and struggle . . .[2]

Tick, tick, tick, tick . . .

Then I read that the psychiatrist, Judith Herman, recognizing that the standing model for PTSD did not capture the 'protean symptomatic manifestations of prolonged, repeated trauma', had introduced a variation: 'complex PTSD'.[3] In his book *Coercive Control*, Evan Stark describes it as:

---

1. Evan Stark, *Coercive Control: How Men Entrap Women in Personal Life* (Oxford University Press, 2007), p. 124.
2. Ibid., p. 125.
3. Ibid.

. . . [recasting] the original symptom categories as hyper-
arousal (chronic alertness), intrusion (flashbacks, floods
of emotion, hidden re-enactments), and constriction, 'a
state of detached calm . . . when events continue to regis-
ter in awareness but are disconnected from their ordinary
meanings'.

I knew all about 'chronic alertness' – I was always ready to
run. Furthermore these symptoms were linked to 'protracted
depression'. And there I was assuming I'd be stuck on antidepressants for the rest of my life.

Finally, and perhaps most significant of all:

The fear elicited by the traumatic events also intensifies
the need for protective attachments, leading some women
to unwittingly move from one abusive relationship to the
next.[1]

At this point I ran out of ticks.

Here was the answer to a question that has always puzzled
me – exactly why many women (myself included) become
unwitting 'serial offenders'.

It takes only two cycles of violence for a woman to suc-
cumb to 'learned helplessness':

a form of depression that gives her an exaggerated sense
of her partner's power and control. She concludes that
escape is impossible and concentrates instead on survival,
employing denial, numbing, or in extreme cases, pro-
active violence to cope.[2]

It takes the same number of cycles to establish PTSD.

---

1. Ibid., p. 126.
2. Ibid., p. 151, 'A Battered Woman's Defense'.

Yes, I was married to one abusive man and lived with another; I think this is what my (sacked) therapist was driving at when she asked how it felt to have a violent father. I had jumped to the traditional stereotype of a man who daily took a strap to his wife and children or came home drunk on a Saturday night and abused them and I was, understandably, hugely offended. I didn't equate her reference to my father, who was strong, kind and loving but disciplined his children in the generally accepted way at the time: spare the rod and spoil the child.

This upbringing contributed to my vulnerability and my passive acceptance of male authority. It wasn't unique to my father. It was society. If I hadn't stormed out perhaps she would have gone on to explain this.

When I married young I was simply following a time-honoured path. I thought I was marrying well – my husband was wealthy and our lifestyle would be comfortable. But although I had escaped my father, I had entered another family dominated by men. I had a husband my father grew to detest for his arrogance, who isolated me from my own family and friends and replaced them with his own. A man who refused to be present at the birth of any of his three daughters; who refused to take me to hospital to see our first child, born prematurely with a life-threatening condition, because it was Christmas and he wanted to be, as always, with his parents and siblings. Desperately ill myself, I hadn't seen my baby since the day after her birth – the week that passed before I saw her again robbed me of the chance to breastfeed her and made it difficult for us to bond. This was a man whose house was full of women but who refused to allow tampons to be stored in the bathroom where they might be seen; who made me look so much like his mother that someone mistook me for her in the street. A man who, when our marriage ended, stalked and harassed me and lied about his income to avoid supporting his own children; who threatened to withdraw his promise to give away (oh, those words!) his own daughter at her wedding if I insisted on attending. A man who has forbidden me from entering the town I grew up in for the simple reason that he now lives there.

My reaction to being filmed at the Women of the World talk was startling and completely unexpected. However it reminded me that my ex-husband still tries to control me and uses his money and our daughters to do it. I was frightened because I thought I'd been found out in an act of non-compliance.

One thing only fell into place very recently. I don't set very much store by the importance and interpretation of dreams except that ever since I can remember I've had a recurring one about a monster. It is always a massive, rampaging Godzilla-like beast and I am always running in terror and hiding from it. The setting is always ruined buildings, sometimes in a city, other times just an isolated building. Sometimes the monster finds me but I wake before I am killed and eaten. Sometimes I stay safely concealed while others are caught. There are times I experience what is known as a waking dream (*hypnagogia*) and as soon as it starts – the setting, the way the 'action' develops – I am able to think, I know this. It's just a dream – but even so I am still terrified. When I am going through one of these dream cycles I can never sleep properly. I have this dream, I now know, when I'm anxious about something.

There is another night terror, which is different and far more troubling. I can never remember what comes before it but I wake up, unable to breathe and struggling. Sometimes

I think I scream as I wake. When I open my eyes I can see a roiling mass, like a dense black cloud, always high up in the corner of the bedroom. It moves slowly towards me. I know it's not real but the panic I feel is. I tell myself not to be stupid but I still have to put the light on, and sleep with it on all night. This doesn't happen very often but when it does I am jumpy for days. Then just the other week I came across a passage in a book I was reading that described my dream exactly: the feeling of suffocation, of something covering me, the gasping for air and panic as I woke, and of seeing something dark, unknown and threatening moving, growing, in the corner of the room. Like me, the woman in the book is terrified.[1]

That's my dream, I thought with astonishment and a prickling scalp. All of a sudden I knew exactly what it was. A whole sackful of pennies dropped. My dream was a re-enactment of the times Franc had tried to strangle me. But now I know what it is I don't think it will bother me again.

I have tried to remember when it first started. Certainly I remember it in my old flat. Each time the dense black cloud was above the wardrobe, by the door. It happened so often I began to seriously consider inviting an exorcist round to check it out. I'm pretty sure it started after that day in August 2010 when the phone rang and a familiar voice said, 'It's me.'

He'd been to my flat once. He had my landline number because he used to call me almost every week. They were the sorts of things he would remember and keep, just in case.

He was on a cycling holiday. He said he'd just come off the ferry and planned to stay the night in London before making his way up to the Midlands to see Jeannie and Dave. He

---

1. Paula Hawkins, *The Girl on the Train* (Doubleday, 2015), p. 157.

carried his bike up the stairs, padlocked it to the railings on my balcony and proceeded to take over the flat. He changed out of his cycling gear, rinsed it and hung it up in the bathroom. He complained that I still didn't have a shower and grudgingly took a bath. Then he got dressed and suggested a trip to the supermarket to buy food for supper.

He waltzed in and occupied my life, just as he always used to. I suggested a couple of times that perhaps I should call one of the hotels in Greenwich or Blackheath and book him a room for the night. I thought that would send a clear signal about how inappropriate this was, but no.

I ended up cooking for him and then he settled comfortably onto my one sofa and turned on the television. I sat on the floor at his feet, still his Sock.

As the evening wore on and it became clear that he had no intention of leaving I went and fetched a spare duvet and pillow, put clean covers on them and left them pointedly on the table. Perhaps he was trying to save money, I thought, too kindly.

At eleven o'clock, I said goodnight and with my two cats (who soundly judged that they should have nothing to do with him) retreated to the bedroom. Just to be on the safe side, I wedged a chair under the door handle. I was very aware of him being there in my sitting room all night but I didn't think I was afraid, although my subsequent night terrors seem to suggest otherwise: of course I was afraid of the door – that was how the 'monsters' got in.

In the morning, when I heard him moving about, I emerged fully dressed and made some coffee. I did nothing that might give him an excuse.

He didn't say much before leaving and when he did get his stuff together and I went downstairs with him to say goodbye he looked sad. Again I felt that little twist in the heart, but this time I ignored it.

*

Franc got inside my head on the day I met him and he never left. Sometimes, when I experience the after-effects, I feel angry or scared or sick. But after all my efforts to understand how and why I got involved with him and stayed with him and took him back, I've arrived at a surprising decision – I shouldn't eradicate him completely.

Why? Because he's taught me how to protect myself. I can spot others like him through their camouflage now. I should, I suppose, thank him for that.

He would like the last word but he's not going to get it.

Look, Franc. Look what you made me do.

Acknowledgements

The thought, 'I'm going to be in so much trouble', has never been far away while I've been writing this book. That thought has stopped me before, as it was meant to. Perhaps what I've written will explain to those who know me why, on occasion, I have behaved in ways they couldn't understand, been unable to do things I should have jumped at, sought solitude at inconvenient times, and so on . . . Thank you for the support you weren't aware you were giving.

Franc's 'encouragement' stopped me from writing for years. Whenever I tried I found I couldn't. The encouragement and friendship of those around me were what got me started again. Thank you for persevering.

I owe an enormous debt of gratitude to my agent, Juliet Pickering at Blake Friedmann, who, when I came up with the idea, completely understood why I felt it was an important book to write and has been tireless in keeping my spirits up.

I send an equally enormous bundle of thanks to Georgina Morley at Macmillan who, in addition to being an utterly brilliant human being, had an instinctive grasp for what I was trying to do – I could not have wished for a better editor.

A lifetime of love and thanks go to Daughters Numbers 1, 2 and 3. Decades of the same go to 'Nina' and 'Lizzie'. You know who you are.

Paul Trueman gets a special mention and a big slice of cake

for setting up the 'Helen Titchener (née Archer) Rescue Fund' and for being my Twitter friend.

The cast and scriptwriters on *The Archers* shone a spotlight into a dark corner of many women's lives and I wouldn't have written this without them.

To my friends at Refuge, Women's Aid and SafeLives, 'thank you' seems a very small word for all you have done and continue to do.

And finally, to any woman who has had similar experiences to those I have described – this book is for you.

Further Reading

The Handmaid's Tale by Margaret Atwood (Jonathan Cape, 1986)

Zero Degrees of Empathy: A New Theory of Human Cruelty and Kindness by Simon Baron-Cohen (Penguin, 2012)

Do it Like a Woman by Caroline Criado-Perez (Portobello Books, 2015)

Witchfinders: A Seventeenth-Century Tragedy by Malcolm Gaskill (John Murray, 2005)

The Girl on the Train by Paula Hawkins (Doubleday, 2015)

Trauma and Recovery: From Domestic Abuse to Political Terror by Judith L. Herman (Pandora, 1992)

Power and Control: Why Charming Men Make Dangerous Lovers by Sandra Horley (Penguin Random House, 2017)

Why is it Always About You? The Seven Deadly Sins of Narcissism by Sandy Hotchkiss (Simon & Schuster, 2003)

Eve Was Framed: Women and British Justice by Helena Kennedy (Vintage, 2005)

The Empathy Trap: Understanding Antisocial Personalities by Dr Jane McGregor and Tim McGregor (Sheldon Press, 2013)

The Fact of a Body by Alexandria Marzano-Lesnevich (Macmillan, 2017)

Rebecca by Daphne du Maurier (Virago Press, 2003)

Big Little Lies by Liane Moriarty (Penguin Books, 2014)

Perfect Wives in Ideal Homes: The Story of Women in the 1950s by
        Virginia Nicholson (Viking, 2015)
So You've Been Publicly Shamed by Jon Ronson (Picador, 2015)
The Psychopath Test by Jon Ronson (Picador, 2011)
The Public Woman by Joan Smith (The Westbourne Press, 2013)
Misogynies by Joan Smith (The Westbourne Press, 2013)
Coercive Control: How Men Entrap Women in Personal Life by Evan
        Stark (Oxford University Press, 2007)